Strangers and Neighbors
Multiculturalism, Conflict, and Community in America

The city of Lewiston, Maine, has struggled since its mills began closing in the 1950s. Historically recognized for its large French-speaking population descended from the Canadians who staffed the city's mills, in the new millennium Lewiston acquired a new identity as "Maine's Mogadishu." Beginning in 2001, substantial Somali immigrant settlement gave Lewiston the largest per capita Somali population in the United States and sparked controversies and collaborations that redefined the city.

In *Strangers and Neighbors*, Andrea M. Voyer shares five years of observations in the city of Lewiston. She shows how longtime city residents and immigrant newcomers worked to develop an inclusive and caring community in which they could all take part. Yet the sense of community developed in Lewiston was built on the appreciation of diversity in the abstract rather than on fostering close and caring relationships across the boundaries of class, race, culture, and religion. Through her sensitive depictions of the experiences of Somalis, Lewiston city leadership, anti-racism activists, and even self-described racists, Voyer reveals both the promise of and the obstacles to achieving community in the face of diversity.

Andrea M. Voyer (Ph.D., University of Wisconsin, Madison) is Assistant Professor of Sociology at Pace University.

D1414209

Strangers and Neighbors

Multiculturalism, Conflict, and Community in America

ANDREA M. VOYER

Pace University

CAMBRIDGE
UNIVERSITY PRESS

CAMBRIDGE
UNIVERSITY PRESS

32 Avenue of the Americas, New York, NY 10013-2473, USA

Cambridge University Press is part of the University of Cambridge.

If furthers the University's mission by disseminating knowledge in the pursuit of education, learning, and research at the highest levels of excellence.

www.cambridge.org
Information on this title: www.cambridge.org/9781107676800

© Andrea M. Voyer 2013

First published 2013

Printed in the United States of America

A catalog record for this publication is available from the British Library.

Library of Congress Cataloging in Publication data
Voyer, Andrea M., 1972–
Strangers and neighbors : multiculturalism, conflict, and community
in America / Andrea M. Voyer.
pages   cm
Includes bibliographical references and index.
ISBN 978-1-107-03993-3 (hardback) – ISBN 978-1-107-67680-0 (pbk.)
1. Lewiston (Me.) – Race relations.   2. Somalis – Maine – Lewiston – Social conditions.
3. Immigrants – Maine – Lewiston – Social conditions.   4. Multiculturalism – Maine –
Lewiston.   5. Community development – Maine – Lewiston.   6. Lewiston (Me.) –
Social conditions – 21st century.   I. Title.
F30.S67V69   2014
974.1′82-dc23   2013003967

ISBN 978-1-107-03993-3 Hardback
ISBN 978-1-107-67680-0 Paperback

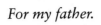
For my father.

The processes of social life, the "how" of everyday interaction and negotiation, the organization of humans into effective working units, the development of specific capacities and powers to move the world, are formed by meaning.

Reed 2011

In every community there are conventional understandings concerning the divisions of mankind, and there are customary procedures governing their social interaction.

Shibutani and Kwan 1965

Contents

Figures and Tables

Acknowledgments

There comes a time in the life of a text when it is time to send it out in the world to see how it fares. For me this is a difficult task – acknowledging that I have taken this about as far as I can and now it is time to let it go. There are still so many ideas I wish I could present more effectively, so many empirical observations I would like to highlight, so many things I would do differently if I could roll back the clock and begin again. This book is not perfect, not by a long shot, but I hope that it will be a sufficient jumping-off point for discussion of a subject that can always use fresh perspectives – immigration, diversity, being, and belonging in modern, multicultural societies. Thank you for reading.

This project would not have been possible without the generous participation of the people of Lewiston, Maine, and my fellow diversity trainers-in-training. Thank you for bringing me in. I hope that I have made good on your trust and honored your good intentions and hard work.

Linnaeus University, the National Science Foundation, University of Wisconsin – Madison, University of Wisconsin System Institute on Race and Ethnicity, and the Center for Cultural Sociology (CCS) at Yale University provided financial and logistical support for this research. Draft portions of the manuscript were presented at the Centre for Cultural Sociology at Linnaeus University; Malmö Institute for the Studies of Migration, Diversity and Welfare; Stockholm University Department of Sociology; University of Wisconsin Politics, Culture and Society Workshop; University of Wisconsin Race and Ethnicity Workshop; University of Wisconsin Social Psychology and Microsociology Workshop; and the Yale University Center for Cultural Sociology. Sections of Chapter 4 appeared in *Ethnic and Racial Studies* 34.11 (2011): 1874–1893.

I owe a tremendous debt of gratitude to those who provided intellectual and procedural guidance to this novice sociologist with a penchant for doing things the hard way. My doctoral advisor, Mustafa Emirbayer, supported this research from its earliest days. Mustafa is an exceptional cheerleader, academic guide, and intellectual coach. He was an indispensable mentor. Jeffrey Alexander provided a community of thought in the Yale CCS and the freedom to apply his theory in an unconventional manner. His belief in the value of this project gave me the strength to persevere when things looked bleakest. Danilyn Rutherford appeared at a serendipitous moment to bring me into a writing fellowship and reinvigorate my commitment to the story of Lewiston. Gary Sandefur provided the early research experiences upon which my later investigations were built. Pamela Oliver was a straight-talking mentor who supported my research and advised me as I pursued a life in academia. I was also guided on my intellectual trajectory by the wisdom and expertise of Shelley Correll, John DeLamater, Nina Eliasoph, Ron Eyerman, Jeremy Freese, Phil Gorski, John Levi-Martin, Paul Lichterman, Doug Maynard, Phil Smith, and Mats Trondman, among others. Many colleagues were conscientious readers of various chapters of this book including Danielle Berman, Ellen Berrey, Matt Desmond, Ben Eastman, Alison Gerber, Aya Hirata, Nora Hui-Jung Kim, Abby Kinchy, Johannes Lang, Anna Lund, Stefan Lund, Emily Manetta, Isaac Reed, Luisa Farah Schwartzman, Jonah Steinberg, Kaelyn Wiles, and especially Vicki Brennan, my writing partner extraordinaire. On my frequent returns to Lewiston, Linda and Joe Ricchio provided a warm place to stay, the support of family, and a forum for heated debate. Sue Duncan, an emotional and intellectual kindred spirit, spent more hours than I can tally talking over this research and my many other life projects. Pat MacClarence and Allen Harden provided love that bridged the gap between my community-of-origin and my adult life.

This book has benefited from the expertise and support of Cambridge University Press and its affiliates. Robert Dreesen responded enthusiastically to the tentative early work of this first-time author and stuck with the project through thick and thin. The manuscript was much improved by the conscientious comments of anonymous reviewers. My thanks to the entire Cambridge University Press team, including editorial assistant Abigail Zorbaugh, production controller James Dunn, production editor Regina Paleski, and copy editor Patterson Lamb.

My life as a sociologist and a whole person is only possible because of the love and support of Jason Czarnezki. We two academic compatriots, explorers, and fellow travelers are on an amazing journey. Thank you for sharing the ride with me. Lauretta and Hazel, my true life's work born in the midst of this research enterprise, make it all worthwhile. I watch with joy as you grow.

As a child playing in the attic, I came across a box of my father's unpublished short stories. I read his work voraciously, in awe that my dad, someone I could not imagine outside out of the mundane world of family life, had created literature. My father's writing and his love of reading instilled in me a reverence for the beauty and power of words on a page. Dad, this book is for you.

Introduction

Strangers in a Strange Land

THE LETTER

On October 1, 2002, Mayor Laurier Raymond released an open letter to African immigrants settling in Lewiston, Maine. In his letter, Raymond maintained that Somali newcomers were overwhelming the city. Endeavoring to protect the economic resources, physical space, and emotional health of Lewiston from what he understood to be the pressure of immigrant settlement, the mayor asked that local Somalis discourage further resettlement in the town. The letter read:

For some number of months, I have observed the continued movement of a substantial number of Somalis into the downtown area of our community. I have applauded the efforts of our city staff in making available the existing services and the local citizenry for accepting and dealing with the influx.

I assumed that it would become obvious to the new arrivals the effect the large numbers of new residents has had upon the existing staff and city finances and that this would bring about a voluntary reduction of the number of new arrivals – it being evident that the burden has been, for the most part, cheerfully accepted, and every effort has been made to accommodate it.

Our Department of Human Services has recently reported that the number of Somali families arriving into the city during the month of September is below the approximate monthly average that we have seen over the last year or so. It may be premature to assume that this may serve as a signal for future relocation activity, but the decline is welcome relief given increasing demands on city and school services.

I feel that recent relocation activity over the summer has necessitated that I communicate directly with the Somali elders and leaders regarding our newest residents. If recent declining arrival numbers are the result of your outreach efforts to discourage relocation into the city, I applaud those efforts. If they are the product of other unrelated random events, I would ask that the Somali leadership make every effort to communicate my concerns on city and school service impacts with other friends and extended family who are considering a move to this community.

To date, we have found the funds to accommodate the situation. A continued increased demand will tax the city's finances.

This large number of new arrivals cannot continue without negative results for all. The Somali community must exercise some discipline and reduce the stress on our limited finances and our generosity.

I am well aware of the legal right of a U.S. resident to move anywhere he/she pleases, but it is time for the Somali community to exercise this discipline in view of the effort that has been made on its behalf.

We will continue to accommodate the present residents as best as we can, but we need self-discipline and cooperation from everyone.

Only with your help will we be successful in the future – please pass the word: We have been overwhelmed and have responded valiantly. Now we need breathing room. Our city is maxed-out financially, physically and emotionally.

I look forward to your cooperation.

Laurier T. Raymond Jr. Mayor, City of Lewiston (Raymond 2002)

The mayor's missive, the first shot in what became a war of words, pit two communities against one another. Raymond characterized Lewiston as a "generous" and "accepting" "community" facing a growing "community" of undisciplined Somali immigrants making undue demands on the city's meager economic resources. Dominant voices in the media maelstrom that followed challenged Raymond's fiscal claims. Local liberals condemned the mayor as racist and mounted public demonstrations in defense of Lewiston's diversity. Meanwhile, individuals and groups calling for racial purity and an end to immigration seized upon the letter and its author as their cause célèbre. Raymond and many city residents appeared taken aback by the magnitude of the response to the letter. The mayor claimed he was misinterpreted and, after a few failed attempts to explain the reasoning behind the letter, withdrew from the media entirely. Somali residents of Lewiston released a letter of reply in which they dismissed Raymond's charges, criticized him for scapegoating them for the city's financial difficulty, and laid out the benefits of immigrant settlement in Lewiston.

Three months later the uproar caused by the letter culminated in a day of competing demonstrations. A homegrown diversity organization, the Many and One Coalition, staged a pro-diversity rally while a national white supremacist organization, the World Church of the Creator (WCOTC), held a recruitment meeting on the other side of town. Legions of journalists and hundreds of protestors stood outside the site of the World Church of the Creator meeting, which was attended by approximately forty individuals. The Many and One event exceeded its 2,000-person seating capacity. An additional 2,000 supporters stood outside in the cold cheering and chanting. Charged with maintaining order and protecting public safety, Lewiston's Chief of Police William Welch created a security plan that called for the largest mobilization of law enforcement in Maine history. Welch's preparation was thorough. There was no violence and only one arrest – that of an anti-racist protestor outside of the World Church of the Creator meeting.

Following the rallies, everyday community building, service provision, and immigrant settlement efforts replaced polarizing rhetoric and demonstrations. As reminders of the social costs associated with bigotry and the mismanagement of diversity, the letter and the tumult that followed continued to loom large in public consciousness. The emerging rhythm of life in post-letter Lewiston included some novel elements. Diversity training programs, community needs assessments and discussions, Somali ethnic festivals, and multicultural celebrations marked the community calendar. Immigrant resettlement services and English language programs joined Lewiston's roster of municipal and social service programs. Sporadic expressions of hostility and bigotry intermittently shattered the calm and mobilized in diversity's defense a newly minted and competent cadre of local activists, law enforcement, and political figures. Old-timers and newcomers continued to negotiate the boundaries of the Lewiston and Somali "communities." In the wake of Mayor Raymond's letter and in the face of continued immigrant settlement, the city and its residents acquired, through a combination of predilection, consent, and coercion, the practices and perspective associated with upstanding residents of a locality characterized by diversity and inclusivity.

The Usual Plot

When Mayor Raymond wrote his letter I was in the early years of graduate school. I happened upon coverage of the letter in my hometown newspaper, Maine's *Portland Press Herald*, which I was reading online from my apartment in Madison, Wisconsin. My initial reaction to the letter was one of contempt and anger. I found the letter offensive, immediately assumed that it reflected the racism of the author, and felt keenly that it also reinforced the view that my home state of Maine, the whitest state in the United States and a place considered by many to be a rural backwater, was populated by bigots. I later learned through conversations with city officials and administrators that Mayor Raymond received a flood of scathing emails, telephone calls, and letters from people who shared my perspective. The major news outlets reporting on events in the city also suggested that something was amiss in Lewiston.

Raymond publicly denied the charge of racism and asserted that his letter was a reasonable and unremarkable response to Somali settlement and the municipality's difficult fiscal situation. He insisted that he did not intend to discriminate, incite debate, or encourage hostility toward the Somalis. I also spoke with many longtime acquaintances of Mayor Raymond who maintained that, while the letter was a mistake, its writer was a good person who made a bad decision. Raymond believed that he was merely acting upon his motivation to explain that Somali settlement had an impact on the city and to communicate necessary information to the Somalis so they could change their behavior. The mayor asserted that he was not an agile public speaker and, thus, often relied on letters to convey information. He considered the case of Somali settlement no different from prior and successful efforts at communicating with city residents through the publication of open letters. Raymond was not alone in this assessment or in his astonishment that the letter became the subject of world news and the springboard for the mobilization of white supremacists and anti-racist activists. In a departure from the mayor's understanding of the letter as benign, some city residents welcomed its publication as long-overdue resistance to Somali settlement and the problematic "politically correct" and misguided "multiculturalist" ideas altering the racial and cultural fabric of the community. Other residents of the city claimed that while the letter proved a troublesome method of intervention, some response to the economic and social crises resulting from Somali settlement was necessary.

As an outside observer who perceived with immediacy and certainty that Lewiston's troubles were the result of racism, the lack of consensus among Lewiston's residents on the meaning of Somali settlement and the merit of Raymond's letter gave me pause. My disquiet only increased as I watched events in Lewiston unfold after the publication of the letter. Despite the unique characteristics of the community, the plot, timing, and cast of characters in the events that followed resembled precisely what one might observe in any social drama involving cultural outsiders and bigoted community members – desegregation squabbles in the South (e.g., Warren 1957), Chicago neighborhoods fighting public housing projects (e.g., Hirsch 1998), community mobilization in the face of a Ku Klux Klan march (e.g., Hall 1993), or tensions around Latino immigrant settlement on Long Island, New York (e.g., Sandoval, Tambini, Camino Bluff Productions, New Video Group, and Docurama (Firm) 2004). City officials, schools, public servants, social service providers, and hospitals with negligible experience in and few policies concerning racial and ethnic minorities and immigration threw their efforts into learning about "best practices" for managing diversity and meeting federal requirements for equal opportunity and accessibility. Liberal white activists, whose limited mobilization experience centered on gay rights, poverty, and religion, organized against racism. Lewiston lacked historical racial diversity but was traditionally a center of population for Maine's long-standing cultural and linguistic underclass, Catholic French Canadians who only a generation earlier were subject to significant pressure to assimilate, were now witnessing a very different kind of orientation to minority language and culture. Somalis eschewed racial classification as African American and, instead, asserted their rights and belonging as immigrants and Somali Muslims bringing diversity to the community.

While my initial interpretation of Lewiston's troubles focused on Mayor Raymond's racism and its impact on Somali reception and the public perception of all Mainers, I learned through observation of the city that there is a story beyond individual bigotry worth telling. In Lewiston, Somali incorporation relied on cultural practices and perspectives that became decoupled from individual actors and took center stage in the negotiation of meaning and membership, identity groups, and self-identities.[1] The analytical approach mobilized in the following pages precludes an emphasis on both individual and institutional racism while acknowledging their role in perpetuating discrimination and inequality. Instead, this book delineates the mechanisms producing Somali immigrant incorporation in a majority Franco-American town in the whitest state in the United States. As the ties between Lewiston's response to Somali settlement and national interventions and discourses demonstrate, the cultural processes I observed in Lewiston provide insight into ideas and approaches characterizing contemporary immigrant inclusion throughout the United States and in other settings oriented toward the positive valuation of cultural heterogeneity.

[1] Jepperson and Meyer maintain that causal accounts do not necessarily need to reason at the level of the individual actor. Instead, the selection of the level of analysis in which causal relationships are observed should be established in relationship to the empirical case (Jepperson, Ronald and John W. Meyer. 2011. "Multiple Levels of Analysis and the Limitations of Methodological Individualisms." *Sociological Theory* 29:54–73).

A CULTURAL SOCIOLOGY OF IMMIGRANT INCORPORATION

This ethnographic and cultural sociological account of immigrant incorporation focuses on the cultural pragmatics of immigrant incorporation – the contextualized meanings and practices characteristic of the fragile inclusion of Somalis in Lewiston. I use the term "cultural pragmatics" to indicate the on-the-ground cultural or symbolic system that shapes immigrant incorporation. Inherent in the term is a shift away from the emphasis on the characteristics and motivations of individuals and groups of actors, and a break with the assumption that meaning as coded in language may be divorced from the context of its employment.[2] I demonstrate the material impact of cultural processes and consider the tight interrelationship between discursive meanings and social action in Lewiston.[3] The cultural pragmatics of Somali incorporation consisted of the establishment of symbolic boundaries[4] that were inclusive of immigrant newcomers; the dissemination of an epistemological orientation consisting of foundational meanings, assumptions, and a related praxis; and a system of disciplinary procedures for managing the challenges mounted by alternative perspectives and practices.

This cultural-structural system enabled and shaped the inclusion of Somali immigrant newcomers, provided the narrative framework for the moral constitution of community, and set the performative parameters for the expression of individual and subgroup identities worthy of community membership. The structures of meaning considered here operated independently of individuals while playing a crucial role in immigrant incorporation. City residents engaged these foundational meanings as they sought to identify the values that they believed defined their community. The broader establishment of an inclusive definition of the city and

[2] Thus, in the sense employed here, cultural pragmatics is distinct from Alexander's consideration of the cultural performances (Alexander, Jeffrey C., Bernhard Giesen, and Jason L. Mast. 2006. *Social performance: Symbolic action, cultural pragmatics, and ritual.* Cambridge, UK: Cambridge University Press).

[3] Smith and Riley (Smith, Philip and Alexander Riley. 2009. *Cultural theory: An introduction.* Malden, MA: Blackwell) note that cultural theories are characterized by a focus on revealing the components of culture, demonstrating the influence of culture on social life, and accounting for the relationship between culture and action.

[4] I focus in this text on the construction and productive potential of symbolic boundaries that underlie epistemological divisions and categorizations. Social boundaries, the ontological categories visible and implicated in the divisions between groups' practices, positions, and treatment, have no necessary relationship to symbolic boundaries, and are of secondary concern here (Lamont, Michèle and Virág Molnár. 2002. "The Study of Boundaries in the Social Sciences." *Annual Review of Sociology* 28:167–195).

its membership was fundamental to Somali immigrant incorporation. The inclusive community was constructed through narratives that centered on the value of diversity and pro-diversity individuals. These core values were associated with particular behaviors, a praxis taken as evidence of a moral uprightness. Widely shared and endorsed understandings that good people welcomed diversity were reified as particular positions, perspectives, and manners of speech. Genuine endorsement notwithstanding, individuals and groups constructed their belonging through the performance of their own inclusivity. Lewiston residents attempted to stake their claim to social membership by demonstrating consistency between those values and their individual characters. City residents struggled to make sense of their community and its moral foundations, producing ongoing heterogeneity and resistance to the meanings and methods of social life. The terms of social inclusion in Lewiston experienced ongoing challenge in the face of the assertion of additional perspectives, complicating facts, and alternative interpretations. Disciplinary procedures of silencing, excluding, and reimagining dissent assisted in the establishment and maintenance of Somali incorporation.

Theory and Method

The following contextual and cultural account of Somali immigrant inclusion in Lewiston demonstrates that incorporation is a process occurring through collective negotiation of the symbolic boundaries of the community and corresponding categorization of those who are included and excluded as members. These negotiations include immigrant newcomers, longtime residents, community leaders, and advocates and experts working across settings and, thus, oriented to macrocultural parameters and national (or regional) social institutions. As I show in the following pages, all of these actors participate in the creation, application, and challenge of symbolic boundaries. Their actions establish the significance of those boundaries for policy and program development, material management of communities, and the orientations people take to one another and their own personal development.

Given the role of group boundaries in the process of immigrant incorporation,[5] I avoid imposing outside categories on my ethnographic data

---

[5] Attention to boundaries is nothing new in the literature on immigrant inclusion and racial and ethnic relations (cf. Alba, Richard D. and Victor Nee. 2003. *Remaking the American mainstream: Assimilation and contemporary immigration.* Cambridge, MA: Harvard University Press; Lamont, Michèle and Virág Molnar. 2002. "The Study of Boundaries in

and dispense with classifying and analyzing my observations in Lewiston in terms of the unity of individual actors or "types" of people (e.g., men and women, racists, Somalis, liberals).[6] In fact, I seek to demonstrate that these very categories are not natural but are instead produced to great effect through selective vision and the negotiation of meaning. I offer only limited attention to individual qualities and biography. To a great extent detaching words from their speakers, I make no attempt to uncover the intentions and motivations of the people I encountered. Alternatively, I emphasize the shared community and cultural context of social inclusion. I listen for evidence of how words and actions take on meanings, how meanings engender categorizations, and how those categorizations have consequences for Somali immigrant incorporation in Lewiston, Maine.

The study of Somali immigrant incorporation in the context of Lewiston, Maine, the United States, in the early years of the twenty-first century uncovered an ongoing cultural process, and variations on this process may be observed in different settings and for different groups of immigrants (Voyer 2013). In the city of Lewiston, Somali and non-Somali residents I observed, encountered, and interviewed; the events I attended; incidents I witnessed; and the accounts I collected provided empirical insight into the cultural pragmatics of immigrant incorporation. As I accumulated ethnographic observations of life in Lewiston, I continued refining the open question that initially guided my research: "What happens when Somali, Muslim, immigrants settle in substantial numbers in a small, Franco-American city in the whitest State in the United States?" I conducted formal interviews and focus groups only as an entrée into enduring contacts and a supplement to my observations as a participant observer and ethnographer in the community.

---

the Social Sciences." *Annual Review of Sociology* 28:167–195; Wimmer, Andreas. 2013. *Ethnic boundary making: Institutions, power, networks.* New York: Oxford University Press.). In this book I consider the process of category construction and application in the context of one city, but I also show the relationship between local categories and more broadly shared meanings and systems of relationships. This approach yields insight into the broader process of incorporation instead of merely highlighting isolated factors that might explain why different individuals, groups, or contexts yield particular trajectories of assimilation.

[6] In other words, I have abandoned what Abbott refers to as "the 'variables' paradigm" in favor of developing an account of a process as it unfolded in context (Abbott, Andrew. 1997. "Of Time and Space: The Contemporary Relevance of the Chicago School." *Social Forces* 75:1149–1182). Variations on this process may be observed in different settings and for different groups of immigrants (Voyer, Andrea. 2013. "Notes on a Cultural Sociology of Immigrant Incorporation." *American Journal of Cultural Sociology* 1:26–41).

Interested in developing insights from empirically rich observation of a given case, never did I attempt to construct a "representative sample" of interview subjects or locations.[7] A researcher motivated to achieve representativeness in the study of immigrant incorporation and multiculturalism would have committed a catastrophic error by ever setting foot in a city as outlying and full of outliers as Lewiston. My project is the study of a unique subject. I selected the case for its specificity and only learned through its examination how closely that specificity was related to more general social processes. While I make no claims to the representativeness of data in the statistical sense, I do maintain that my assessment of the process of immigrant incorporation in Lewiston offers unique and valuable insight into the similar processes unfolding in new destination cities and towns throughout the United States.

Listening for the meanings circulating in Lewiston required me to utilize mixed methods of social research. I gathered data primarily through participant observation and ethnography. Given its strength as a tool for detailed observation of cultural interpretations, routine behaviors and the underlying forces that motivate them, and the interaction between the local and larger systems of meaning and practice, ethnography is a research method well suited to the consideration of the cultural pragmatics of Somali immigrant incorporation in Lewiston (Fetterman 1998; Katz 2001, 2002; Marcus 1998). As an ethnographer in the city I uncovered the routines and rhythms particular to that place. I was able to observe the relationships between community life and extralocal practices and perspectives. Furthermore, ethnographic research provided the opportunity to take a long view on the research process and draw information from a variety of sources. Over a period of more than five years I observed Lewiston, supplementing data collected during visits to the field with other observational data garnered through interviews and newspapers as well as information gleaned through continued contact with folks in the fieldsite.

I began ethnographic fieldwork in Lewiston in July 2003. During the 2003–2004 academic year, I immersed myself in the community. I engaged Lewiston and its residents though everyday activities: purchasing groceries, clothes, and other supplies at local stores; getting my hair cut at the salon; going to the movies; and taking my laundry to the

---

[7] I concur with Small regarding the futility of forcing ethnographic work to adopt quantitative notions of validity, sampling, and representativeness (Small, Mario Luis. 2009. "'How Many Cases Do I Need?' On Science and the Logic of Case Selection in Field-Based Research." *Ethnography* 10:5–38).

Laundromat instead of doing it at home. I attended the city's biweekly city council meetings, school sporting events, a host of diversity training sessions, professional hockey games, high school musicals, protests and demonstrations, meetings of community organizations, and any and every ethnic and cultural event I could jam into my calendar. In addition to the informal discussions that I had with locals in these venues, I carried out interviews and focus groups with local residents, both Somali and non-Somali. I also conducted semistructured interviews with public officials, service providers, and other public figures – journalists, academics, individuals considered Somali spokespeople, community organizers, and other people active in local civic life and thus considered community leaders. For the purposes of analysis, I privilege naturally occurring talk over my interview data. I returned to the site for follow-up data collection several times between 2003 and 2005, including two three-week visits to the community in February and May 2005. During my research I took detailed field notes and recorded most interviews.

Throughout my time in the field, I honed my focus upon the meaning of community emerging in the town, and the successes and challenges of Somali incorporation. I noted the manner in which city residents referenced or did not reference ideas about population diversity. As my research progressed, I grew increasingly aware of the influence of diversity professionals coming from outside Lewiston. A core group of community members served as local "watchdogs" identifying and challenging bigotry and discrimination in the city. Somali organizations and individuals did significant "pro-diversity" outreach by offering cultural festivals and sitting on advisory boards and panels. However, outside diversity professionals representing several different federal agencies, and national and international organizations provided crucial administrative and didactic expertise. Traveling from locales such as Portland, Maine; Boston; Seattle; Los Angeles; and Toronto, Canada, diversity consultants advised the city on its hiring practices, service plans, school organization, accessibility policies, and community-building efforts. Diversity trainers offered frequent seminars geared toward increasing participants' multicultural skill sets. The trainings variously targeted city personnel, social service providers, and laypeople.

Increasingly interested in the relationship between Lewiston's local characteristics and more generic and mainstream ideas about race, culture, and immigration, I followed diversity professionals out of Lewiston and into diversity train-the-trainer programs. Using Dunieier's (2001) extended place method and "empirically following the thread of cultural process" (Marcus 1998, p.80), I stepped out of Lewiston in order to understand the encounter between local and specific practices of Somali immigrant incorporation, and generalized, systemic techniques for understanding and managing immigrant inclusion and racial and ethnic relations. I conducted research in a high-profile corporate diversity train-the-trainer series offered by Corporate Org, one of the United States' largest professional development organizations, and staffed by representatives of an agency known as a global leader in diversity consulting. In addition, I trained as a diversity trainer with well-established Rights Org, an international civil rights organization conducting a widely used school- and community-based diversity program. My observations in diversity train-the-trainer programs provided crucial insight into the cultural pragmatics of Somali incorporation in Lewiston.

In both theory and method, this book represents a departure from research on immigration and diversity as it is often conducted in the early twenty-first century. Existing studies generally seek to characterize the immigrant experience by focusing on the aggregate cultural attitudes, motivations, adaptations, challenges, and political and institutional encounters of individuals identified as representative of or in close contact with the group in question.[8] Such individual-level research sheds light on otherwise unexposed aspects of social life. When it comes to the quest for thorough sociological explanation, however, a field consisting of isolated examinations of immigrant identities, culture, subjectivity, and even immigrants' own accounts of the American mainstream runs the risk of overemphasizing individualism, psychologism, and the impact of immigrant group particulars at the expense of insight into cultural and structural elements of the contexts of immigrant reception and more general processes of inclusion and exclusion that also shape immigrant outcomes.[9]

---

[8] Some standout contributions in this voluminous literature include Marrow, Helen B. 2011. *New destination dreaming: Immigration, race, and legal status in the rural American South*. Stanford, CA: Stanford University Press; Massey, Douglas S. and Magaly Sánchez. 2010. *Brokered boundaries: Creating immigrant identity in anti-immigrant times*. New York: Russell Sage Foundation; Portes, Alejandro and Ruben G. Rumbaut. 2001. *Legacies: The story of the immigrant second generation*. Berkeley: University of California Press; Waters, Mary C. 1990. *Ethnic options: Choosing identities in America*. Berkeley: University of California Press; Waters, Mary C. 1999. *Black identities: West Indian immigrant dreams and American realities*. New York: Russell Sage Foundation.

[9] In much of the research on immigrant incorporation, macrolevel factors should be considered as the "context of reception" (Portes, Alejandro and Min Zhou. 1993. "The New Second Generation: Segmented Assimilation and Its Variants." *Annals of the American Academy of Political and Social Science* 530:22). In practice, however, context generally

A growing number of sociologists are responding to this overemphasis on immigrant group particulars by turning their attention to more detailed study of the contexts of immigrant reception.[10] Contexts of immigrant reception studies generally consider characteristics of the national context encountered by new immigrants – the particular racial and ethnic history, established groups, and intergroup relations; the characteristics of the labor market and other social institutions; government policies regarding immigration and diversity; and the relationship between the national setting, global migration, and international relations (Reitz 2002). Notable in this emerging literature is Massey and Sánchez's (2010) study of the development of immigrant identities that are reactive to "objective conditions in American society" such as a difficult economic situation and the "war on immigrants." But how are objective macrostructural and macropolitical conditions implicated in day-to-day encounters, experiences, and categories of understanding (and vice versa)?

Wimmer has developed a detailed sociology of ethnic boundary making (Wimmer 2013). His theory is designed to explain the emergence and trajectory of ethnic boundaries. Wimmer also claims to have an approach that adequately accounts for the struggles between actors seeking to establish and emphasize particular group boundaries. The cultural pragmatics of immigrant incorporation developed in this book has some commonalities with the ethnic boundary approach, namely, a view that

---

receives only limited analysis (cf. Marrow, Helen B. 2011. *New destination dreaming: Immigration, race, and legal status in the rural American South*. Stanford, CA: Stanford University Press; Portes, Alejandro and Ruben G. Rumbaut. 2001. *Legacies: The story of the immigrant second generation*. Berkeley: University of California Press; Waters, Mary C. 1990. *Ethnic options: Choosing identities in America*. Berkeley: University of California Press; Waters, Mary C. 1999. *Black identities: West Indian immigrant dreams and American realities*. New York: Russell Sage Foundation).

[10] Cf. Ajrouch, Kristine J. and Abdi M. Kusow. 2007. "Racial and Religious Contexts: Situational Identities among Lebanese and Somali Muslim Immigrants." *Ethnic and Racial Studies* 30:72–94; Alba, Richard D. and Victor Nee. 2003. *Remaking the American mainstream: Assimilation and contemporary immigration*. Cambridge, MA: Harvard University Press; Bloemraad, Irene. 2006. *Becoming a citizen: Incorporating immigrants and refugees in the United States and Canada*. Berkeley: University of California Press; Hein, Jeremy. 2006. *Ethnic origins: The adaptation of Cambodian and Hmong refugees in four American cities*. New York: Russell Sage Foundation; Jaworsky, B. Nadya. 2013 "Immigrants, Aliens and Americans: Mapping Out the Boundaries of Belonging in a New Immigrant Gateway," *American Journal of Cultural Sociology* 1: 221–253; Massey, Douglas S. and Magaly Sánchez. 2010. *Brokered boundaries: Creating immigrant identity in anti-immigrant times*. New York: Russell Sage Foundation; Reitz, Jeffrey G. 2002. "Host Societies and the Reception of Immigrants: Research Themes, Emerging Theories and Methodological Issues." *International Migration Review* 36:1005–1019.

group boundaries have both categorical and behavioral implications, are amenable to change, and are embedded within the institutional and political context of reception. However, I do not share Wimmer's underlying assumptions of intentional and strategic boundary-making, and view that ethnic boundaries as, at root, political. Most important, my discussion of immigrant incorporation is focused on civil inclusion and considers the civil sphere as a symbolically bounded group that is analytically (even when not substantively) independent of ethnic boundaries.

This work builds upon and extends consideration of the contexts of immigrant reception by moving past consideration of national context, whether conceived in terms of macrolevel policies, discourses, attitudes, and institutions (cf. Bloemraad 2006; Massey and Sánchez 2010), or, alternatively, in terms of the local construction of national political identity (cf. Brubaker 2006; Miller-Idriss 2009). The varying role of political boundaries and supranational identities in local processes of social inclusion is a factor frequently left unexplored in research, yet the tightness of fit between local and national identities is a subject that requires empirical investigation. In Lewiston, Maine, Somali incorporation is a matter of becoming a member of the local community – a status that only obliquely and weakly references national identity and legal membership.[11]

Why Lewiston?

The case of Lewiston, Maine, and its Somali residents is a tale of uncommon immigrants in an unlikely location. Such "least likely" cases of immigrant incorporation and cultural diversity are increasingly common in the United States.[12] In 2008 approximately 12.6 million legal permanent residents (LPRs) or green card holders (Rytina 2009), 15 million foreign-born U.S. citizens (U.S. Census Bureau 2008b), and approximately 12 million undocumented residents (Hoefer, Rytina, and Baker 2009) made their home in the United States. In the same year, nearly

---

[11] While there is significant divergence between the parameters for and process of local and national belonging in Lewiston, my subsequent research on immigrant inclusion in Malmö, Sweden, suggests that immigrants are incorporated almost exclusively into a national, instead of a local, collectivity (Voyer, Andrea. 2013. "Notes on a Cultural Sociology of Immigrant Incorporation." *American Journal of Cultural Sociology* 1:26–41).

[12] "In general, the strongest possible supporting evidence for a theory is a case that is least likely.... Theories that survive such a difficult test may prove to be generally applicable to many types of cases" (George, Alexander L. andnd Andrew Bennett. 2005. *Case Studies and Theory Development in the Social Sciences*. Cambridge, MA: MIT Press, 121).

13 percent of U.S. residents were not born in the United States – the highest proportion of foreign-born residents since 1920 and double the foreign-born population in the 1950s and 1960s (U.S. Census Bureau 2008a). Contemporary immigrants come to the United States from many countries. In both academia and the mainstream, discussion of U.S. immigration focuses primarily on Mexican and other Western hemisphere immigrants, often considering the impact of of immigration within major cities and traditional settlement hubs. Yet, the top ten nations sending immigrants account for only half of the substantial immigrant population in the United States, and immigrants are increasingly settling in cities, suburbs, and small towns that have not historically been home to substantial immigrant populations (Singer 2004). This diversity is felt on the ground and influencing everyday life in communities across the United States. In the 1980s and 1990s, Hmong immigrants settled among German and Polish Americans in Wausau, Wisconsin, where they encountered some initial discrimination and segregation (Koltyk 1998). Hmong now are about 12 percent of the Wausau population (U.S. Census Bureau 2010). Immigrants from Africa and South East Asia have transformed Greeley, Colorado (Green 2009). During Ramadan, Dearborn Michigan's Fordson High School holds their football practices from 11 P.M. to 4 A.M. in order to accommodate the fasting of their many Muslim players (ESPN. com news services 2010). In Portland, Maine, only thirty minutes from Lewiston, 25 percent of the public school enrollment in 2005 consisted of children speaking one of sixty languages other than English (Portland Public Schools Multilingual and Multicultural Center 2011).

Lewiston is one of a growing number of small towns and minor cities seeking to incorporate nonwhite, non-Christian immigrant newcomers, and Somali immigrants stand alongside many immigrant groups shaping modern America. Despite the increasingly typical nature of this case, in many ways Lewiston and its Somali newcomers diverge from common conceptions of immigrant America, race, and diversity. The city is not one of the bustling metropolitan centers typically associated with the United States' immigrant settlement and population diversity. Somalis emigrate from Africa and thus, in comparison with the substantial population of Mexican and other Latino immigrants, are part of a proportionally small African diaspora. However, Somalis' recent African emigration separates them from African Americans and even other "new world" African diasporic immigrants who, like many African Americans, are descended from slaves forcibly removed from Africa and denied full social and political membership upon arriving in the Americas. Somalis are typically Muslim and are frequently involuntary migrants – refugees practicing a maligned religion (Esposito and Kalın 2011; Gottschalk and Greenberg 2008) and from a failed nation that is considered an important battleground in the United States' War on Terror (Elliott 2009b). Despite, or perhaps because of, these particulars, sociological observation in Lewiston and among Somalis is highly relevant inquiry explicitly engaging current debates in the fields of cultural sociology, immigration and transnationalism, racial identification, and multicultural theory.

The details of local life in Lewiston encountered a cultural-structural system of recognition and incorporation that linked the community to the larger American public. The cultural pragmatics of Somali incorporation visible in the town arose from everyday practices and practical necessity, federal policy regimes, and widely shared structures of meaning. Observing the work that local public officials and administrators did to ensure that their programs, practices, and perspectives were defensible to a larger public, I also document the way in which national policies and politics, programs, and discourses became a part of local practices in a new immigrant destination. In considering the way that Somali immigrants laid claim to local belonging, I also detail the efforts and dilemmas of a few of the many new nonwhite immigrants challenging historical American racial categories and arguing for acceptance and inclusion. By following diversity education and management practices out of Lewiston and into the organizations where they were developed and distributed, I uncover widely shared cultural meanings and discursive practices. I consider the implications of those meanings and practices for understanding and addressing the immediate complexities of immigrant settlement, cross-cultural contact, and community identification in new and old immigrant destinations throughout the United States and beyond.

OUTLINE OF THE BOOK

The book contains six chapters.

Chapter 1, "Ellis Island South and Main's Mogadishu," provides crucial cultural, demographic, and historical information about Lewiston and Somalia. I indicate the ways in which Lewiston and its Somali newcomers, because of the ways they diverge from typical understandings, indicate the taken-for-granted nature of immigration, racial and ethnic relations, and religious diversity. The chapter introduces the theoretical contribution of the book, the cultural sociology of immigrant incorporation. This model of immigrant incorporation identifies three aspects of Somali inclusion in

Lewiston: the assertion of a definition of the Lewiston community and its members that could be inclusive of Somali newcomers; the reification of unquestioned truths and legitimated behaviors seen as naturally related to the definition of community; and procedures for managing challenges to these aforementioned symbolic boundaries and practices.

Chapter 2, "The Meaning of Somali Settlement and the Boundaries of Belonging," considers the shift from the view that the Somalis endangered the well-being of Lewiston to the perspective that the Somali presence in the city was an element of life "as usual." The changed meaning of community and belonging in relation to Somali settlement is visible in common narratives woven through the accounts I collected in my field research. Through analysis of public talk, I identify three diversity-affirming narratives celebrating Somali contributions to the city on the basis of the economic prosperity, cultural richness, and global stature accompanying immigrant settlement. I also identify four different narratives employed in explanations of diversity troubles, the challenges of immigrant incorporation, and the causes of community tension and turmoil related to the Somali presence in Lewiston. The predominant narrative of diversity troubles cites inexperience as the primary challenge to the community. Additional narratives of resource limitations, exploitation, and racism attributed trouble to porous community boundaries that allow interlopers, gain-seekers, and racists to exploit Lewiston. The everyday public acceptance of Somalis arises from the conception of Lewiston as a moral community of loving, accepting, and reasonable people who must defend the place against the threats of exploitive, irrational, and hateful individuals who would not accept Somali newcomers. Discursive meanings produce material consequences as Lewiston residents draw on both diversity-affirming and diversity-troubling narratives to understand and manage community relations.

Chapter 3, "Being the Inclusive Community," examines Lewiston's programmatic efforts directed toward becoming a welcoming and diverse community. I observe the rise of several responses to Somali settlement in the town. The city took action to assist the various elements of Lewiston in welcoming its new residents. Local officials and service providers developed policies and programs that complied with legal mandates and standards for accessibility and equality. Additional programmatic efforts provided cultural competence training to Somali newcomers and diversity education programs that educated community service providers about aspects of Somali culture and guided laypeople in examining the impact that their biases have on their behavior. Efforts in the city were characterized by a reorientation away from community debates and difficulties and toward the individual psychological and emotional work required in overcoming intolerance. In observing the material responses to community diversity and the relationship between the meaning of community and the boundaries of belonging, we witness the manner in which the moral values associated with community membership become associated with a legitimated praxis consisting of manners of speech, vocabularies, and perspectives.

Chapter 4, "Disciplined to Diversity," follows common interventions in Lewiston into the world of diversity trainers. That chapter shows how the values associated with community membership become reified in standardized practices and perspectives – an epistemology making sense of diversity and an associated praxis. Through their participation in diversity training, trainees learned what they may say about diversity and how they may say it. The work that trainees did to discipline their talk to the rules of discourse accomplished more than indicating their skill as trainers. "Successful" trainees assured their status as champions for the cause of diversity and allies in the fight against prejudice. Diversity training framed the complexity of cross-cultural contact in highly psychological terms. The curriculum depicted individuals as cultural products, biased in favor of their own cultures, and saw prejudice as the root of all discrimination and hostility. In this view, successful elimination of prejudice is achieved through personal contact and establishment of common ground.

Chapter 5, "Familiar Strangers," discusses the manners in which Somalis were engaged as familiar strangers – carriers of diversity whose distinctiveness must be consistent with hegemonic truths and practices. Members of Lewiston's Somali immigrant community performed complicated roles as they sought to make a home for themselves in their new country. Two contrasting narratives made sense of Somalis in Lewiston as both outsiders and insiders – actively highlighting the intractable alterity of Somalis as refugees, Muslims, and newcomers to the community while simultaneously tempering Somali's otherness with allusions to their place as immigrants in a nation of immigrants, people of faith, and parents, homeowners, and workers hoping to live the American dream. The position of Somalis as familiar strangers influenced the nature of Somali incorporation and the development of Somali American culture and identity in Lewiston.

The Conclusion, "Cultural Scaffolding," ends the book by recounting the way in which events in Lewiston ten years after the beginning of Somali settlement reveal both the success and the fraught nature of Somali incorporation. Multicultural incorporation of newcomers takes place through (1) the establishment of a meaning of community that is inclusive of newcomers and the association of the appreciation for diversity with the deep moral values underwriting community membership; (2) the reification of moral values in epistemology and praxis; and (3) the disciplining of individuals and communities to those particular social truths. This cultural scaffolding enabled the inclusion of immigrant newcomers, provided the framework for the symbolic constitution of community, set the parameters for the performance of individual and subgroup identities worthy of inclusion, and managed contestation and conflict. This chapter considers the implications of and rationale for this system of incorporation.

Ellis Island South and Maine's Mogadishu

Clarkston, Georgia, lies about fifteen miles from the center of metropolitan Atlanta. With a population of about 7,000 in 2000 and estimated at 7,800 in 2010, Clarkston houses many of Metro Atlanta's recent immigrants and immigrant service organizations. The city is nearly 7 percent Somali, 56 percent black, and 34 percent foreign-born. Approximately 41 percent of residents speak a language other than English at home – all characteristics that have earned the town the label "Ellis Island South" (Bouchard 2002b; U.S. Census Bureau 2009). The nature of Clarkston as an immigrant hub has exerted a lasting pull on some of the Somali immigrants who have settled the area since the early 1990s. However, other Somalis in Clarkston felt the strain of the high costs of living, a lack of access to educational opportunity and social services, and police harassment. Others worried that Somali culture was in jeopardy, endangered by pan-Muslim mosques in which Somalis worshipped alongside immigrants from Bosnia and Afghanistan and public schools in which parents felt children were being lost to "the lure of hip-hop music, clothes and attitudes that are so popular among African-American youth" (Bouchard 2002b, p. 1A). Those who were not satisfied turned their gaze elsewhere.

Lewiston, Maine, is 1,230 miles from Clarkston, Georgia – the trip is about thirty-two hours by Greyhound Bus, a common mode of transportation for Somali travelers. Heading north on Interstate 95, a lonely highway sign directs vehicles to Lewiston, a city sitting on the edge of the Maine woods, the largest contiguous forested area east of the Mississippi River (Sierra Club n.d.). The city center is not visible from the tree-lined exit. In February 2001, Somali immigrants began making the journey from Clarkston and its multinational immigrant population representing over fifty nations and more than 50 percent of the local population to wintry Lewiston, Maine, a regional population center with no immigrant community to speak off.

During my research I collected several different accounts of the initial impetus for Somali settlement in Lewiston. Some early media stories claimed that a few Somalis at a community center in Clarkston did an internet search, looking at crime rates and school quality to locate a better community. The group reportedly sent a team to visit potential sites and decided upon Lewiston.[1] Many civil servants and immigrant service providers dismissed that story as myth. They claimed that because of a dearth of apartments in Portland, Maine, Somali refugees who were being settled by official resettlement organizations in Portland were temporarily placed in Lewiston (e.g., Nadeau 2011). This reportedly introduced Portland-based Somalis to a community with comparatively more readily available apartments, underutilized social services, and vacant buildings for establishing businesses. Many business and Somali leaders dismissed both of these accounts and claimed that Lewiston, only thirty minutes from Portland, would inevitably be settled as Portland's booming economy and tight housing market put the cost of rental apartments in the city out of the reach of many. In this view Somali settlement was merely one aspect of population movement to a town destined to become a bedroom community of Portland.

However it began in 2001, by the summer of 2002 Lewiston was known within the global Somali diaspora as a desirable location with a low cost of living and crime rate, tolerance of religious diversity, little racial conflict, and the opportunity to avoid the intergroup conflicts that characterized Somali settlement in many other cities (Huisman 2011; Mott 2009). Self-sustaining migration developed as Somalis throughout the country heard about Lewiston's good schools and generous welfare benefits (Bouchard 2002b; Huisman 2011). The city increasingly drew Somalis aware of Lewiston's substantial Somali community known for its small and largely homogeneous immigrant enclave (Harkavy 2007; Huisman, Hough, Langellier, and Toner 2011) characterized by religious conservatism and high levels of parental oversight of their children's

---

[1] Although I never encountered anyone who admitted participating in such a community search, scouting of this sort is not uncommon among Somalis (Huisman, Kimberly A. 2011. "Why Maine? Secondary Migration Decisions of Somalis in Maine." Pp. 23–47 in *Somalis in Maine: Crossing cultural currents*, edited by K. A. Huisman, M. Hough, K. M. Langellier, and C. N. Toner. Berkeley, CA: North Atlantic Books).

educational and moral development (Huisman 2011).² The information about the community, how to get there, and where to go for settlement assistance upon arrival in town passed by word of mouth, postings on various Somali internet chat rooms, and, according to Somalis I spoke with in Lewiston, even bulletin boards in Somali community centers in Clarkston. Although Lewiston had no Somali population in 2000, between the summer of 2001 and October 2002 more than 1,200 Somali immigrants relocated to the city.³ By 2004, the Somali population of the community hovered around 3,000, leading some to claim that the city of 37,000 was home to the highest per capita concentration of Somalis in the United States (Harkavy 2007).

Somali settlement in Lewiston did not result from an explicit recruitment strategy in which local organizations contracted with U.S. Department of State's Bureau of Population, Refugees and Migration to resettle refugees from Africa. On the contrary, Somalis relocated to Lewiston of their own accord and in pursuit of a better life, distance from African Americans, and the opportunity to establish Somali-specific ethnic community and religious institutions. While many of Lewiston's Somali residents did come to the United States as refugees, they arrived in Lewiston as secondary migrants (Bennett and Nadeau 2002), free-movers without financial and social support from the refugee resettlement agencies that oversaw their initial placement in the United States.⁴

In the wake of Somali settlement, Lewiston drew the interested gaze of researchers, government officials, and the press. After the media frenzy stretching from the October release of the letter to the January rallies, Lewiston dropped almost completely from the national news. Over the ensuing years the unique demographic character of the city brought about by the Somali influx led to intermittent attention from the press (e.g., Fahrenthold 2006; Finnegan 2006; Jones 2004). Foremost in much of the attention to Somali settlement is the question of why Somalis would choose to settle in such a "white" community. The persistence of this preoccupation with why Somali immigrants would select Lewiston reveals

---

² Samatar (2004) documents that Somalis settling in the Minneapolis area appreciate the city for very similar characteristics.

³ Lewiston had no documented Somali population before that time.

⁴ Bloemraad (Bloemraad, Irene. 2006. *Becoming a citizen: Incorporating immigrants and refugees in the United States and Canada*. Berkeley: University of California Press) notes that, relative to dynamics of inclusion of typical immigrants, the incorporation of refugees is assisted by the material resources provided for refugee resettlement and adjustment services.

underlying assumptions about what a place like Lewiston is and where people like Somali immigrants belong. Such background expectations are the focus of this research.

LITTLE CANADA

Although it may be imagined by outsiders as a provincial, white, rural backwater, Lewiston, the political, economic, and cultural center of the Maine interior, has historically been considered an ethnic minority city (see Figure 1.1). With a 2000 population of approximately 37,000, the city was the second largest in the State – second in size only to Portland. Largely cleared of its prior Native American Androscoggin settlers and French trappers after the 1763 conclusion of the French and Indian War, the land that would become Lewiston was first settled by colonists in 1770. Beginning in the late 1830s, Lewiston and its sister city on the other side of the river, Auburn, underwent rapid growth and industrialization with the construction of five textile mills and a supporting series of canals and dams. The mills brought significant prosperity to the towns, particularly during the Civil War when previously amassed stockpiles of southern cotton allowed the mills to continue to produce textiles (Hodgkin 2008). Growing wealth in the area led to the founding of what would become Bates College as well as the establishment of a substantial downtown urban area characterized by grand buildings, prestigious houses, and a lively commercial district. The tides of fortune began to turn in Lewiston in the late 1950s when the city's Androscoggin Mill ceased operating. By the mid-1980s, all the mills had closed, leaving behind an economically devastated city, a declining population, and legions of former millworkers living with lower household incomes and higher rates of poverty than the state and national averages (U.S. Census Bureau 2003). Many of these out-of-work and underemployed individuals were descended from French Canadians who arrived to work at the mills shortly after their founding.

Initially staffed by "Yankee farm girls" (Hodgkin 2008), the mills moved on to employ Irish immigrants in the 1840s and, in the 1860s, turned to a larger workforce – French-speaking Quebecers and northern (Acadian) Mainers migrating to industrializing New England (Levine 2003; Parker 1983). Although later waves of Irish, Greek, and Italian immigrants came to Lewiston, the city's French-speaking population dwarfed these groups. It is estimated that the population of Lewiston was nearly 46 percent Franco by 1900 – an ethnic minority that that

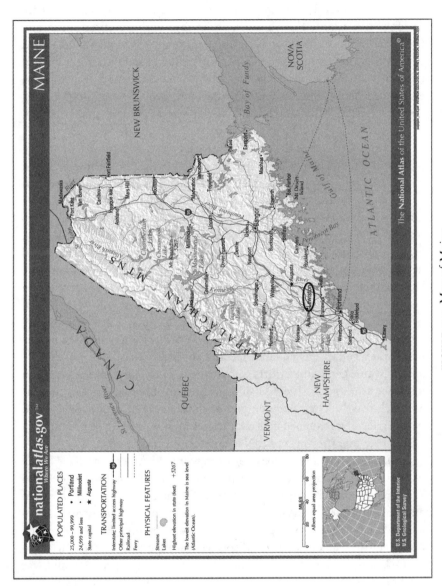

FIGURE 1.1 Map of Maine.

Source: http://nationalatlas.gov/printable/reference.html#Maine

soon became the majority. With more than 61 percent of the community French-Canadian in 1971, Lewiston had the largest per capita Franco-American population in the United States (Parker 1983). Thus, the small British and Scotch-Irish "settler" population came very quickly to share the city with a large French-speaking enclave with significant back and forth migration between Lewiston and their sending regions – Quebec and New Brunswick. French-Canadians also settled in significant numbers in other industrial cities in the northeastern United States and Franco laborers moved between settlements in Lewiston, Providence, Rhode Island, and Springfield, Worcester, Lowell, and Salem, Massachusetts, in pursuit of work (Belanger and Belanger 1999).

Throughout much of their Maine history, Franco-Americans occupied a persistent underclass position characterized by lower household incomes, low-skilled employment in agriculture and manufacturing, and depressed educational attainment in comparison with Yankee neighbors (Levine 2003; Parker 1983). Lewiston remained socially and linguistically seg-regated through the 1960s, 150 years after the initial Franco settlement. Francos and Yankees lived and conducted everyday affairs in segregated neighborhoods, separate churches, schools, and hospitals (Parker 1983). Despite their large numbers, Franco-Lewistonians primarily occupied an area known as Little Canada. Lewiston's French Canadians were dogged by a view that labeled the group as lazy, intellectually inferior, and more interested in the pursuit of pleasure than the acquisition of wealth and sta-tus (Parker 1983). French language and culture were ridiculed in the city and in Maine generally. Efforts were made to eliminate Franco-American influence from public life. Outside perception of the city of Lewiston as a French town elicited the prejudice of those in other locales. Believed to be a carrier of a maligned culture, the community held a poor reputation within the state (Levine 2003; Nadeau 2007; Parker 1983).

Many negative stereotypes regarding Franco-Americans have given way since the 1960s, and the sharp ethnic boundary that once governed social relations in the city no longer holds. French-Lewistonians have gen-erally acculturated to the mainstream, moved into many occupations, and acquired educational parity with other city residents; they have moved out of Little Canada and are dispersed throughout the area (Richard 2008). All the same, in 2000 Franco-American culture persisted and was celebrated in the city while the memory of past persecution lingered. In addition to Franco-American heritage celebrations and cultural festivals, French language still circulates. I spoke with many Lewiston residents over fifty years of age whose parents spoke French exclusively. Currently the majority of Franco-American residents of Lewiston speak English proficiently, but many are still most comfortable with French. In the year 2000, a full 25.5 percent of the population spoke French at home (U.S. Census Bureau 2000). The city's major Roman Catholic Church conducts mass in French, local doctors and dentists advertise their services with the plug "Ici, on parle francais," and one need only wait in line at the service counter at the local sites of the Canadian restaurant franchise, Tim Hortons, to learn that the French language continues to flourish in the city. The Lewiston Maineiacs, the popular local hockey team (housed in the Lewiston Colisée), the sole professional sports team in town and the only Quebec Major Junior Hockey League team in the United States, further cements ties to French Canada. In light of the persistence of a self-consciously minority Franco-American culture, language, and identity in the community, Lewiston is certainly outside the American white-ethnic mainstream.

The Whitest State

Lewiston's Franco-American identity places the town on the fringes when it comes to white ethnic identity. The same may be said of the area's racial diversity. As of the 2000 United States Census, Maine was the whitest state in the union. Ninety-seven percent of the state's population identified as white on the census. In 2000 Lewiston, was 96 percent white,[5] slightly less racially homogeneous than the state of Maine as a whole (U.S. Census Bureau 2008b). Table 1.1 presents data on the racial background of Lewiston residents between 1800 and 2007. Lewiston is a historically white community, more than 96 percent[6] white every year until 2005. Furthermore, the black population of Lewiston has generally been quite small, not exceeding 100 persons or 0.3 percent of the city's population each year before 1990 in which a census was taken.

By most accounts, Lewiston and the state of Maine lack a substantial African American population and black institutions. While it is true that Maine has no large and cohesive African American community, the account of African American involvement in Lewiston and the larger community is as long as the history of settlement. The early years of the twenty-first century witnessed a resurgence of interest in documenting

---

[5] Ninety-six percent of Lewiston residents reported being only white. When including individuals who report being white alone or in combination with other races, the figure rises to 97 percent.

[6] See note 5.

Table 1.1 *Race and Hispanic Origin for Lewiston, Maine: Earliest Census to 2007*

Year	Race					
	White		Black		American Indian, Eskimo, and Aleut	
	Number	Percent	Number	Percent	Number	Percent
2005–2007[a]	34 581	91.5	2947	7.8	3 242	8.5
2000[a]	34 726	97.3	561	1.6	351	1.0
1990	39027	98.2	267	0.7	92	0.2
1980	40046	98.9	131	0.3	44	0.1
1970	41601	99.6	63	0.2	26	0.1
1960	40756	99.9	25	0.1	9	–
1950	40927	99.9	28	0.1	4	–
1940	38564	99.9	8	–	4	–
1930	34893	99.8	25	0.1	1	–
1920	31714	99.8	54	0.2	–	–
1910	26190	99.8	47	0.2	–	–
1900	23705	99.8	47	0.2	–	–
1890	21653	99.8	40	0.2	2	–
1880	19031	99.7	52	0.3	–	–
1870	13581	99.9	19	0.1	–	–
1860	7424	100.0	–	–	–	–
1850	3583	100.0	1	–	(NA)	(NA)
1840	1801	100.0	–	–	(NA)	(NA)
1830	1549	100.0	–	–	(NA)	(NA)
1820	1312	100.0	–	–	(NA)	(NA)
1810	1033	100.0	–	–	(NA)	(NA)
1800	948	100.0	–	–	(NA)	(NA)

- Represents zero or rounds to 0.0 in data cells. In first column, represents greater than 100 for national rank and greater than 3 for state rank. (X) Not applicable. (NA) Not available.

[a] Race alone or in combination with one or more other races

Source: Adapted from U.S. Census Bureau, Historical Tables, Table 20. Maine – Race and Hispanic Origin for Selected Large Cities and Other Places: Earliest Census to 1990, Internet Release Date: July 13, 2005; U.S. Census Bureau, Census 2000 Summary File 1, Matrices P1, P3, P4, P8, P9, P12, P13, P,17, P18, P19, P20, P23, P27, P28, P33, PCT5, PCT8, PCT11, PCT15, H1, H3, H4, H5, H11, and H12; U.S. Census Bureau, 2005–2007 American Community Survey.

Asian and Pacific Islander		Other race		Hispanic origin (of any race)		White, not of Hispanic origin	
Number	Percent	Number	Percent	Number	Percent	Number	Percent
288	0.8	306	0.8	555	0.5	37252	98.5
416	1.2	130	0.4	448	1.3	35242	98.7
274	0.7	97	0.2	284	0.7	38831	97.7
133	0.3	127	0.3	239	0.6	39841	98.4
56	0.1	33	0.1	(NA)	(NA)	(NA)	(NA)
13	–	1	–	(NA)	(NA)	(NA)	(NA)
15	–	–	–	(NA)	(NA)	(NA)	(NA)
22	0.1	(X)	(X)	(NA)	(NA)	(NA)	(NA)
29	0.1	(X)	(X)	(NA)	(NA)	(NA)	(NA)
23	0.1	(X)	(X)	(NA)	(NA)	(NA)	(NA)
10	–	(X)	(X)	(NA)	(NA)	(NA)	(NA)
9	–	(X)	(X)	(NA)	(NA)	(NA)	(NA)
6	–	(X)	(X)	(NA)	(NA)	(NA)	(NA)
–	–	Black					
–	–	Total		Free		Slave	
–	–	–	(X)	–	(X)	–	(X)
(NA)	(NA)	1	100.0	1	100.0	–	(X)
(NA)	(NA)	–	(X)	–	(X)	–	(X)
(NA)	(NA)	–	(X)	–	(X)	–	(X)
(NA)	(NA)	–	(X)	–	(X)	–	(X)
(NA)	(NA)	–	(X)	–	(X)	–	(X)
(NA)	(NA)	–	(X)	–	(X)	–	(X)

"Maine's visible black history" (cf. Lee 2005; Price and Talbot 2006). The state's early African Americans came in first as free settlers and as slaves acquired primarily through the sea trade with the West Indies, and later as employees of the railroads and runaway slaves settling along the underground railroad (Lee 2005). Once in Maine, African Americans worked in an integrated labor force, worshipped in integrated churches, visited the same hospitals, and attended the same schools as other Mainers (Lumpkins 2006). Residing primarily in the major cities of Maine, African Americans largely escaped the ethnic violence and discrimination that arose intermittently in smaller towns and more rural areas and was typically directed at Native Americans, Irish Catholics, French Canadians, and Jews (Lumpkins 2006). This is not to suggest that black Mainers did not experience discrimination, but the exclusion and inequality were quiet and insidious – not written into the letter of the law, the structure of social institutions, or the nature of cultural discourse undergirding social membership.

It is often argued that a "one-drop rule" in which the presence of any African American heritage is sufficient to indicate blackness characterizes the black-white racial boundary in the United States (Omi and Winant 1986). In Maine, however, the remembrance of founding African American settlers who married whites demonstrates the atypical and fluid nature of racial identification. Some Lewiston and Maine residents who are not "visible" African Americans assert and celebrate their multiracial heritage as descendants of an African American settler (cf. Bragdon 2006; Talbot 2006). When I first arrived in Lewiston I would often find myself surprised by the assertions of Lewiston residents in their sixties and seventies who believed, as did one lifelong area resident in his sixties, that "just like it happened with the Greeks and the Irish," the Somalis would intermarry with other Lewiston residents and "in 20 or 30 years everyone will be so mixed up they won't know who is who."

With too few African Americans to constitute a segregated community, just as whites did not maintain segregated institutions, so, too, has the notion of traditionally black institutions failed to take root. For example, Maine currently has three chapters of the National Association for the Advancement of Colored People (NAACP) – one, the Maine State Prison chapter, has a white president and is currently a favorite of the national organization (Thompson 2009). When asked why he joined the NAACP, chapter president Billy Flynn "explains that it seems better than the Jaycees and the Longtimers, the only other organizations the prison allows" (Thompson 2009).

In addition to having a historical, albeit minuscule, African American population, a tradition of recognizing individual African American citizens as founding residents, and an uncharacteristically fluid notion of racial identity, in the last decades of the twentieth and first decades of the twenty-first centuries, Lewiston has been the home of one of the state's most influential black leaders, John Jenkins. Raised in a working-class family in Newark, New Jersey, Jenkins attended Lewiston's Bates College from 1970 to 1974 and returned to the community in 1980. He established a successful and influential business and, in 1993, was elected mayor – the first African American mayor of Lewiston and the second African American mayor in Maine history. In 1995 he was elected to the state senate as the first African American senator in Maine history. In 2010 Jenkins made an unsuccessful write-in bid in the gubernatorial race but vowed to continue his political involvement in the region.

The Local Context of Reception

Somalis settling in Lewiston did not encounter an ethno-cultural vacuum nor did they find themselves entering a context that was indistinguishable from nationwide political, economic, and social conditions. Lewiston offered a demographic landscape built upon a particular ethnic and racial history. As will be discussed in Chapter 2, the city's initial reaction to Somali settlement arose in the context of a city characterized by economic decline, a dearth of immigration since the 1920s, without strong racial boundaries, a lack of a visible and politically organized racial minority population, and the cultural and demographic centrality of a white ethnic group with an underclass status that declined only in the second half of the twentieth century. Correspondingly, just as the early context of reception in Lewiston was derived from the particular character of the city, so, too, did the Somalis bring a unique culture and background to Lewiston.

SOMALI DIASPORA OF THE UNITED STATES

With their self-identifications and settlement choices, Somali immigrants challenged typical categorical understanding of what it means to be an immigrant, a Muslim, and black. Somalis are black but not African American in the commonsense meaning of the term. They are Muslim but not Arab. They are immigrants but not Latinos. After a brief introduction of the cultural background Somalis carried to the United States and the conditions of Somali emigration from Somali, we will get a first glimpse of the ways Somali newcomers to the United States have, with their aggregate residential choices and mode of engaging the culture of the mainstream, actively charted a course for social inclusion.

Settling in increasing numbers since the late 1980s, immigration statistics suggest that by 2005 more than 100,000 Somalis resided in the United States (Department of Homeland Security 2009). At .005 percent of the foreign-born population of the United States in 2005 (U.S. Census Bureau 2000), Somali immigrants attracted little widespread attention in public debates and discussions of immigration. Yet, Somali immigrants have emigrated from a nation with continued foreign policy significance. This leads to the ongoing involvement of Somali Americans in the United States domestic anti-terror efforts.

The Horn of Africa

Located in Eastern Africa on the coast of the Indian Ocean, in 2005 the area known as the Horn of Africa was home to approximately 10 million Somalis (Central Intelligence Agency 2009) (Figure 1.2). Additional ethnic Somalis resided in the adjoining regions of Kenya, Ethiopia, and Djibouti. The majority of territory within the region is arid savanna. The people inhabiting the area traditionally lived as pastoral nomads, primarily herding camels, goats, sheep, and horses. In the southern part of the country, an arable region between the Juba and Shebelle rivers historically contained more sedentary farming communities as well as the ethnic and linguistic minority (Somali) Bantu population, brought to that area as slaves in the nineteenth century. The Juba valley was considerably depopulated as a result of violence and periodic droughts that began affecting the area in the 1980s (Lewis 2002; Menkhaus 2003).

Formed through the union of two colonies, British Somaliland and Italian Somalia, Somalia peaceably gained its independence from colonial powers in 1960. While the two former colonial possessions joined on the basis of shared language and culture, unification failed to include much territory that could be considered ethnically Somali, namely, the Ogaden and Haud regions of Ethiopia, the Northern Frontier districts of Kenya, and French Somaliland, now Djibouti. The nascent Somali government made the unification of all the Eastern African territories inhabited primarily by Somalis an early, unattained goal (Lewis 2002).

Somalis have generally considered themselves an ethno-national group (Kymlicka 2001). While regional differences in everyday language and

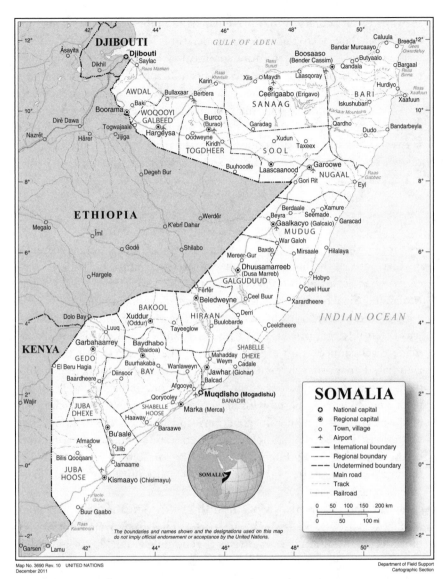

FIGURE 1.2 Somalia.
Source: United Nations; http://www.un.org/Depts/Cartographic/map/profile/soma-lia.pdf

culture can be found, the Somali people generally share the ability to speak standard Somali, a well-developed oral tradition, the practice of Islam, and a history of cultural contact with the Arab world (Lewis 2002). Somalis recognize their common ethnic and cultural heritage. However, they are also members of four principal clan families, each consisting of a number of clans. Clan and subclan associations have traditionally under-written Somali social organization, political association, and legal protec-tion and obligations (Lewis 2002). In both historical and contemporary practice, elders – esteemed older male members of the group – controlled day-to-day operation of the clan. Somalia's patrilineal clans have tended to be associated with particular regions of the country. This association between land and clan does not hold fast, particularly in more agrarian regions and urbanized areas (Bjork 2007; Kusow and Bjork 2007; Lewis 2002; Luling 2006).

People without a Nation

It is ironic that a nation formed on the basis of ethnic solidarity should devolve into both internecine and clan-based conflict but this is pre-cisely what occurred in Somalia upon the 1991 overthrow of President Mohamed Siad Barre. The dictator had ruled Somalia since a military coup placed power in his hands in 1969. The young Somali government was ostensibly free of clan-based loyalties, and, in fact, for a time Barre made discussion of clan affiliation illegal (Lewis 2002). All the same, clan-based coalitions characterized political representation and employ-ment throughout the history of the Somali nation. In the later years of his presidency, Barre dispensed with his desire to eradicate clan attachments and was instead drawn into coalitions and conflicts based upon clan affiliations (Lewis 2002). Somali refugees began to come to the attention of the United Nations High Commissioner for Refugees (UNHCR) in the mid-1980s as Barre waged war against many northern Somali clans (Menkhaus 2007).

By the time Barre fled Mogadishu in 1991, Somalia was in a state of chaos (Kusow 2004; Menkhaus 2003). The strength and social sig-nificance of traditional clan divisions rebounded quickly as individu-als sought to fill the gap left by the failure of the state (Lewis 2002). Warlords, to whom others gave allegiance based upon clan membership, began programs of clan-based ethnic cleansing in Mogadishu. The vio-lence quickly spread throughout the south, the region that had formerly been Italian Somalia (Menkhaus 2003).

In early 1992, Somalia first received international intervention in the form of United Nations Security Forces (UNISOM I). The United Nations (UN) peacekeepers were quickly overwhelmed. By December 1992 the United States and UN reached an agreement for the deployment of

25,000 American troops (Operation Restore Hope) as the lion's share of a unified force (UNITAF) (Central Intelligence Agency 2009). As depicted in the book and subsequent film "Black Hawk Down" (Bowden 1999; Scott 2001), these peace-keeping operations in Somalia foundered and cost the lives of eighteen American military personnel. The United States has been intimately involved with the country since that time. In 2006, George W. Bush's administration made the decision to topple an emerging functional government, the first evidence of stability and order in much of the country since the early 1980s. Led by the Islamic Courts Union (ICU), an organization with presumed ties to al-Qaeda, the new Somali government troubled the Bush administration who saw it as a threat to the United States' attempts to eliminate al-Qaeda and other terrorist networks (Reuters 2006). The White House consequently supported an Ethiopian invasion and occupation of Mogadishu (Mazzetti 2006). Ethiopian forces successfully removed the ICU and reestablished the United Nations-sponsored but ineffective transitional government in the Somali capital.

Ousted from Mogadishu, the ICU fractured and its most radical faction, Al-Shabab, rose to power (Perry 2009). In the wake of the U.S.-backed invasion, Al-Shabab openly claimed affiliation with Al-Qaeda. The group established control over much of the country, using draconian measures enforce their rule– banning bras, music and television; and using stoning, maiming, and other violent acts to punish rule infractions. The group also operated an active insurgency – staging suicide bombings and attacks on individuals and sites associated with the transitional government. In July 2010, Shabab extended its operations out of country with two coordinated suicide attacks during World Cup festivities in Uganda. Killing more than seventy individuals, Shabab claimed the attack was retribution for the presence of Ugandans among the African Union peace-keepers in Somalia and threatened further attacks on African nations involved in peacekeeping efforts (Kron and Ibrahim 2010). Attempting to thwart Al-Shabab, the African Union, United Nations, and United States incorporated less violent and more moderate Islamic groups, many of the same groups that made up the ousted Islamic Courts Union, into the transitional goverment. It was the hope that supporting these groups will lead to moderate rule and more humane treatment of the Somali people (Gettleman and Ibrahim 2010).

At the time of this writing, Somalia has experienced two years of relative stability. The Somali transitional government typically controlled no more than a few blocks of Mogadishu and was propped up by African

Union troops, American military support, and United Nations aid (Gettleman 2010a). Recently, the transitional government has enjoyed increased authority within Somalia. The United States officially recognized the government and the African Union has successfully ousted Al-Shabab from most cities. Some Somalis in the diaspora have begun to return to their home country (Gettleman 2012).

Although local rule by warlords and the tyrannical rule of religious extremists was the norm in southern Somalia for more than two decades, northern Somalia has been much more politically and economically stable (Gettleman 2007; Kristof 2007; Lewis 2002; Menkhaus 2003). In the former British colony of Somaliland, local clan-based leaders joined together to fill the void left by the disintegration of the national government. The region declared itself the independent nation of Somaliland in 1991, a few short months after Barre was deposed. Despite the fact that international support flowed primarily to the war-torn South, Somaliland developed a functioning government and services. In 2010 the breakaway nation held its fourth elections and successfully saw the second peaceful transfer of power in its brief history (Gettleman 2010b). After his election the new president vowed to seek international recognition for the emerging democratic nation (Agence France-Presse 2010).

The Somali northeast, a region known as Puntland, also remained free of much of the destruction and violence occurring in the south although the region had some troubles. Somali pirates operating out of Puntland became the focus of international anti-piracy efforts. Pirates grew increasingly aggressive in seizing ships in the Indian Ocean and the Gulf of Aden. Despite coordinated international attempts to maintain safe shipping routes, in 2009 Somali pirates attacked over 200 vessels, ultimately hijacking 47 and ransoming 12 (McDonald 2009). In 2008, a year with significantly fewer attacks, piracy brought about $100 million into the country (*New York Times* 2010). Piracy emerged as the economic lifeblood of Puntland – a well-organized economic and occupational juggernaut financed in part by a "stock market" in which individuals invested in the pirates' operations and received a dividend when ransom was paid (Kraska 2010). In addition to its dependence on the international scourge of piracy, in the end of the first decade of the twenty-first century, Puntland increasingly experienced violent clashes between various Islamic factions – some claiming loyalty to the Shabab and a desire to bring the rule of the Shabab to the region and other more moderate groups engaged in local power struggles (Gettleman and Ibrahim 2010; Ibrahim and Gettleman 2010).

Displaced People

In the 1990s Somalia emerged as its own national disaster and the wider world's international conundrum. After twenty years of international intervention, the country remained unstable, many of its people left impoverished and traumatized by a lifetime of deprivation and unpredictable violence (Gettleman 2010c). Difficult conditions within Somalia drove people from their homes and created a widely dispersed Somali diaspora.

The Office of the United Nations High Commissioner for Refugees estimates that, between 1991 and 2008, sectarian strife in Somali resulted in the death of 300,000 individuals as well as the displacement of over 1 million others. A decrease in violence in the late 1990s led nearly 500,000 Somalis to seek repatriation, primarily in the stable regions of the north. Increasing violence beginning in 2006 and escalating in the waning months of 2008 and into 2009 prompted a resurgence in Somali movement. In January 2009, nearly 1.3 million Somalis were displaced within Somalia as they fled to find safety in other regions and nearly 600,000 individuals sought refuge outside of Somalia (United Nations High Commissioner for Refugees 2009). Although living primarily in refugee camps in neighboring Kenya, this substantial and growing Somali diaspora was nonetheless dispersed over many nations.

Data limitations make it difficult to estimate the complete Somali population of the United States in the first decade of the twenty-first century. While approximately 35,000 Somalis were admitted into the country as refugees by the year 2005 and these refugees accounted for a significant portion of foreign-born Somali residents, this number dramatically underestimates the number of Somalis in the country. Other sources of Somali population include the nearly 400 additional Somalis admitted as permanent legal residents each year between 1991 and 2005 under classes of admission besides refugee (immediate relatives of U.S. citizens being a major contributor), a substantial diaspora of Somalis who arrived before 1991 (early political refugees and part of the African "brain drain" (Arthur 2000)), and the well-established Somali American second generation (the growing population of children born in the United States). Therefore, Somali American population estimates varied widely, with the figure of 100,000 serving as the conservative estimate offered by the Office of Immigration Statistics (Table 1.2).

During this period, Somalis in the United States appeared to participate in the labor force at slightly higher rates than the national average.

Table 1.2 *African and Somali Persons Obtaining Legal Permanent Resident Status: Fiscal Years 1950 to 2008*

Region and Country of Last Residence[a]	1950 to 1959	1960 to 1969	1970 to 1979	1980 to 1989	1990 to 1999	2000	2001
Total	2,499,268	3,213,749	4,248,203	6,244,379	9,775,398	841,002	1,058,902
Africa	13,016	23,780	71,408	141,990	346,416	40,790	50,009
Percentage of total African	1	1	2	2	4	5	5
Somalia	—	—	—	747	18,061	2,393	3,007
Percentage of total				1	5	6	6

Region and Country of Last Residence[a]	2002	2003	2004	2005	2006	2007	2008
Total	1,059,356	703,542	957,883	1,122,257	1,266,129	1,052,415	1,107,126
Africa	56,002	45,559	62,623	79,697	112,100	89,277	100,881
Percentage of total African	5	6	7	7	9	8	9
Somalia	4,535	2,444	3,929	5,829	9,462	6,251	10,745
Percentage of total	8	5	6	7	8	7	11

— represents zero or not available.
[a]Data refer to country of last residence.
Note: Immigrant aliens admitted for permanent residence.
Source: U.S. Department of Homeland Security.

In 2009, the unemployment rate among Somali legal permanent residents was 7 percent, compared to a rate of 9.7 percent for all immigrants and 8.6 percent for the native-born population (Camarota and Jensenius 2009; Department of Homeland Security 2009). On the ground in Lewiston, however, the employment situation of Somalis was not so rosy. According to Maine Department of Labor data, only 39.7 percent of Somali immigrants in Lewiston worked consistently for at least one year without interruption between 2001 and 2006 and only 50 percent worked at any time after their entry into the state's employment and social services (Rector 2008). Unfortunately, there are few data available on Somali American household income or occupational attainment.

While there is substantial ambiguity around population size, earnings, and education, Somali immigrants to the United States clearly demonstrated distinct settlement patterns, often residing in areas with little history of recent nonwhite immigration and where they made up a substantial proportion of the immigrant community. Waters and Jimenez (2005) note that contemporary immigration is characterized by movement to "new immigrant gateways" as immigrants settle in cities and small towns with little prior immigration experience. In this manner, Somalis in the United States passed over traditional urban areas and immigration centers, choosing instead states such as Minnesota, Ohio, Washington, Tennessee, and Maine – places not commonly associated with immigration. Table 1.3 presents data on the states of residence of legal permanent residents of the United States in 2008. In 2008, more than half of newcomers to the United States settled in just four states – California, New York, Florida, and Texas. Somali immigrant settlement is concentrated primarily in Minnesota, Ohio, and Washington State. Six of the top ten states of Somali settlement are not primary settlement sites for the majority of other legal permanent residents.

With the exceptions of Columbus, Ohio; Clarkston, Georgia; and Minneapolis,[7] in 2008 Somali residents tended to live outside major urban areas. In locations such as Lewiston, Maine, recent Somali arrivals resided in communities where there are no other immigrant groups to speak of. Table 1.4 depicts the proportion of Somali immigrants in Lewiston and the largest centers of Somali residence, Minneapolis and Columbus, compared with the total population of legal permanent residents. In Minneapolis, Somali immigrants are the largest of many

---

[7] The metropolitan statistical area of Minneapolis includes many suburban and exurban areas home to Somali settlement.

Table 1.3 *Most Popular States of Residence, Persons Obtaining Legal Permanent Resident Status by Region or Country of Birth: Fiscal Year 2008*

All Legal Permanent Residents		African		Somali	
Rank / State	Total Pop	Rank / State	Total Pop	Rank /State	Total Pop
1/ California	238,444	3/ California	7,7834	4/ California	498
2/ New York	143,6791	1/New York	11,020	—	—
3/ Florida	133,445	—	—	—	-
4/ Texas	89,811	5/ Texas	7,458	8/ Texas	339
5/ New Jersey	53,997	9/ New Jersey	5,144	—	—
6/ Illinois	42,723	—	—	—	—
7/ Massachusetts	30,369	6/ Massachusetts	5,543	10/ Massachusetts	256
8/ Virginia	30,257	7/ Virginia	5,5361	—	—
9/ Georgia	27,769	8/ Georgia	5,248	9/ Georgia	257
10/ Maryland	27,062	2/ Maryland	8,406	—	—
		4/ Minnesota	7,659	1/ Minnesota	3,372
		10/ Ohio	4,302	2/Ohio	1,303
				3/ Washington	782
				5/ Tennessee	470
				6/ Arizona	378
				7/ Maine	346

— represents zero or not available.
Source: Adapted from U.S. Department of Homeland Security Yearbook of Immigration Statistics 2008.

Table 1.4 *Somali Immigrants as a Proportion of All Legal Permanent Residents in Minneapolis, MN; Columbus, OH, and Lewiston, ME; Fiscal Year 2008*

Minneapolis			Columbus			Lewiston		
Total	13,372	Percent	Total	5,401	Percent	Total	395	Percent
Somalia	2,565	19	Somalia	1,279	24	Somalia	194	49
Ethiopia	1,096	8	Ghana	368	7	Kenya	125	32
Liberia	1,006	8	India	313	6	China	13	3
Thailand	627	5	Kenya	284	5	Ethiopia	11	3
Mexico	570	4	China	246	5	Philippines	6	2
India	545	4	Ethiopia	243	4	Ghana	5	1
Vietnam	519	4	Mexico	134	2	Iraq	5	1
Kenya	517	4	Mauritania	108	2	Albania	4	1
China	508	4	Liberia	105	2	Canada	3	1
Laos	500	4	Nigeria	89	2	Jamaica	3	1
Nigeria	256	2	Sierra Leon	82	2			
Philippines	234	2	Pakistan	76	1			
Korea	206	2	Russia	74	1			
Russia	200	1	Canada	71	1			
Guatemala	172	1	Korea	70	1			
Cambodia	167	1	Morocco	62	1			
Burma	165	1	United Kingdom	61	1			
Cameroon	156	1	Philippines	60	1			
Canada	147	1	Jordan	54	1			
Pakistan	131	1	Vietnam	54	1			

Source: Office of Immigration Statistics, U.S. Department of Homeland Security.

groups of immigrants in a substantial city, comprising 19 percent of the population of legal permanent residents in the area. Somalis make up an even larger share of the immigrant population in Columbus – nearly 30 percent of the immigrant population when including those born in Kenya, a group largely consisting of ethnic Somalis born inside Kenyan refugee camps. In many smaller towns home to sizable Somali populations, there are few other immigrant groups. In Lewiston, Maine, 81 percent of legal permanent residents in 2008 were Somali or Kenyan born.

In their settlement patterns, Somalis in the United States have demonstrated a general desire to maintain their distinctiveness and establish self-sufficiency. The nature of Somali immigrant incorporation is bound to be influenced by the decision to reside in smaller communities where being an immigrant means being Somali (Waters and Jimenez 2005). As will become apparent, the decision to settle in Lewiston provides Somalis the opportunity to construct a Somali enclave, develop a distinct group identity, and nurture responsive relationships with political structures and bureaucratic organizations in the city.

Settlement in new destinations has significant impact on political and economic incorporation and the construction of the immigrant-American identity. In comparing immigrants from identical sending countries who settle in major cities with those settling in small towns and rural areas, Hein (2006) concludes that those living outside major urban centers are more likely to acquire citizenship and to view citizenship as an element of becoming American. Alternatively, urban immigrants seek naturalization less frequently. When they do pursue citizenship, they tend to offer more pragmatic reasons for the decision: for example, in order to acquire a United States passport so they can more easily travel internationally. Leitner (2004) observes that Somalis in rural Minnesota who plan to acquire citizenship reference both the ease of international travel and the opportunity to run for local political office as motivating factors while others plan to return to Somalia as soon as possible and do not intend to become U.S. citizens. In her research on Latino immigrants settling in the rural South, Marrow (2011) observes that such settlement eases economic integration of newcomers because of the lower socioeconomic status (SES) of the general population, results in more rigid social boundaries between racial and ethnic groups, and hinders political integration because of the lack of political representation of newcomers. Waters and Jimenez (2005) suggest several other ways in which new immigrant destinations might impact the immigrant experience including more freedom for immigrants to define their place in the social structure, un- and under-developed immigration services, and less social isolation from other groups.

Transnational Ties

In the contemporary United States, many Somali Americans hope to return to Somalia once stability is restored to that country. There is evidence that the desire to return is greater among Somalis than among some other refugee and immigrant groups (Samatar 2004). Somali Americans often remain involved in far-flung conflict in Somalia through continued contact with political and clan entities and through sending remittances to family and communities. Remittances were estimated at $US790 million in the year 2006 alone (International Fund for Agricultural Development 2007).

There are even those who return to present-day Somalia with the hope that expertise and resources they have acquired in the United States will make a difference in the destitute country. A Somali American, Mohamed Abdullahi Mohamed, was offered the post of prime minister and returned to Somalia for the first time in twenty-five years to accept it (Ibrahim 2010). Managing the transitional government, Mohamed joined president Sheik Sharif Sheik Ahmed, a former high school teacher who led the Islamic Courts Union to power and oversaw the brief period of stability that ended with the U.S.-backed invasion. Mohamed held the post for one year and was then forced to resign due to political infighting. Mohamed was not the only Somali American to return to help the ailing Somalia. Mohamed Aden, an individual in his mid-thirties, moved with his wife and children from the Minneapolis suburbs to the drought-stricken village of Adado. Aden intended to stay just long enough to help during the drought and ended up being appointed village president by the local elders. At the time of this writing he remains in Adado, presiding over a relatively peaceful community but also fending off violent attacks by Islamist militias seeking to take control of the area (Gettleman 2009; Gettleman and Ibrahim 2010).

Somali American involvement in conflicts in the Horn of Africa has also taken a more insidious form. Increasing evidence of al-Shabab recruitment among Somalis living in the United States further highlights the ongoing transnational ties of Somali Americans. In February 2009, Federal Bureau of Investigation (FBI) director Robert Mueller announced that more than twenty young Somali American men who vanished from their Minneapolis homes between 2007 and 2009 had been recruited by al-Shabab for terrorist training and to fight in Somalia. One of those men, U.S. citizen Shirwa Ahmed, killed thirty people in a suicide bombing in Somalia in 2008 (Johnston 2009). According to sources close to the recruits, six others had died in Somalia as of 2011, although the United States identified only the remains of Ahmed and one other Minneapolis recruit (Elliott 2009c). In an ongoing investigation, the FBI charged four-teen Somali Americans with providing aid to terrorists through their U.S.-based recruitment for Al Shabab (Elliott 2009b). The men were detained shortly after their return from Somalia (Elliott 2009a). The charges are part of an ongoing inquiry into the recruitment of Somalis in the United States by Islamic extremists and into the whereabouts of American Somalis recruited by Al-Shabab. At the time of this writing, all evidence indicates that Somali Americans are recruited to fight in Somalia, not the United States. However, the presence of terrorist-trained U.S. residents and citizens is considered a national security threat (Elliott 2010).[8]

Challenging Perceptions, Being Imperceptible

Despite the ongoing security and strategic implications of developments in Somalia, the active position of Somali Americans in domestic and inter-national anti-terrorism efforts, and the fact that Somalis generally prac-tice Islam, a religion whose adherents are currently held in low esteem among the American public at large (Goodstein 2010), Somalis in the United States receive little attention in public discussions of immigration, race, and Islam, and outside of a small circle of Somali studies scholars, little is known in Lewiston or elsewhere of the challenges faced by Somali immigrants seeking to make a life in the United States.[9] For example, the

[8] In November 2010, the Federal Bureau of Investigation arrested a young Somali American suspected of plotting to detonate a bomb during a holiday tree lighting in Portland, Oregon. Although the suspect sought contact with Islamic extremists in planning his attack, he was not recruited or trained within Somalia and is not tied to Somali terrorist organizations (McKinley, Jesse and William Yardley. 2010. "Suspect in Oregon Bomb Plot Is Called Confused," *New York Times,* November 29, 2010, p. A17).
[9] The best documentation of the experience of Somali residents of Lewiston, told primarily in the voices of those residents themselves, is *Somalis in Maine* (Huisman, Kimberlly A., Mazie Hough, Kristin M. Langellier, and Carol Nordstrom Toner. 2011. *Somalis in Maine: Crossing cultural currents.* Berkeley, CA: North Atlantic Books), an edited volume that combines the autobiographical accounts of Somali residents of Lewiston with more aca-demic and policy-oriented considerations of Somali leadership, the service needs of Somalis, and the process of establishing a collaborative Somali Narrative Project. For more general reading, the most comprehensive consideration of the Somali diaspora is found in Kusow, Abdi and Stephanie R. Bjork. 2007a. *From Mogadishu to Dixon: The Somali diaspora in*

previously described FBI investigation into terrorist recruitment among Somalis in the United States constituted the largest domestic terrorist investigation since the terrorist attacks on the United States on September 11, 2001. Yet the topic escaped all but perfunctory media coverage.[10]

a global context. Trenton, NJ: Red Sea Press. See also Ajrouch, Kristine J. and Abdi M. Kusow. 2007. "Racial and Religious Contexts: Situational Identities among Lebanese and Somali Muslim Immigrants." *Ethnic and Racial Studies* 30:72–94; Berns-McGown, Rima. 1999. *Muslims in the diaspora: The Somali communities of London and Toronto.* Toronto: University of Toronto Press; Collet, Bruce Anthony. 2006. "Migration, education, and perceptions of a national identity among Somali immigrants in Ontario, Canada." Ph.D. Thesis, Loyola University, Chicago, IL; Farah, Nuruddin. 2000. *Yesterday, tomorrow: Voices from the Somali diaspora.* New York: Cassell; Ford, Richard. 2004. "Somali Pastoralists in Lewiston, Maine: Searching with Participatory Tools for a New Life." Pp. 59–77 in *Somalia: Diaspora and state reconstitution in the Horn of Africa,* edited by A. O. Farah, M. Muchie, and J. Gundel. London: Adonis & Abbey; Hopkins, Gail. 2006. "Somali Community Organization in London and Toronto: Collaboration and Effectiveness." *Journal of Refugee Studies* 19:361–380; Kusow, Abdi M. 2004. "From Mogadishu to Dixon: Conceptualising the Somali Diaspora." Pp. 34–42 in *Somalia: Diaspora and state reconstitution in the Horn of Africa,* edited by A. O. Farah, M. Muchie, and J. Gundel. London: Adonis & Abbey; Kusow, Abdi M. 2006. "Migration and Racial Formations among Somali Immigrants in North America." *Journal of Ethnic and Migration Studies* 32 (3): 533–551; Leitner, Helga. 2004. "Local Lives, Transnational Ties, and the Meaning of Citizenship: Somali Histories and Herstories from Small Town America." *Bilhaan: An International Journal of Somali Studies* 4: 44–64; Lindkvist, Heather L. 2008. "The Reach and Limits of Cultural Accommodations: Public Schools and Somali Muslim Immigrants." In *Just schools: Pursuing equality in societies of difference,* edited by M. Minow, R. A. Shweder, and H. Markus. New York: Russell Sage Foundation; Luling, Virginia. 2006. "Genealogy as Theory, Genealogy as Tool: Aspects of Somali 'Clanship.'" *Social Identities* 12:471–485; Rector, Amanda K. 2008. "An Analysis of the Employment Patterns of Somali Immigrants to Lewiston from 2001 through 2006." Augusta: Maine Department of Labor and Maine State Planning Office; Roble, Abdi and Douglas F. Rutledge. 2008. *The Somali diaspora: A journey away.* Minneapolis: University of Minnesota Press; Samatar, Ahmed I. 2004. "Beginning Again: From Refugee to Citizen." *Bildhaan: An International Journey of Somali Studies* 4:1–17; Shepard, Raynel Mary. 2005. "Acting is not becoming: Cultural adaptation among Somali refugee youth." Ed.D. Thesis, Harvard University, Cambridge, MA; Shepard, Raynel Mary. 2008. *Cultural adaptation of Somali refugee youth,* edited by S. J. Gold and R. G. Rumbaut. New York: LFB Scholarly Publishing; Shio, Thadeus Joseph. 2006. "Housing experiences of Somali immigrants in the Twin Cities, Minnesota: A housing careers perspective." Ph.D. Thesis, University of Minnesota, Minneapolis. For information on African refugees including Somalis see Mott, Tamar. 2009. *African refugee resettlement in the United States.* El Paso: LFB Scholarly Publishing.

[10] Huisman et al. (Huisman, Kimberlly A., Mazie Hough, Kristin M. Langellier, and Carol Nordstrom Toner. 2011. *Somalis in Maine: Crossing cultural currents.* Berkeley, CA: North Atlantic Books) do not appear to share my opinion that Somali immigrants remain largely untouched by media and public scrutiny and condemnation. They claim that, despite their limited numbers, Somalis have experienced significant negative press in and out of Lewiston. I believe that their evaluation is skewed by their own research interests in Somalis and their location in Maine where Somalis are a large immigrant group representing a significant portion of the visible diversity.

Public inattention to Somali immigrants derives in part from the challenge that the group poses to the cultural meanings of immigrants, Muslims, and people of African descent in the contemporary United States. In terms of deep-seated American cultural categories underwriting conceptions of social membership and civil inclusion, Somalis defy classification. While Somalis are overwhelmingly Muslim, a group that is increasingly stereotyped as uncivil, un-American, and undemocratic (Goodstein 2010; Gottschalk and Greenberg 2008), their darker complexion and East African origin set them outside of stereotypes about Muslim immigrants as originating in the Middle East.[11] Although African with dark complexions, Somalis' newcomer status casts them outside of commonplace understandings of African Americans that draw upon the legacy of slavery, Jim Crow segregation, and the civil rights movement. Furthermore, Somali arrival from Africa sets the group apart from more visible African diasporic immigrant communities from the Caribbean and Latin America who, like African Americans, are tied to the history of slavery in the new world. As immigrants, Somali Americans may claim their place in this "country of immigrants" and their claims generally escape challenge by blistering anti-immigrant rhetoric focusing upon Mexicans and other Latinos who are more likely to be undocumented and constitute a much larger and linguistically cohesive bloc of newcomers.

As new immigrants choosing Lewiston, Somali newcomers did not seek to be assimilated into conservative national identity and a priori racial categories. Instead, creative dynamics of identification, incorporation, and distinction characterize Somalis who live in the intersections of national, religious, racial, and historical (colonial and clan) identities. As I will show, Somalis exercised significant impact on the meaning of relevant subgroups – contesting the culture, color, and geography associated with immigrant status, African American-ness, and Islam. Somali immigrants

---

[11] Public aversion to Islam depends so heavily upon erroneous racial and regional stereotypes that, during a 2010 diplomatic trip to India, President Obama canceled a visit to a Sikh Temple. In order to enter the Temple, he would have been required to wear a turban. In the United States, Sikh turbans are often mistaken for Muslim garb and the Obama administration chose not to further fuel insidious claims that he is Muslim by providing an image that, in the eyes of many, would confirm that claim (Polgreen, Lydia. 2010. "A Question of Appearances: Obama Will Bypass Sikh Temple on Visit to India." *New York Times*, October 20, 2010, p. A6). Most books and media coverage of Muslim immigrants focus on Arabs (e.g., Abdo, Geneive. 2006. *Mecca and Main Street: Muslim life in America after 9/11*. New York: Oxford University Press; Emmerson, Nick, Jennifer O'Connell, and Dan Peirson, producers. 2011. *All-American Muslim*. Film. Distributed by Discovery Communications.)

in Lewiston developed and adopted a Muslim-Somali-American identity founded upon core American values of hard work, faith, family orientation, and economic self-sufficiency. However, that identity was also sensitive to a mandatory group-ness and the requirement that the Somalis' American-ness emphasize a benign and easily assimilable Somali-ness, and its linguistic, cultural, and religious particulars as quintessential distinctiveness and diversity.

THE CULTURAL PRAGMATICS OF INCORPORATION

The unique history and prior cultural heterogeneity in Lewiston, while not conforming to expectations regarding the landscape of American immigration history and race relations, provided the context of Raymond's chilly reception of Somali newcomers. The Somalis' unique characteristics prompted their decision to move to Lewiston and caused them to "slip through the cracks" of typical classifications as Muslim and African American. These unmet background expectations, much like the assumption that people like Somalis do not belong in places like Lewiston, hint at the existence of structures of meaning that were exogenous to Lewiston and Somali Americans – a widely shared web of meanings, categories of perception, moral distinctions, and manners of speech pertaining to nation, immigration, race, Islam, and small-town America. Research into Somali immigrant settlement in Lewiston exposes the interactions between this cultural system and the local, particular characteristics of Lewiston and Somalis.

Somali immigrant incorporation in Lewiston was achieved through the establishment of a social solidarity in which immigrants were considered members of society, as defined by its constituents. I observed three cultural mechanisms by which the process of immigrant incorporation was achieved:

1. Symbolic Boundaries: Widely shared narratives established the boundaries of society (Alexander 2003; Alexander 2006; Alexander 2010). These boundaries were drawn by characterizing the "we" of that community vis-à-vis others who did not belong. Immigrant incorporation in Lewiston was based on the characterization of Somalis as possessing socially desirable and morally correct attributes while characterizing those who objected to Somalis as being unacceptable, morally and socially problematic.

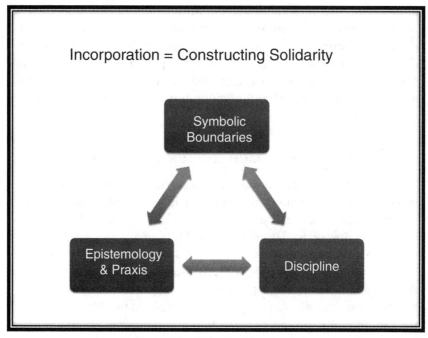

FIGURE 1.3 The Culture of Incorporation.

2. Epistemology and Praxis: Symbolic boundaries of belonging were reified in a particular theory of intercultural relations and a corresponding praxis.[12] Epistemology operated as a theory that made sense of the merits of diversity and identified the root causes and remedies for diversity troubles. Practices were identifiable orientations and behaviors seen as organically and irrevocably associated with predominant narratives and the fundamental values they evoked. In Lewiston, epistemology and praxis guided the speech and actions of Somali and non-Somali individuals, the development

[12] My analysis of the role of epistemology and praxis in Somali immigrant incorporation holds much in common with readings of Barthes (e.g., Billig, Michael. 1991. *Ideology and opinions: Studies in rhetorical psychology*. Newbury Park, CA: Sage; Billig, Michael. 1995. *Banal nationalism*. Thousand Oaks, CA: Sage; Ricoeur, Paul and George H. Taylor. 1986. *Lectures on ideology and utopia*. New York: Columbia University Press) that parlay his understanding of modern myth into conceptions of ideology as constructed and naturalized "habits of behavior and belief" (Billig, *Banal nationalism*, p. 37). However, the concepts of epistemology and praxis are better suited to my interest in considering beliefs and behaviors as separate but interrelated facets of meaning-making.

of municipal policies, and the construction of diversity education programs for nonimmigrants.

3. Discipline: Disciplinary procedures (Foucault 1972, 1977) maintained the terms of social solidarity, epistemological orthodoxy, and the hegemony of legitimated praxis. Immigrants and others were disciplined through the receipt of implicit and explicit instruction in the vocabulary, outlook, and style of communication associated with moral worth in an inclusive community. These reifications operated as seemingly imposed and exterior forces on the public construction of selves, identity groups, and communities (Kymlicka 2007; Voyer 2011a).

These mechanisms of incorporation are laid out in the pages that follow (see Figure 1.3). Although observed in the particular case of Somali settlement in Lewiston, the consistency between my observations in Lewiston and the epistemology, praxis, and discipline operating in extra-local diversity train-the-trainer programs suggests that the cultural pragmatics of immigrant incorporation is a process observable in other settings in which the ideals of the multicultural inclusion of newcomers are widely endorsed in public talk, political debate, and policy formation.[13]

Somali incorporation occurred through application of the values underlying social inclusion, the establishment of legitimate performances, and the ongoing negotiation of meaning. Officials attempting to restore the good name of the city and meet the needs of its constituents, non-Somali community members seeking to show genuine welcome, Somali newcomers constructing public notions of Somali American-ness, and even individuals hoping to express their hostility to the changing face of Lewiston could not understand or demonstrate their positions and intentions de novo. They all accounted for the space between the particularity of their own experiences and perspectives and the generally meaningful – the infinite detail of everyday life and the black and white simplicity of that which can and cannot be expressed.

---

[13] In later research, I have observed a similar mechanismsa underlying the process of immigrant incorporation in Sweden (Voyer, Andrea. 2013."Notes on a Cultural Sociology of Immigrant Incorporation." *American Journal of Cultural Sociology* 1:26–41).

2

The Meaning of Somali Settlement and the Boundaries of Belonging

COMMUNITY IN CRISIS

The initial cultural context of reception of Somalis was visible in early public responses to Somali settlement. Emerging narratives included a range of perspectives – from those who decried all immigration to those who championed Somali settlement as the key to a prosperous future for Lewiston. Most characteristic of early official responses to Somali immigration, however, was the perspective that Somali settlement was a burden for the city, that the flow of newcomers was out of control, and that Somalis lacked the self-discipline required if Lewiston was to be successful. This was the understanding presented in Raymond's letter:

I have applauded the efforts of our city staff in making available the existing services and the local citizenry for accepting and dealing with the influx.

I assumed that it would become obvious to the new arrivals the effect the large numbers of new residents has had upon the existing staff and city finances and that this would bring about a voluntary reduction of the number of new arrivals – it being evident that the burden has been, for the most part, cheerfully accepted, and every effort has been made to accommodate it....

This large number of new arrivals cannot continue without negative results for all. The Somali community must exercise some discipline and reduce the stress on our limited finances and our generosity. (Raymond 2002)

Far from entering the scene as a shocking challenge to local understandings of Somali settlement, Raymond's letter was consistent with other early

Author's note: I would like to thank Jaworsky for introducing me to this term (Jaworsky, B. Nadya. 2013. "Immigrants, Aliens and Americans: Mapping Out the Boundaries of Belonging in a New Immigrant Gateway," *American Journal of Cultural Sociology* 1: 221–253.)

assessments of Somali settlement. Somalis were widely believed to be a drain on the city's coffers and a challenge to historical conceptions that ethnic and linguistic minorities receive limited cultural accommodations. In establishing a distinction between local citizenry and Somali newcomers, public talk emphasized the importance of hard work, self-discipline, and a commitment to community demonstrated by tenure in the area. Despite the regular assertions that there was nothing personal, racial, or religious about seeing Somali settlement as a problem, anti-Somali hostility was increasingly observed by city and social services officials, local law enforcement, and members of the public who took the time to read the opinion pages in the local daily newspaper, the *Lewiston Sun Journal*.

In April 2002, *The Portland Press Herald* published an article about what the author referred to as "Lewiston's Somali surge." The article discussed Lewiston's Somalis and their progress toward settling in the community. Somali newcomers had already opened three halal markets and a mosque in the city. At that time, Somali city residents had recently staged a culture night for the public in the interest of fostering goodwill with other locals. The article also mentioned tensions surfacing in the community. Some Lewiston residents believed Somalis were receiving more than their fair share of social services while others in the community who were struggling economically went without. Some Lewiston residents reacted with hostility to the use of public money for translation services and other cultural accommodations for Somali immigrants. Lewiston's Mayor Raymond expressed what he believed to be public feeling on the issue:

"There is an undercurrent of resentment of people who are coming," said Mayor Laurier Raymond. "I don't think it's racial. I don't think it's religious. I think its dollars and cents. I think the citizenry is genuinely concerned about the impact on their taxes. We probably should be flattered they've picked Lewiston. Unfortunately, many of them don't come with any money and they don't have jobs, and there is some resentment of that." (Bouchard 2002b, p. 1A)

In understanding Somali settlement as a burden for the city of Lewiston, Raymond made sense of Somali settlement and its relationship to community membership and moral behavior. Somalis, Raymond claimed, were a financial burden for the citizens of the city. Raymond's decision to refer to taxpayers as citizens, while inaccurate, reflected a meaningful distinction many Lewiston residents perceived between themselves and Somalis. In this view, legitimate Lewistonians demonstrated their commitment and contributions to the community through tenure and personal responsibility. The very well-being of this community was endangered by (Somali) newcomers who failed to demonstrate their personal responsibility by requiring services and accommodations out of proportion to the city's means, practical necessity, and the Somalis' perceived right to limited resources. This moral distinction between citizens and residents circulated in much of the public discussion of Somali settlement in Lewiston.

On May 3, 2002, five months before Mayor Raymond distributed his letter, community leadership took steps to diffuse increasing tensions in Lewiston. Working closely with a variety of stakeholders, including the department of education, local hospital administrators, and welfare and immigrant service providers, the city organized an open-format town hall meeting in which Lewiston residents could come to learn about Somali migration to the community and the steps the city was taking in adjusting to population changes. Organizers publicly touted the meeting as a chance for people to pose questions to a panel of experts when it came to Somali settlement. The panel included Somali residents of Lewiston, immigration and refugee service providers and policy analysts, and city officials. The meeting organizers hoped that the forum would diffuse tensions and quell persistent rumors about the Somalis. Among stories in wide circulation were those that the Somalis were known to keep livestock in their apartments and roast goats in their bathtubs, that Somali students at the school washed their feet in the water fountain, and that Somalis received priority in the provision of welfare and access to subsidized housing.

Approximately 500 individuals attended Lewiston's town hall meeting, an exceedingly large turnout for an event of this sort. In the estimation of those with whom I spoke and as indicated by exit interviews conducted by the city of Lewiston, the meeting was a failure (Nadeau 2011). Attendees expressed little interest in hearing the details of U.S. refugee resettlement or asking questions about Somali culture. Instead, people wanted to know why their community had suddenly changed so dramatically. Why, attendees asked, were they surrounded by so many neighbors who did not speak the same language that they did and who dressed and behaved so differently? When were the problems in Somalia going to be resolved so that the Somalis in Lewiston could go home?

A refugee services case manager I interviewed shed tears as she described the polarizing effect of the town hall meeting. According to her account and corroborating statements made by others, prior to that night tensions and hostility in Lewiston had remained largely latent, an uncomfortable undercurrent that found occasional expression in outlandish rumors and snide comments. After the meeting, however, she reported, "folks just walked away feeling right. They said, 'See. These Somalis are costing us a lot of money and the people in Washington are just going to let them keep coming until we have nothing left.'" Furthermore, while those predisposed to understand Somali settlement in Lewiston as a problem held their views with greater conviction, Somalis in attendance and on the panel carried dismal reports of the event back to other Lewiston Somalis. "Before I would sometimes talk with my Somali friends about a particular person that said something wrong to them and we would talk about how that was a bad person," the case manager reported. "After that meeting, my Somali friends were like, 'Everyone in Lewiston is like that. You're the only one who doesn't hate that we are here.'"

Instead of easing community tensions and dispelling rumors, the May town meeting contributed to an air of crisis – increasing hostility and tension in the city, greater attention from regional and local media, and the immediate formation by Maine governor Angus King of the Governor's Immigrant/Refugee Task Force charged with developing statewide policies for the management of problematic situations like the one in Lewiston (Nadeau 2003b).[1] In October 2002, Mayor Raymond claimed his letter was a necessary response to the crisis of the Somali influx that he believed was draining Lewiston's coffers and testing the goodwill of the city. In other words, the letter expressed the same meaning of Somali settlement as the public outcry heard in May.

LIFE AS USUAL

Despite initial preoccupation with Somali migration to Lewiston as a social problem, by the time I arrived in the town in the summer of 2003, talk of crises in Lewiston no longer referred to Somali settlement, which continued unabated. Instead it referenced the period between the publication of the letter and the Many and One and WCOTC rallies, a period in which most Lewiston residents believed that the city was beset by frenzied forces from outside – the glare of the media spotlight, the intervention of racists and anti-racists, and judgment at the hands of those who did not know or understand the community. In the aftermath of the uproar and despite the ongoing arrival of Somali newcomers, many Lewiston residents, both Somali and non-Somali, expressed a keen interest in returning to normalcy. A participant in a series of community conversations

[1] The task force had not made any public progress on their charges before Mayor Raymond published his letter.

conducted in the spring of 2003 reported, "the truth is that most people are going on with their lives as usual" (Nadeau 2003a, p. 12).

In many ways the rhythm of life that emerged in Lewiston represented a new normal. Open expressions of hostility to the Somali presence and discussion of the costs of Somali settlement virtually disappeared. As Ahmed, a Somali employee of the city remarked in 2005, "Here in Lewiston it is much better than before. The negative voices are declining. Everyone knows that the Somali people are here to stay and that they are part of the community." Discussion of Mayor Raymond's letter and the growing Somali immigrant community persisted in muted form as academics and advocacy groups replaced journalists. City leaders fielded frequent requests for interviews with researchers, like myself, interested in immigration and diversity, the future of Lewiston, Somali cultural adaptations, and the relationship between community diversity and social capital (e.g., Braverman 2002; Lindkvist 2008; Putnam 2007). Human and civil rights groups, community organizing and immigration specialists, and consultants specializing in improving services in health care, law enforcement, employment, and education contacted the city to offer their expertise or to inquire into the city's current practices. Through their exposure to continued scrutiny from the outside, people in Lewiston understood, oftentimes begrudgingly, that the noteworthy nature of the city's demographic mix and recent history would continue to keep the community in the view of the larger public.

How did Somali settlement, which had been considered a crisis, become a noteworthy but unproblematic characteristic of Lewiston? The changed meaning of community and belonging in relation to Somali settlement is visible in common narratives woven through the accounts I collected in my field research. This chapter considers these cultural narratives that enabled the shift from the view that the Somalis endangered the well-being of the community to the perspective that the Somali presence in Lewiston was an element of life "as usual." I identify three diversity-affirming narratives that celebrate Somali contributions to the city on the basis of the economic prosperity, cultural richness, and global stature accompanying immigrant settlement. I also identify four different narratives employed in explanations of diversity troubles, the challenges of immigrant incorporation, and the causes of community tension and turmoil related to the Somali presence in Lewiston. The predominant narrative of diversity troubles cited inexperience as the primary challenge to the community. Additional narratives of resource limitations, exploitation, and racism attributed trouble to porous community boundaries that allowed interlopers, gain-seekers, and racists to exploit Lewiston.

These thoroughly localized narratives were built upon established and conflicting "modes of incorporation" (Alexander 2001) and within a national cultural context that had already assigned potential meanings to diversity and imagined the possible outcomes of immigrant incorporation. According to Alexander (2001), there are three modes of incorporation: assimilation, hyphenated incorporation, and multicultural incorporation. In the first century of the United States, outsiders seeking inclusion in the social collective did so through assimilation, by abandoning any public trappings of their membership in marginal groups. Eventually this mode of incorporation gave way to hyphenated incorporation, in which collective identity and character is understood as a product of the incorporation of the qualities of multiple groups. In such a system, minority groups and individuals are a special (hyphenated) type of member of society whose foreignness is perceived as ethnic difference that, although tolerated, is not central to civil life. According to Alexander (2006), in the final decades of the twentieth century and beyond, these erstwhile ascendant modes of group incorporation into the American social collectivity were increasingly replaced by the historically unique multicultural mode of incorporation. While previous modes of incorporation involve recasting stigmatized groups as the same in terms of collective values, the multicultural mode of incorporation recognizes and accepts differences as "variations of the sacred qualities of civility" (Alexander 2006, p. 452).

The centrality in Lewiston of positive valuations of diversity in accounts of Somali settlement (the diversity-affirming narratives described later in the chapter) demonstrates that multicultural incorporation, as Alexander describes it, does indeed characterize the general orientation to Somali immigrant inclusion. However, the multicultural mode still encountered considerable challenge and backlash.[2] Hyphenated and assimilative incorporation maintained roles, both through institutional structures predating multiculturalism and through the existence of considerable hostility to positive valuations of Somali culture. Different modes of incorporation and contestation in the terms of inclusion produced shifts and conflicts in

[2] See also Glazer, Nathan. 1997. *We are all multiculturalists now*. Cambridge, MA: Harvard University Press; Lynch, Frederick R. 2002. *The diversity machine: The drive to change the "white male workplace."* New Brunswick, NJ: Transaction Publishers; Michaels, Walter Benn. 2006. *The trouble with diversity: How we learned to love identity and ignore inequality.* New York: Metropolitan Books; Wood, Peter. 2003. *Diversity: The invention of a concept.* San Francisco: Encounter Books.

techniques for discussing the character of the Lewiston community and its members.[3]

In other words, the narratives emerging in Lewiston yielded particular understandings, not just of the meaning of Somali settlement and diversity troubles, but of the nature of those who constituted the Lewiston community. Lewistonians employed these narratives and the meanings they engendered to make sense of the past, present, and future of the city. The everyday public acceptance of Somalis arose from the conception of Lewiston as a moral community of loving, accepting, and reasonable people who defended the place against exploitive, irrational, and hateful individuals who would *not* accept Somali newcomers. The moral boundaries of belonging visible in Lewiston were mobilized retrospectively to embrace diversity and to exile those who failed to demonstrate that acceptance. However, collective meanings produced material consequences as Lewiston residents drew on both diversity-affirming and diversity-trouble narratives to understand and manage new community tensions. The practical consequences of narrative forms are visible in two moments of tension and high ritual discussed in the next sections.

Diversity-affirming Narratives

By the time I arrived in Lewiston in summer 2003, most public observations and accounts of the meaning that Somali settlement and the turmoil of the past had for Lewiston defined the Somali presence in the community as an unquestionable good because of the value of the "diversity" they brought to Lewiston. For example, public officials, bureaucrats, local journalists, and social service providers I interviewed demonstrated this epistemological orientation when they turned quickly to discussing the benefits of Lewiston's Somali population. When conversation allowed, they would repeat and reemphasize the positive aspects of Lewiston's increasing population diversity, drawing upon common themes and

---

[3] Thomas Faist (2009. "Diversity – A New Mode of Incorporation?" *Ethnic and Racial Studies* 32:171–190), suggests that "diversity" be understood as a distinct mode of incorporation separate from multiculturalism and assimilationism on account of what he claims is its emphasis on societal and organizational response to increased cultural and demographic diversity. In this view, the end goal of diversity as a mode of incorporation is the organization of society to take advantage of the unique strengths of its various groups. However, Faist's description of the diversity mode of incorporation does not differ significantly from hyphenated incorporation. Furthermore, in characterizing diversity as a structural mode of incorporation, he neglects the discourse of diversity's focus on individual bias as the problem and overcoming said bias as the repair (see Chapter 4).

narratives of economic prosperity, cultural cosmopolitanism, and global stature. The Somalis, they claimed, were a boon to economic development in the region and contributors to the rich cultural fabric of the city; also, they were in a unique position to provide new and important links to the global community. Three diversity-affirming narratives emerged in my data from the field. These narratives cast Somali settlement as benefiting the Lewiston community at large.

Economic Prosperity

One common narrative account focused on the positive economic impact of Somali settlement in Lewiston. According to a city official with whom I spoke, Lewiston's economic standing was on the upswing prior to the arrival of the Somali newcomers. Community leaders claimed that Somali settlement yielded clear payoffs, providing a diverse workforce that buoyed municipal attempts at wooing business investments. Urban redevelopment projects combined with local corporate job training programs and the construction of a Wal-Mart distribution center and several big box stores to make the Lewiston economy one of the most rapidly expanding local economies in the state. Lewiston's "arrival" as a city was further cemented in 2007 when the city took the National Civic League's coveted All-America City Award, an annual award honoring communities that work productively to address critical needs.[4] The city administrator claimed that he sought the award as a way to heal the community and restore its public image. Lewiston's application for All-America City status included the way it had successfully addressed the challenges of Somali immigrant incorporation.

In focusing on the economic advantages of community diversity, folks in Lewiston echoed arguments made in the corporate world by diversity trainers and consultants, human resource managers, and others spearheading the movement to harness the potential of an increasingly diverse U.S. labor market: diversity yields economic payoff (Gardenschwartz and Rowe 1998; Herring 2009; Hough and Toner 2011). An elected city official whom I interviewed in 2003 summed this view up nicely when he said:

The city of Lewiston has been lacking economic development for many, many years but it's probably one of the most heavily developed areas in the State of Maine right now. There's construction going on everywhere. It's just booming....

---

[4] For more information about the All-America City Award, see the National Civic League's website: http://ncl.org/.

We think about [diversity] all the time because we see it all the time. When I was brought up you were either Franco or Irish or Greek or Polish and that was about the limit of it. As the years go by, for the last several years, you see a lot more diversity. And it's good for the community, you know. Diversity brings economic development. I mean, you know, whether they be Somalis or, you know, whatever. Whatever their nationality or whatever culture they are. (city official, in interview)

Within the economic prosperity narrative, not all diversity was valued equally. Visible diversity was recognized as the type of heterogeneity with positive economic ramifications. In the prior quotation, the city official who was speaking made an implicit distinction between Lewiston's prior diversity, white ethnic heterogeneity, and the type of diversity "you see a lot more of," the visible racial and cultural diversity that the Somalis supplied.

Embracing Somali relocation on account of its contributions to the economic well-being of Lewiston, many of the people I encountered in the city claimed that Somalis also improved the local economic climate through their roles as consumers and their contributions as workers. Somali immigrants provided a necessary boost to the economic engine of an aging community with a declining population. Prosperity accounts emphasized that immigrant settlement increased consumer demand for housing, services, and specialty products. For example, citing the positive impact of Somali settlement, the administrator of local public housing reported that with the arrival of newcomers the vacancy rate in the city decreased significantly for the first time since the textile mills and shoe factories began closing in the 1970s.

Cosmopolitanism

In addition to the perception of Somali settlement as an engine of economic development, I observed the widespread use of a narrative in which Somalis bring sophistication and cosmopolitanism to cultural life in the city. Citing their appreciation for the increased "color" of local life, many Lewiston residents recognized the cultural contributions of Lewiston's newest residents. They claimed the city was livelier on account of the Somali businesses and institutions that filled previously vacant storefronts on downtown Lisbon Street. Lewiston residents had access to henna tattoos, exotic attire, Somali dance and music showcased at various "culture nights," and other celebrations. This narrative of cosmopolitanism held that Lewiston's cultural palette was enriched by the Somali presence. As one elected official noted in an interview, "[Somalis] have something to contribute to the city of Lewiston also. They have their culture, their food, their customs."

The narrative of appreciation for increased cultural richness in the community focused on the presence of Somalis at some distance removed from the speaker's own life. Thus, when describing the increased cultural richness of the community, those talking about the Somali newcomers' cultural contributions typically referred to the presence of the cultural artifacts brought to Lewiston by Somali residents. Even those who were unlikely to enjoy eating regularly at Red Sea, one of the city's Somali restaurants, recognized the merits of adding the venue to the list of dining establishments available in town.

Global Stature

Yet another narrative extended the growing cosmopolitanism of the city's cultural offerings to include the improved national and global stature of Lewiston and the increased global savvy of its non-Somali residents. According to many people with whom I spoke, the Lewiston Somalis' international ties forged new connections between the town and the global community. Not mentioned in most regional guidebooks, Lewiston was largely unknown outside of Maine prior to the Somali migration. Even within the state the city had a dubious reputation as a community with relatively high poverty and crime rates. Aware of the marginal status of the place, many people believed that Somali settlement placed the city "on the map." In one-on-one conversations and public talk, people proudly emphasized the many distinguished visitors Lewiston hosted: journalists and researchers interested in the community's progress; foreign dignitaries such as Ali Khalif Galaydh, former prime minister of Somalia; and state and federal politicians who believed that developments in the city represented the cutting edge of immigrant settlement.

In the global narrative, Lewiston's new Somali population and the diversity Somalis conveyed provided Lewiston with notoriety unconnected to the city's undesirable reputation as a struggling mill town. The presence of the Somalis also transformed ordinary residents into global citizens who, as a result of increased cross-cultural contact, found themselves well versed in world geography, international relations, and Islamic civilizations. As a result, in the context of this narrative, Lewistonians were described as better prepared for employment in the global workforce. In the following quotation, a local educator talked about the global connections fostered by Somalis enrolled in public postsecondary education in the community.

We have a number of Somali students here. They've helped us develop our course offerings on globalism and Islam. We've had additional guest speakers and short term courses. It's been wonderful. (community college administrator, in interview)

Understanding Somali settlement as contributing to the city's global stature and population of individuals with broad knowledge of world cultures and events, the global narrative further connected the city to the global community by creating obvious and tangible ties to national and international events. The local daily newspaper offered routine front-page coverage of current events in Somalia. The flag of Somalia was displayed in city community centers and at public events. Many city residents, new and old, were quick to express their opinions on immigration debates and post-9/11 fears of Muslim extremists within the nation's borders. Community residents offered their opinions with the understanding that the existence of Lewiston's Somali community legitimated their views, lending them the credence of someone who experienced the realities of U.S. immigration policy and other homeland security issues firsthand.

"Happy Talk"

To the extent that they extolled the merits of diversity in the community while holding diverse newcomers at arm's reach, these narratives of economic prosperity, cultural cosmopolitanism, and global stature were characterized by what Bell and Hartmann (2007) refer to as "happy talk," the propensity "to exoticize, criticize, trivialize and compartmentalize the cultural objects of people of color as contributions to the enrichment of whites." While happy talk would likely be seen by many as an improvement over segregationist and discriminatory sentiments routinely expressed in other times and other places, the incorporation suggested by happy talk was partial and contingent nonetheless. The focus on embracing the contributions of Somali newcomers instead of the Somalis themselves was simultaneously productive and descriptive of the social distance between Somali and most non-Somali Lewiston residents. Few of the non-Somali city residents and public officials I interviewed had formed close friendships with any Somali community members. Only those city and state officials in the position of providing a direct service to members of the Somali community or supervising Somali employees could speak of any relationship at all with Somali residents of Lewiston.

To be fair, establishing relationships required extra effort on the part of many Somali and non-Somali residents. With few exceptions, at the time of my interviews Lewiston's Somali newcomers, although considered a large group, were relatively invisible outside of frequent local media coverage and the downtown neighborhood where many of them resided. The other city residents sharing neighborhoods with Somali inhabitants tended to be in economically disadvantaged positions relative to community activists and the folks working at city hall, the local newspaper, and private social service agencies. Although a substantial number of Somali newcomers also lived in the Lewiston Housing Authority's outlying Hillview Housing Project, a development integrated into a small neighborhood consisting largely of modest single-family homes, Hillview was removed from the sight of all but those who resided in the immediate vicinity. The lack of intergroup relationships surely reflected the organization of everyday life but it also indicated the lack of cultural emphasis on making such connections and on identifying and communicating across social divisions tied to inequality in the distribution of power and material resources.

Beyond speaking to the reality of limited cross-cultural contact, happy talk in Lewiston affected shared understandings of what Somali incorporation should look like. The emphasis on embracing cultural diversity as a consumable and welcomed element of the cityscape corresponded to a lack of attention to the importance of identifying material need and fostering personal connections between Somalis and non-Somalis and achieving a cohesive community. These goals were rarely mentioned in my formal interviews and informal discussions with Lewiston residents. The primary exception occurred in my interview with a public housing employee whose responsibilities included the day-to-day operation of a large housing project with a significant number of Somali families. This employee believed that successful community management requires fostering relationships.

Bell and Hartmann (2007) suggest that happy talk is used primarily by whites. Indeed, diversity-affirming narratives underwrote the white public's embrace of Somali newcomers to Lewiston, but these narratives also provided the platform from which Somali Lewistonians defended their residence in the community. In responding to expressions of hostility toward their presence, Somalis focused on their economic, cultural, and status contributions to the city of Lewiston. Take as evidence the following excerpt from the letter Somali elders penned in response to Mayor Raymond's controversial letter (reproduced here as originally printed).

Officials [with whom we have met] indicated their satisfaction with our coming to live here in the state, they say, is sparsely populated and need to attract more residents as both manpower and future electorates. Those officials, after listening to us, applauded our efforts to try and "Fit in" as much as we can....

Apartment units located in the Lewiston downtown area which were abandoned many years ago, were suddenly refurbished and made livable as the arrival of Somalis generated funds and put money in the pockets of landlords. This also raised the market value of real estate. Somalis were hired to work in businesses and plants making them to be able to contribute to the local economy as taxpayers. (Elders of the Somali Community 2002a)

Diversity-affirming narratives supporting the claim that Somalis were a welcome addition to the Lewiston community because of their contributions as bearers of diversity led Somalis to exoticize themselves in order to "fit in" and legitimate their claims for inclusion. The precarious and coercive cultural context of Somali belonging is discussed in greater detail in Chapter 5.

In understanding the pro-diversity narratives of economic prosperity, cultural enrichment, and global stature, it is important to consider the lack of cultural engagement characterizing the emerging meaning of the Somali presence in Lewiston. Accounts of the benefits of Somali settlement did not emphasize Somali cultural particulars or, for that matter, the way of life that characterized Lewiston before the Somali influx. In their open letter to Mayor Raymond, Somali elders suggested that their contributions to the city derived from economic and status benefits they brought purely on account of their designation as diverse instead of the inherent value or merit of Somali culture, history, heritage, language, and religion.

Diversity-affirming narratives used widely in the public talk of both Somali and non-Somali residents of Lewiston diverged from understandings that see Somalis as newcomers with limited community membership whose immigration ushered in social and economic crises for the city. Given the sense of imminent threat which prompted the town hall meeting and led Mayor Raymond to write his letter, I was surprised to observe that during my time in the field, and particularly in conversations with local political and community leaders, pro-diversity narratives were ubiquitous. The economic, cultural, and prestige benefits of the Somali influx punctuated the vast majority of accounts of life in the increasingly diverse city. As we shall see, accounting for the difficulties of cross-cultural interaction and the tensions that surfaced in the wake of Somali settlement in Lewiston proved a more difficult and risky task.

Diversity Troubles

In interviews and in routine conversations, people in Lewiston rarely provided unsolicited accounts of problems and challenges associated with the incorporation of a large number of Somali newcomers. Therefore, in seeking to learn how individuals made sense of the difficulties surrounding the mayor's letter and of Somali immigrant settlement, I frequently introduced the topic of the city's "diversity troubles" by asking what challenges Somali settlement posed to the city and why the crisis of the letter and the World Church of the Creator meeting had occurred. In discussing the challenges faced in Lewiston, people drew upon three dominant narratives – inexperience, exploitation, and racism.

Narrative accounts of diversity troubles differed significantly from the diversity-affirming narratives discussed earlier. While the emphases of diversity-affirming narratives were implicitly inclusive – reflecting positively on the growth of the community and increased cultural contact with the outside world – accounts of diversity troubles were necessarily exclusive, creating and reifying boundaries based upon geography, tenure, mental fitness, and moral worth. Reflecting on potential diversity troubles and the promise and changes wrought in their community by the influx of visible minorities, people in Lewiston drew upon narratives attributing community problems to internal "growing pains" resulting from a lack of experience with and exposure to difference, limited resources for managing the needs of Somali newcomers, exploitation at the hands of outsiders, or the racism of a problematic few.

Inexperience

When reflecting on the challenges of Somali settlement and the causes of the turmoil around the time that Mayor Raymond's letter was published, many people in Lewiston expressed the belief that the community's prior difficulties and future challenges should be attributed to a lack of exposure to new cultures and limited experience with recent immigrants. The narrative of inexperience that emerged in the accounts of challenges and troubles held that through the process of working to meet the needs of a diverse population, any city would expect to increase its expertise in providing support to Somali residents and managing cross-cultural challenges. The narrative also maintained that Somali newcomers had a great deal to learn about American society and that, in time, they would come to understand the American system and Lewiston's way of life.

The following quotation provides a common example of the narrative of inexperience.

It's a learning process on both sides. It's a learning process for the city, the city officials as well as for the Somali community because culturally it's totally, totally different. (city official, in interview)

Narratives of inexperience generally took Lewiston and, sometimes, the state of Maine as the primary point of reference – the protagonist, as it were, in a story of rapid change after a long period of isolation and demographic continuity. It is no wonder, this narrative posits, that the city was not initially prepared to deal with the needs of the Somali arrivals. Lewiston had little familiarity with best practices for managing racial diversity and had not received substantial immigration for nearly a century. Claiming they were caught off guard by new nonwhite immigrants, city officials and long-time residents acknowledged that they had never imagined that "something like this," meaning the arrival of people as different from them as Somalis, would ever happen in Lewiston. A Somali city employee offered an optimistic account of the city's troubles very much in line with the narrative of inexperience:

Things are much better in Lewiston. The community-at-large is more tolerant now. If a view like the one in the letter came out now it would show the opposite effect. It just takes time. If 1,500 people had moved to one town in Somalia, the same thing would have happened. (city employee, in interview)

While suggesting the universality of learning to be a diverse community and seeing the adoption of outside management techniques as important, the inexperience narrative also asserted the boundary of place by emphasizing the unique culture, history, and culturally rich character of Lewiston. Inexperience accounts might dismiss outright the applicability of national and international perspectives for making sense of immigration and race relations. Emphasizing the local, the narrative of inexperience reified the geographic and historical boundaries of Lewiston, calling into question the relevance and accuracy of perspectives and programs coming from the outside. In the following excerpt from a published report written by a city administrator, we see the assertion of local particularity.

Local officials often found themselves discussing Somali arrivals within the context of national/international immigration and refugee policy. Unfortunately, national policy discussions rarely provided more insight for local residents who tried to understand issues at a local level. (Nadeau 2003b, p.49)

Accounts such as these maintained that Somali settlement posed unique challenges within the city's unique circumstances. The situation, therefore, required locally derived solutions. Lewiston, this narrative suggested, was best left alone to draw upon local knowledge and resources to incorporate new residents.

An emphasis on the boundaries of place notwithstanding, the inexperience narrative was consistent with the inclusive and optimistic nature of diversity-affirming narratives and, therefore, frequently occurred in tandem with accounts of diversity as an enriching aspect of Lewiston life. While noting a lack of preparedness and practice in being an inclusive community, the inexperience narrative referenced an optimistic end goal that echoes diversity management in the corporate world: the efficient operation of the community and success in identifying and meeting the particular needs of city residents. Inexperience accounts generally maintained that managing the challenges posed by community diversity was an ongoing accomplishment characterized by openness to and emphasis on continued learning about oneself and others. If inexperience was the problem, the remedy was time and effort: attention devoted to learning what works, and energy invested into putting the needed services in place.

The inexperience narrative also obviated the ability to lay blame for problems in the city on any single set of actors. Talk of inexperience implicitly acknowledged that well-intentioned individuals were susceptible to mistakes and missteps, but such people were also quick to admit their shortcomings. Ultimately, as discussed in Chapter 3, the processual, developmental perspective embodied by the narrative of inexperience was the most productive frame used to make sense of diversity troubles in Lewiston. While there was no laying of blame, claims of inexperience did keep the responsibility for managing diversity troubles within the community. The perspective that Lewiston and its residents could learn to be a welcoming community for Somalis and other newcomers mapped a path to progress and strategies for action through the successful adaptation and application of guidelines and laws for accessibility and equal protection. For most city officials and social service providers, measures of compliance with national standards for managing diversity provided the clearest indicators of success in overcoming inexperience.

Resource Limitations
Additional accounts of the challenges the Somali influx presented for the city of Lewiston drew upon the narrative of resource limitations.

Echoing in muted form the crisis claims that characterized early resistance to Somali settlement, this narrative alluded to three types of resources: fiscal; programmatic – a lack of qualified support staff and appropriate immigrant adjustment services; and a dearth of guidance from state and federal agencies. Indeed, Mayor Raymond drew upon this narrative when in his letter he argued for a hiatus in relocations to the city on the basis of scarce resources.[5] Resource concerns were prima facie race-neutral, allowing those who raised them to sidestep charges of bigotry and point the finger of blame elsewhere. For example, in the following quotation, a city administrator who bore significant responsibility for diversity management criticized the state and federal governments for failing to offer guidelines, laws, or support to Lewiston as it navigated the uncharted territory of diversity and the secondary migration of refugees.

My shock came as a result of learning that the state has absolutely no policy with respect to what is happening. (city employee, in interview)

Narrative accounts of the city's limited resources for managing the demands of Somali settlement were also at risk of running afoul of diversity-affirming accounts because they might draw upon assimilation-based ideas that saw group differences not as valuable but, instead, as something that must be overcome if the community was to function successfully. One city official made clear the potential assimilationist undercurrent of the resource narrative with the following statement:

---

[5] It is not the goal of this chapter to examine the veracity of claims regarding scarce resources. These claims have been dismissed in the media and were even dismissed within my interviews. However, others offer substantial support for the assertion that rapid Somali settlement presented significant and immediate costs for the city of Lewiston (Nadeau, Phil. 2003b. "The Somalis of Lewiston: Community Impacts of Rapid Immigrant Movement into a Small Homogeneous Maine City," p. 59. Paper presented at the Brown University Center for the Study of Race and Ethnicity, Providence, Rhode Island, August 14, 2003). True or not, the reality of the perception of resource competition and its implications for intergroup relations has long been understood in social science (Blumer, Herbert. 1958. "Race Prejudice as a Sense of Group Position." *Pacific Sociological Review* 1:3–7; Bobo, Lawrence and Vincent L. Hutchings. 1996. "Perceptions of Racial Group Competition: Extending Blumer's Theory of Group Position to a Multiracial Social Context." *American Sociological Review* 61:951–972.). Further, it cannot be denied that the city budget needed to be changed to reflect changing needs in the community (e.g., in less than one year the city went from having virtually no need (or budget) for English language instruction in city schools to having more than 200 students for whom English was a second language).

People look at this and say the city of Lewiston. Well, it's not just the city of Lewiston. We have very limited resources. This is also a state issue and it's a federal issue. If the federal government says to these people "We'll bring you to this country and find you a community to live," I think the federal government should be willing to part with some dollars until, you know, these people are settled down. Settled down and, you know, melted into the community. And, I mean, you know, now they're part of the community, but [pause] you know. (city official, in interview)

While the person speaking initially offered an assimilation-based view of social inclusion, at the end of the quote (which also marked the end of his statement on the matter) he struggled to express the relationship between financial and programmatic needs associated with immigrant incorporation and a view of the relationship incorporated immigrants have with the rest of the community. This comment demonstrates the direct competition between two narratives that assigned a different valence to the Somali presence in the community – a multicultural desire to welcome and preserve Somali distinctiveness and an assimilationist desire for Somali distinctiveness to fade. After suggesting that Somalis should be "melted" into to the community, the speaker paused, producing an awkward moment I understood to arise from his recognition that his statement was inconsistent with the notion that Somalis and the "diversity" they bring are valuable to the community. The public official searched for the words to bridge the gap between affirming diversity, embracing the presence of the Somalis, and the objecting to the costs of Somali settlement for a community that did not ask to become diverse and imagined a time when Somalis were indistinguishable from other Lewistonians. When discourse failed him, he appealed to me, the person with whom he was speaking, with a "you know" appearing to indicate a host of ideas and experiences that he expected I could fathom even if he could not express them clearly.

In Lewiston, resource narratives that focused on the Somali newcomers as the cause of and solution to the community's resource problems characterized early interpretations of Somali settlement. Resource narratives conflicted directly with the diversity-affirming emphasis on the economic benefits of Somali settlement. They also ran the risk of positing an indefensible community boundary – one that excluded Somali residents. Evidence on the ground suggested that such resource claims would likely be challenged, as in the case of Mayor Raymond's letter and early attempts by city officials to defend Raymond against charges of racism. The following quotation offers an early defense of resource claims.

Faced with a possible tax rate last spring of $32 per $1,000 in property value, city officials cut a variety of programs, including Little League funding and 12 positions. Bennett had to lay off eight people.

"And we're not done," [city administrator] Bennett said. "I was lucky to get (the tax rate) down to $28.85. It's not the Somalis' fault, but those are the facts. It's not about skin color. It's about resources." (Bouchard 2002a, p. 1A)

The narrative of resource limitation proved problematic because it suggested that Somali newcomers fell outside the boundaries of the community of people deserving of limited resources. Accounts drawing upon a narrative of resource limitations such as the one made by City Administrator Jim Bennett in the preceding quote were open to attack because they posited decidedly exclusive group boundaries as markers of symbolic belonging and value. To claim that Somalis were unduly taxing the resources of the community was to make an implicit distinction between unworthy and worthy recipients of city funds, pitting All-American Little League against new immigrants, newcomers against old-timers, and the well-being of homeowners against the settlement of Somalis.

The tension between diversity-affirming narratives and narrative explanations of diversity troubles that focused on resource limitations left the legitimacy of resource claims and the authority of the claimants open to challenge and censure. In their written response to Mayor Raymond, Lewiston's Somali elders resisted the "othering" of resource narratives. They demanded equal inclusion and asserted equal rights to city resources.

While we thank the city of Lewiston, and the general public for their understanding and accepting us in their midst, we would nevertheless like to bring to your attention and to the attention of others in your line of thinking, that we are citizens and/or legal residents of this country. (Elders of the Somali Community 2002a)

Somali residents of the United States, they claimed, could live where they chose and are entitled to the same benefits and protections as other Americans. Inclusion and access to the rights that accompany it did not depend upon tenure in the community, naturalization, language acquisition, or a welcoming reception from the community they had selected.

Exploiting Others

While talk of resource limitations tended toward conflict with diversity-affirming narratives, another common narrative, the narrative of exploitation, provided meaning to diversity troubles without questioning the benefits of diversity or the social membership of Somalis. According to the narrative of exploitation, the community had no problems incorporating the Somali newcomers. Any troubles the town experienced resulted from exploitation of the city by outsiders and self-interested people using the situation in Lewiston to further their own unrelated agendas. Exploitation accounts delineated the moral and geographic boundaries of the Lewiston community, extending membership to those with a physical presence and pro-community orientation.

The narrative of exploitation attributed community tensions, persistent rumors, and the difficulties surrounding Mayor Raymond's letter to a variety of individuals and groups, and many of the reported troublemakers were actually community residents depicted as socially or morally deficient. Within this narrative, two groups typically shouldered the blame for Lewiston's diversity troubles – an economically driven media and self-interested geographic or morally problematic outsiders with no concern for the well-being of the community, exploiting turmoil in order to push forward their own agendas.

Talk of media exploitation was ubiquitous in accounts of exploitation. City officials with whom I spoke claimed that the media sensationalized a few minor problems in Lewiston to sell news. They believed that the press, looking for "juicy" stories, contributed to the perpetuation of tensions in the city and was responsible for the WCOTC decision to visit Lewiston. Whereas, if the media had chosen to ignore Mayor Raymond's letter, as I was told in an interview with a high-ranking city official, "it would have all blown over in a couple of days."

In addition to finding fault with the media's attention to the situation in Lewiston, the narrative of exploitation highlights the meddling of outsiders who made the drama what it was or even, as demonstrated in the following quotation, constituted the entire cast of characters in a drama in which Lewiston and its residents served as the backdrop.

I was amazed by how many outsiders took advantage of the city of Lewiston to promote their own personal agendas and that was from all sides. Even the Somalian population will tell you that a lot of people that were on camera who were Somalian weren't from this community and really weren't expressing the views of the actual Somalian people that were living here. We had people flying in from Minnesota that were national Somali representatives, [and other Somalis] from Alabama and Atlanta, and then we had the white racists and then the Canadian group that came down ..., and we had the Boston group that came up here and just wanted to take everything over and everyone that's sitting here in Lewiston is going, where are all these people coming from? That was surprising to me. It wasn't community driven. (law enforcement official, in interview)

The narrative of exploitation points the finger of blame for the community's diversity troubles outside Lewiston. Instead, the city was victimized by the disingenuous and self-interested behavior of outsiders who used the location as a stage to enact their own dramas. When I followed up on discussions of this sort by asking how the community might best respond to diversity troubles resulting from outsider meddling, the answer was frequently to ignore the disruptive presence of intruders.

Claims of exploitation were not limited to blaming community outsiders. In some cases, informants claimed that derogatorily labeled "multiculturalist" Lewiston residents exploited the Somali presence and Mayor Raymond's letter to push for increased acceptance and recognition of other groups, most notably for some, the city's lesbian, gay, bisexual, and transgendered (LGBT) population.

> It wasn't even Somalis who made the fuss. It was all the activists who jumped in.... They were having a meeting that was going to form the Many & One Coalition, right? So they go to this meeting. I think it was at one of the churches. They thought it was a coalition to show support for the Somalis, right, and suddenly these people from gay groups and transgender and all this crazy stuff start standing up and talking about their persecution. (local journalist, in interview)

Current conceptions of diversity generally incorporate a variety of factors including race, ethnicity, gender, disability, sexual preference, gender orientation, and religion. While this may be a typical "diversity package," many people in Lewiston, both Somali and non-Somali, were decidedly anti-gay. For many, the desire to show support for the Somalis without condoning homosexuality required action outside of the very public work being done by the nascent Many and One Coalition, a group with a leadership containing openly homosexual members and that explicitly condemned homophobia and discrimination on the basis of sexual orientation. The best example of the impact that the inclusion of sexual orientation in Many and One's platform had on community involvement in the group's activities was the alternative event to show support for the Somalis and condemnation of the WCOTC. The Greek Orthodox Church hosted an interfaith prayer vigil on the evening of January 10, 2003, the night before the other events. The event was attended by some individuals who played a role in the Many and One rally and by several others expressing discomfort with, as a leader of the event reported, "some of the aims of Many and One."

The narrative of exploitation holds that the city's diversity troubles resulted exclusively from exploitation, be it the intervention of folks from away who care little for the people of Lewiston, media sensationalism, or the machinations of immoral and activist Lewiston residents seizing upon the Somali influx for their own benefit. Ironically, conceptions of diversity tying the inclusion of Somalis to acceptance of homosexuals apparently eroded public support for inclusivity and even led to a backlash against and social exclusion of "multiculturalists" and "pluralists" heralding the value of diversity (see Chapter 5 for more information on the impact of homophobia on the incorporation of Lewiston's Somali residents).

Naming Racism

An additional narrative accounted for diversity troubles by pointing the finger of blame at problematic people – bigoted, racist, xenophobic, and ignorant residents of the community. According to the narrative of racism, community tensions resulted from persistent rumors regarding special treatment for the Somalis that some "less-informed" people spread and never bothered to verify. The narrative of racism held that every community must expect bad apples and that Lewiston had its fair share of old-fashioned and close-minded neighbors resistant to seeing the city change. A Somali Lewiston resident who participated in the University of Maine's Somali Narrative Project summed this up nicely when she said, "Lewiston is a great city, and most of the Somalis there don't face racism. This does not mean that racism is not an issue. There is always that one person or group in every community in the United States" (Huisman 2011, p. 35).

Unlike the calculating and selfish individuals characterized within narratives of exploitation, within the narrative of racism, psychologically troubled and mentally limited local racists and ignorant undesirables were the actors who brought the underlying cynicism and hostility into Lewiston. Racists were depicted as bothersome, irrational individuals with a questionable grasp on reality. According to this narrative, the rehabilitation of racists was a difficult enterprise. In short term, the community was best served when problematic people were dismissed and denied the opportunity to have significant impact on community relations and public discourse. Through the identification and exclusion of problematic people, the narrative of racism established community boundaries based on moral and psychological fitness.

A particular racist character – an individual with cultural attributes typically held in low esteem – generally populated narratives of racism. As evident in the following examples, the narrative of racism accounted for diversity troubles by affixing the racist label to those who objected to the Somali presence. Racists were often performed by putting on a heavy Maine accent and mockingly referring to Somalis as Somalians, characteristics more common among those with less education and from lower economic classes, when repeating the claims associated with racism and ignorance.

> Over the last two or three years, I'll hear things like, [mock heavy Maine accent] "You guys get paid twenty thousand dollars to move in a Somali family." Where the heck is that coming from? I don't even listen to them. (city employee, in interview)
>
> The [mock accent] "*Somalians*" this and the "*Somalians*" that. I can't stand the stupidity of the racists in this town. (local activist, in interview)

In the preceding quotations, the individuals with whom I spoke made use of the narrative of racism in making sense of diversity troubles. These quotations are telling when it comes to understanding the construction of a racist persona – someone identifiable by accent and vocabulary, lacking intelligence and rationality, and whose ideas are off base and dismissible. While folks with whom I spoke acknowledged that people fitting that description certainly roamed the streets of Lewiston, it was clear in accounts using the narrative of racism that such individuals did not represent the city but, instead, spoke for themselves only.

At a community screening of *The Letter* (Hamzeh 2003), a documentary film covering Lewiston's diversity troubles, many members of the audience chuckled and snorted disdainfully each time beliefs based upon rumors about the Somalis and hostility toward the Lewiston's new residents were expressed by individuals appearing in the film. Quite frequently the individuals depicted in the film *did* have heavy Maine accents and refer to Somalis as Somalians, and, therefore, personified the type of individual interviewees presented as troublesome: lower-class and less-educated Mainers, particularly those living in Lewiston's downtown and in public housing. In fact, to a great extent Hamzeh's film did justice to the reality I observed during my time in the field. Although I encountered poor and working-class, white, downtown residents who were active in the Many and One Coalition and other pro-diversity activities, the unabashedly anti-Somali actions and comments I observed came exclusively from those lower-income and less-educated Lewiston residents living in close proximity to Somalis and with limited access to and participation in the venues where other city residents acquire competence in diversity talk (see Chapter 3).

Whether the racist label stuck on account of the social class characteristics or was earned by the explicit expression of racial or anti-Somali prejudice, the narrative of racism provided an understanding of diversity troubles that emphasized the adverse impact of a problematic few residents. By highlighting the existence of racism and racist individuals expressing it, the narrative of racism acknowledged the tension and discord in Lewiston without qualifying the diversity-affirming conclusion that the Somalis, representing diversity, were a boon to the community.

"From Away"

Narratives of diversity troubles that emerged in Lewiston did more than assign meaning to tensions surrounding Somali settlement; they also asserted understandings of community membership based on categorical distinctions between times, places, people, perspectives, and moral orientations. While residence in the community arose as the first criterion of membership in most narratives of diversity troubles, being there often proved insufficient to indicate belonging. Tenure, intellect, commitment to place, psychological health, and moral worth all emerged as individual characteristics mobilized to denote the symbolic boundaries of belonging.

As a researcher "from away,"[6] I learned through experience that skepticism of the perspective, involvement, and advice of outsiders, however they might be construed, persisted long after the crisis of the rally passed. In discussing difficulties in the community, folks in Lewiston generally contextualized their expertise by making a claim to community membership. Individuals frequently referenced their tenure in the community. In our conversations about Somali settlement, community members required no prompting to note that they "were born and raised in Lewiston," "had lived here all of [their] adult lives," or "consider Lewiston home" even if they lived forty minutes away in Portland. Even when they could not claim protracted residence, both Somali and non-Somali people in Lewiston professed their love for the place and the commitment they had made to the city through their choice to live there, community involvement, and efforts to lay down lasting roots.

---

[6] The expression "from away" was widely used in Lewiston. In my data "from away" variously referenced out-of-staters who descend upon Maine over the summer months; instances when out-of-state individuals feel that Mainers need intervention on the part of "city folk" from, for example, Boston or New York; recent transplants (which can be construed in terms of years or generations) to the community seeking an active role in local issues; and those from other localities within Maine levying an opinion on the situation in the community.

The emphasis on belonging indicates, in relief, the importance of identifying those who do not belong. On September 11, 2003, a local weekly newspaper, the *Twin City Times*, announced two projects: a two-day project on race relations sponsored by the Maine chapter of a nationwide anti-racist organization, and an assessment of the needs of Lewiston's Somali community conducted by researchers from Clark University, located in Worcester, Massachusetts. An editorial in this same issue of the paper noted these developments and sardonically lamented the continued meddling of people from away in the lives of this mill community of "horrible white people" (Steele 2003). This preoccupation with the definition of Lewiston and its people acted as the background condition for Somali immigrant incorporation.

INCLUSION AND EXCLUSION

The narratives emerging in Lewiston were more than idle words and convenient plotlines that individuals mobilized to talk about diversity in the abstract. In assigning meaning to Somali settlement and community tensions, the narratives drew upon widely shared structures of meaning and deeply held cultural and moral values. While much of the literature on multiculturalism and immigrant incorporation considers the way in which immigrants assimilate by traversing group boundaries and creating hybridized group identities (e.g., Alba and Nee 2003; Kivisto 2005; Portes and Zhou 1993; Raymond and Modood 2007; Waters 1990, 1999), my observations in Lewiston suggest that social inclusion in Lewiston hinged less upon the changes in the content of any given category than the shifting application of the boundaries of belonging. Alba and Nee claim that the social boundaries altered in the process of immigrant assimilation "are almost always associated with numerous concrete social and cultural differences between groups" (2003). I observe, however, that the process of boundary construction enabling Somali incorporation in Lewiston was oriented toward characterizing the common characteristics of community. As will be discussed in Chapters 3 and 5, Somali cultural particulars were not generally considered and sometimes they were actively ignored. In addition to making sense of community diversity and diversity troubles, diversity-affirming narratives and narratives of diversity troubles did not so much define the Somalis as they narrated the moral boundaries of the community and established the criteria for social inclusion.

"Who We Are and Where We Are"

In observing diversity-affirming and diversity-trouble narratives in Lewiston, we also observe the first element of the cultural pragmatics of incorporation. If Somalis were to be incorporated into the broader community, their presence must be recognized as a unproblematic fact of community life and their group identities must be considered compatible with the identity and values associated with membership in the broader "circle of we" (Alexander 2006). This aspect of incorporation took place through the definition of place and the corresponding establishment of moral parameters of the community. Making meaning around Lewiston's diversity necessitated establishing the meaning of community – of, as one city resident noted, "who we are and where we are." Somali incorporation in Lewiston occurred through the application of diversity-affirming and diversity-trouble narratives emphasizing diversity as a social good and tying the endorsement of diversity to deeply held social values. These social values acted as the boundaries of belonging, the moral criterion for social inclusion.

The boundaries of belonging appeared most obviously during moments of high ritual such as the Many and One rally on January 11, 2003. The event coincided with the meeting of the white-supremacist World Church of the Creator. In addition to showing community support for Somalis, the Many and One rally offered a platform from which participants could mobilize a moral definition of Lewiston and its people. The event featured a lineup of prominent speakers and guests including John Jenkins, African American activist and former mayor of Lewiston; Governor John Baldacci; U.S. senators Olympia Snowe and Susan Collins; and the reading of a letter in support of the Somalis by Muhammad Ali, whose 1965 fight with Sonny Liston was hosted by the city of Lewiston (Ali 2003).

"Defining moments. This is something we all have in our personal lives and in the life of any community. Defining moments. This is a defining moment in Maine's history. For all of us" stated master of ceremonies and former Lewiston mayor John Jenkins as he stood before the people in attendance at the Many and One rally. "We're sending a very clear message about who we are and where we are." The attendees responded to Jenkins with thunderous applause. The overflow crowd, the air of goodwill, and the frenzy of mass collective action in a place better known for quiet disengagement all contributed to the euphoric feeling of success surrounding the rally in repairing the damage done by Mayor Raymond's letter and countering the message that the people of Lewiston were bigots who would support the racist, anti-immigrant stance of the World Church of the Creator.

In his remarks to the crowd, Governor John Baldacci also emphasized the idea of identity. He announced, "This is not a haven for any hate group or any racist organizations and Maine stands in opposition to that kind of thing.... This is a great State. It has wonderful natural resources but it has something even more wonderful than that. It has the best people in the world."

Steven Rowe, attorney general of the state of Maine, joined the procession of public figures addressing the crowd. Rowe explicitly engaged the moral division between the people of Lewiston, represented by those in the room, and the racist, exploitive outsiders meeting on the other side of town.

Certain individuals have come to this community for the express purpose of infecting it with a vile disease: a disease of hatred, of bigotry and of racism. These individuals hope to leave the germs of that disease behind when they leave. They hope these germs will infect the residents of this community and throughout this state. You are wasting your time here. You are wasting your time! Your germs of hatred and bigotry and racism and discrimination will not survive here. They will just not survive. But let me tell you what will survive and that is the message that we – all of us at this event today and those that are standing outside and those that have already left – that is the message that all of us are sending to the world today. Our message is that we respect one another. That we care for one another and that we love one another.

As the preceding quotes indicate, accounts assigning meaning to Somali settlement and diversity troubles in Lewiston also narrated the boundaries of Lewiston, the place and people deemed worthy of inclusion. More specifically, diversity-affirming, exploitation and racism narratives circulating in Lewiston relied upon implied deep values of love, respect, unity, equality, and concern. In making sense of Somali settlement as a social good and diversity troubles as the unfortunate result of inexperienced but well-intentioned people, exploitation at the hands of outsiders, and the racist actions of a few bad apples, these narratives constructed a Lewiston community that evaluated social membership through commitment to the community and moral criteria hinging upon the expression of enthusiasm for Somali settlement and other forms of diversity.

The moral and symbolic boundaries were not merely a by-product of "happy talk." On the contrary, these narratives and the discourse of which they are a part were fundamentally preoccupied with establishing the epistemological and discursive foundations of social membership. Alexander's work on the civil sphere provides the theoretical frame with which to understand the centrality of the meaning, membership, and boundaries of the Lewiston community as they were constructed through talk (Alexander 2003, 2006, 2010). According to Alexander, "just as there is no developed religion that does not divide the world into the saved and the damned, there is no civil discourse that does not conceptualize the world into those who deserve inclusion and those who do not" (Alexander 2006). These divisions are made by understanding social members as in possession of socially desirable and morally correct attributes and characterizing those who are not worthy of social membership as being unacceptable, morally and socially problematic. Both pro- and anti-civil classifications draw upon binary codes defining the pro-social characteristics, relationships, and institutional structures that characterize healthy and worthwhile communities in a "discourse of liberty" while laying out the opposite, anti-civil elements in "a discourse of repression." In Lewiston, diversity-affirming and diversity-trouble narratives indicated the sacred and profane values forming the bases of social cohesion and promulgating the boundary conditions for membership in the civil sphere of Lewiston.

In order to make sense of the nature of Somali settlement and diversity troubles, individuals in Lewiston drew upon the multicultural discourses of liberty and repression in applying abstract and generalized understandings of collective life, individual character, and institutional structure. Narratives offered a binary understanding that contrasted the sacred inviolability of commitment to community and diversity as social goods with the racist, exploitive, and unstable natures of those who made diversity problematic. As one community activist put it: "I don't think things in Lewiston are ever going to change as long as [city official] and [city official] are [in their positions]. I know there is a little bit of racism in me. I was in the same [diversity training] group as [city official] and [city official]. They wouldn't even admit that they had racism in them." In this web of meanings in which the moral good associated with Somali settlement stood juxtaposed with evil individuals, the eruption of tensions and expressions of anti-Somali sentiment offered the opportunity for the symbolic expulsion of immoral people and the ritualized purification of the "Lewiston community." Long-time Lewiston resident Brent Mathews provided just such an opportunity.

Head of a Pig

During evening prayer on July 3, 2006, Brent Matthews rolled a frozen pig head down the center aisle of Lewiston's mosque. This act, which would be disturbing and disgusting in most any circumstance, was particularly problematic in the Lewiston-Auburn Islamic Center. In Islam, pork is *haram*, or forbidden. In subsequent investigation of the case, Matthews claimed that he was not aware of this fact, and that the pig head "slipped" from his hands. His claims were met with skepticism. Matthews was quickly apprehended and arrested on misdemeanor charges of desecrating a house of worship. The Lewiston Police Department referred the case to the U.S. Department of Justice and the state attorney general as a possible hate crime (Tice 2006).

In less than forty-eight hours, Lewiston found itself again at the center of a media blitz and widespread expressions of disapproval and skepticism (Taylor 2006a). Brent Matthews's actions sparked a flurry of anti-Somali activity. Vandals targeted a downtown Somali restaurant shortly after the incident and a woman was arrested after she confronted a Somali man, spat on him, and shouted racial epithets (Taylor 2006a; Williams 2006b). A host of anti-Somali and anti-immigration letters filled the opinion pages of the *Lewiston Sun Journal*.

In a departure from the silence that reigned after Mayor Raymond penned his letter, the city sprang into action. Within days, Police Chief William Welch met with the leaders of the mosque and held a press conference to update the public on the investigation of the mosque incident. Welch's conference focused on Matthews to the exclusion of other expressions of hostility. Welch characterized Matthews as emotionally unstable by providing information on his former encounters with local law enforcement and his spotty employment record. Welch also discussed police efforts to protect the public from Matthews by monitoring his activity subsequent to his release on bail. The chief provided the details of the FBI investigation into Matthews's action as a hate crime (Williams 2006a). Meanwhile, the Many and One Coalition and representatives of some area churches organized a news conference and a rally to show support for the city's Somali residents and mosque members.

By the end of the summer, Matthews faced civil rights charges in the Maine Superior Court and remained under threat of federal litigation. However, the public tension and flurry of anti-Somali activity had subsided. Representatives of Lewiston's mosque reported the pig head incident to be an isolated event perpetrated by a disturbed individual. The

Sun Journal ran a cover story quoting Somali residents' assertions that they felt at home in Lewiston despite occasional harassment at the hands of "bullies" (Taylor 2006b). A middle-aged Somali participant in the University of Maine's Somali Narrative Project believed public response to Matthews demonstrated the goodness of the people of Lewiston:

Recently, somebody threw a frozen pig head into the mosque while people were praying. We actually found a lot of people helping us, taking part in our outrage. The community in general, whether they are Muslims or non-Muslims, acted positively and showed solidarity in support for us. Everyone from the mayor to the governor – they all came to our support, and they all showed respect for our culture and our religion. (Huisman, Hough, Langellier, and Toner 2011, p. 262)

Drawing parallels between Mayor Raymond's letter and the "pig-bowling incident," a *Sun Journal* editorial characterized the event as another learning experience for the community:

When former Mayor Larry Raymond penned his now infamous letter urging Somali families to slow their immigration to Lewiston, world reaction was poor. The letter, written in defense of taxpayers, divided this community, yet we've learned a great many lessons in tolerance and acceptance since then....

Was Matthews wrong? Absolutely....

However, the same senses surged around Raymond's letter, touching off frank discussions, community awareness and widespread support and acceptance of the Somali immigrants.

Matthews' act was vile, but we look at it as an opportunity to continue those discussions and for people of all cultures to focus on acceptance of one another. (Rhoades 2006, p. A6)

While it may be true that the desecration of the Lewiston-Auburn Islamic Center left Lewiston a more supportive and accepting community, it also made Brent Matthews an outsider in his hometown. Ultimately the Federal Bureau of Investigation chose not to charge Matthews with a hate crime. The civil suit resulted in an injunction requiring that Matthews stay away from Islamic houses of worship. According to those close to him, Matthews was ashamed by the media attention and the public discussion of his troubled history that followed his act (Tice 2007). Feeling his reputation sullied, he moved away from Lewiston but returned, homesick, within a few months. He continued to struggle with the notoriety he had acquired as the person who rolled the pig's head into the mosque, finding it difficult to obtain work because of his reputation. On April 11, 2007, in an apparent copycat crime, a white Lewiston Middle School student tossed a ham sandwich on the cafeteria table where some Somali students were eating lunch. The incident touched off another period of media scrutiny and public activism and renewed active public memory of Matthews's desecration of the mosque. Ten days later, Matthews committed suicide.

The discursive construction of community is at stake in the nature of the cultural pragmatics of immigrant incorporation emerging in Lewiston. The meanings that characterized common narratives had practical and material effects on the lives of community residents. I do not intend to suggest that the symbolic meanings that excluded Matthews from community membership on the basis of his assault on the Mosque are the sole cause of his untimely death. However, based upon accounts of the crime, punishment, and remaining few months of his life, it appears that Matthews did not anticipate that his decision to roll a pig's head down the center aisle of the Lewiston-Auburn Islamic Center would cost him his community membership.

Acting the Part

Narratives of racism identified problematic bigoted or racist individuals as a cause of diversity troubles in the town. Through the exclusion of individuals, practices, and perspectives that were not properly inclusive themselves, naming racism proved an important aspect of the construction of an inclusive Lewiston and a group of Somali newcomers worthy of membership in that community. Lewiston residents did not all quietly accept the new terms of community membership, however. In the following field note, area resident George offers an alternative conception of moral community and maintains that Somalis are not members in good standing. He claims the virtues of fair play and commitment to community should indicate the boundaries of belonging. Aware that his perspective would be considered racist, George accepts the label. Fish (1997) contends that multicultural speech codes should be considered an occasional strategy in the campaign against racist morality. While individuals who do not wish to be labeled and excluded as racists utilize, honestly or in self-interest, the vocabulary of the discourse and espouse its corresponding worldview, George's monologue demonstrates that symbolic boundaries can lead to the creation of "racists" who may decide to act the part.

"Somalians come over here with nothing. They come over here because their own country fell apart. They fucked that up and now they are bringing their fighting and their drugs over here. You know that neighborhood down in Portland where they are all living? What's it called?"

"Kennedy Park?" I replied, grateful for a momentary lull in my conversation with George, a white, gregarious, lifelong area resident working for a public utilities company who was eager to share his views on Somali settlement in Maine.

"Yeah, that's it. You know the cops are down there every fucking night. Drugs and fighting and all that shit. It's not safe down there because of them Somalians."

"I don't know about that, George. It has always been a rough area. Back when I was in high school if there was trouble that's where it was."

"Shit, I'm so tired of that liberal bullshit. Look, they don't give a shit about us. They don't call it home. They are just waiting here until things settle down back in Somalia. Back in the day, when my grandfather came from Italy, them immigrants came to become American and to make a better life. Them Somalians are just here because it's the best deal they can get right now and if they can get more money somewhere else, they're gone. And you know what really pisses me off? The special treatment. Here I am, a real, hard-working American. I don't want any special treatment but, shit, I took my daughter to court for something stupid she did when she was just eighteen, right? Here she was facing criminal charges and no one wanted to give her a break but you should have seen the way the lawyers and the judges were treating the Somalians. (mockingly) 'Oh you broke the law? We're so sorry that our laws are not sensitive to you. Please do whatever you want.' Here they were in court for breaking the law and they were being treated like everyone else was wrong but my daughter, forget about her. They won't be happy 'til we're all speaking Somalian and all that shit. And you know what I think? I think that they should all be shipped the hell out of here. If that's racist, then I'm a mother-fuckin' racist."

In arguing against Somali settlement and incorporation, George offered a different moral compass, one calibrated to enduring loyalty and patriotism, equality, and cultural conformity. When I challenged his initial claims that crime and violence came in the wake of Somali settlement, he shifted his emphasis to the moral constitution of community. Citing the hard work of himself and his family and the fact that they were treated as unexceptional in the face of the law, George claimed that Somalis lacked patriotism and attachment to Maine and engaged in rule-breaking behavior that was enabled by the special treatment they received. For these reasons, George felt that Somalis fell outside the moral pale. George acknowledged and dismissed the dominant moral and symbolic boundaries as "liberal bullshit" and sought to defang the assessment of his view of Somalis as racist by applying the term to himself while defending his own moral stance against the exclusion the racist label would typically carry with it.[7]

"DEFINING MOMENTS"

When 500 people attended the town hall meeting to discuss the impact that Somali settlement would have on Lewiston, the venue offered a platform for the expression of a particular definition of community – a community that remained untouched by new cultural and linguistic diversity. In asking to be delivered from the changes wrought by Somalis, participants in the meeting drew upon an implicit desire to maintain the cultural continuity of Lewiston and the boundaries of their society. For those residents who wanted the city to stay the same, Somali settlement contributed to an air of crisis, the demise of a way of life.

In his well-known polemic *Who Are We?* Huntington (2004) argues that the American national project is in jeopardy. Huntington asserts that U.S. national identity, cultural core, cohesion, and global supremacy are declining, in part as a result of the efforts of multicultural "deconstructionists" endorsing subgroup identification and thus undermining the national cultural heritage and core principles of individualism and equality. American cohesion is similarly thwarted by failed immigrant assimilation due to the non-European origins of many contemporary immigrants and the corresponding rise of "ampersands" who fail to identify historical core values because they maintain dual nationalities and close contact with their countries of origin.

Many contemporary scholars of immigration share Huntington's expectations that the present-day trajectory of immigrant incorporation

---

[7] Although not the focus of this particular research project, my observations and the research of others suggests that the meaning and praxis of the category "racist" is a social construct that motivates individuals (Hartigan, John Jr. 1999. *Racial situations: Class predicaments of whiteness in Detroit*. Princeton, NJ: Princeton University Press; Miller-Idriss, Cynthia. 2009. *Blood and culture: Youth, right-wing extremism, and national belonging in contemporary Germany*. Durham, NC: Duke University Press; van Gelder, Elles and Ilvy Njiokiktjien. 2011. "Afrikaner Blood." Pp. 08:26). Thus, racist self-identities, much like the antiracist identities discussed in Chapter 4, are not merely the expression of anomie (Blazak, Randy. 2001. "White Boys to Terrorist Men: Target Recruitment of Nazi Skinheads." *American Behavioral Scientist* 44:982–1000) or empirical manifestations of an ontological category referring to a particular type of "mind" (Ezekiel, Raphael S. 1995. *The racist mind: Portraits of American Neo-Nazis and Klansmen*. New York: Viking). Instead, the racist identity is wilfully enacted through the adoption of the associations, behaviors, and fundamental "truths" associated with the identity.

and the impact that immigrants have upon American society will diverge from melting-pot accounts of past immigrant assimilation. Citing contingencies ranging from new immigrants' histories as colonial subjects, observance of non-Christian religious traditions, and status as racial minorities in the United States, to the fact of ongoing immigration maintaining segregated immigrant enclaves that resist incorporation, to the availability of technological advances ensuring continued communication and economic ties between immigrants and their sending societies, students of immigration have expressed their doubt regarding the nature and scope of the Americanization and assimilation of new immigrants (cf. Faist 2000; Portes and Zhou 1993; Suarez-Orozco 2002; Tienda 1999).

The misgivings of academics find little expression in Lewiston where alternative and contemporary conceptions of "who we are" supplanted understandings that would require the total assimilation or symbolic exclusion of Somali newcomers. In the city, Somali settlement came to be identified as bringing positive growth that enriched Lewiston instead of endangering it. This diversity-affirming sense of the meaning of Somali settlement was inseparable from foundational definitions of community and the moral criteria for membership. Lewiston was no longer to be understood solely in relation to tradition, history, or the tenure and self-discipline of its citizens. The city and its residents worthy of inclusion were characterized primarily by their commitment to the community; their individual natures as welcoming, accepting, and caring; and by the global connections, economic promise, and cultural potential of the setting. Lewiston was a community that had stood in the face of bigotry and hate and demonstrated that racism and prejudice would not find fertile ground within its confines. Somalis were welcomed. It was those who would not or could not accept the new neighbors and the community they engendered who did not belong.

3

Being the Inclusive Community

On October 3 and 4, 2003, I attended my first diversity training conference in Lewiston, Maine. I learned of the event through the sarcastic editorial discussed in Chapter 2, in which the editor of the conservative weekly paper, the *Twin City Times*, suggested that outsiders considered Lewiston a town of racist "horrible white people" requiring reeducation. I sought out registration information for the event and found a description of the "Lewiston and the Two Towns of Jasper Project" on the website of the Maine chapter of the international anti-racist organization[1] hosting the event:

[We, the organization] invite community members to an open discussion about race.

On June 7, 1998, in Jasper, Texas, James Byrd Jr., an African American man, was brutally murdered – dragged behind a pick-up truck. The crime became the basis for a documentary film about race in America – "Two Towns of Jasper ..."

We will provide a forum to watch the film ... and discuss the similarities and differences between Jasper, Texas and Lewiston, Maine. We will then lead a process to explore a controversial issue that has caused division in the city enabling people to find common ground, move forward, and find solutions. In addition to the opportunities for dialogue, we will provide a day for individuals to learn about welcoming diversity into their lives."

---

[1] The organization, founded in 1984, offers prejudice reduction workshops for corporations, communities, and universities throughout North America and Europe. It has been recognized in the national media as a leader in combating racial discrimination and ameliorating racial tensions and prejudices. The Maine chapter began offering leadership training, conflict resolution, and prejudice reduction programs in the late 1980s. While the international organization still exists, the Maine chapter has disbanded in the years since they offered the training session.

I registered for the two-day project, paying the requested fee and explaining my status as an ethnographic researcher in Lewiston to the program leaders and, on the first day of the event, to the other conference participants.

The program commenced on a Friday morning. The three program organizers and training leaders stood before the small number of attendees, fourteen in all. The group consisted of a few city and state officials – high-ranking law enforcement officials; leaders from city, county, and state offices of labor management and social services, and a couple of refugee resettlement case managers; bankers who were taking the training in fulfillment of their professional development training requirements associated with their positions in local and regional branches of a nationwide bank; and three community members, all of whom were involved in the Many and One Coalition. One participant was a lower-class resident of the city, a member of the group most at risk for being labeled racist, who self-identified as an unemployed former drug addict who was now quite involved in the Many and One Coalition and other community-building initiatives. All the other participants appeared to be educated and employed members of the middle class. There were no Somalis present and there was only one nonwhite individual in attendance, an African American and longtime Mainer employed by a state agency with an interest in diversity management.

The training leader lamented the limited and relatively homogeneous turnout for the event. They had expected at least sixty participants, she claimed. They wanted a diverse group including Somalis, representatives of the largely Latino Rural Workers' Coalition, Asian restaurant owners, and representatives from Bates College and other educational institutions. In planning the event, they had hoped to capitalize on the anti-racist energy and enthusiasm generated by the Many and One Rally of the previous winter. Unfortunately, the program leader claimed, *Twin City Times'* negative publicity had extinguished community interest in their project. They had been forced to engage in substantial damage control, scrounging for participants and pressuring city and state agencies to send their leadership for training.

After describing the ways in which the Two Towns of Jasper Project was not the event she had hoped for, the training leader noted that there was still significant learning that could occur if we, the participants, were honest about our own strengths and weaknesses and open to the perspectives of others. We didn't need a diverse group, she stated, to become more aware of racial issues, to work together to identify trouble in Lewiston, and to make progress toward healing the divisions in the community.

With this introduction, the training leader began the film, *The Two Towns of Jasper* (Dow, Williams, Independent Television Service, National Black Programming Consortium, Two Tone Productions, and PBS Home Video. 2004), a feature-length documentary focusing on the town of Jasper, Texas, where the gruesome murder of James Byrd Jr. by three men with ties to white supremacist groups provided fertile ground for the examination of strained race relations and persistent segregation. Focusing on the fence separating the black and white cemeteries and on public support for rodeo days in the town and hostility toward celebrating the Martin Luther King Jr. holiday, the film observed the relationship between Jasper's segregated African American and white communities. *The Two Towns of Jasper* interrogated the social institutions, practices, and perspectives that maintained segregation in Jasper.

The post-film discussion made it clear that the program planners intended participants to hear the echoes of Lewiston's recent drama in the story of Jasper. The conversation moved quickly from a discussion of the details of the film to life in the community. What, the program guide asked, were some of the similarities between Jasper and Lewiston when it came to racial issues? In Jasper, the cemetery fence demonstrated how segregated groups were. What barriers kept people in Lewiston apart? What institutions kept those fences up? As individuals, what were our prejudices – our own personal fences?

As a relative newcomer to the community and stranger to most of the other project participants, I grew increasingly uncomfortable with the latent tensions I sensed in the room. I was sitting next to a high-ranking city official, Ms. Smith,[2] whose responsibilities included much of the day-to-day management of Somali settlement in the city. Early in the day we had chatted amicably about my research and the challenges of her position. In those first conversations I noted that she emphasized the fiscal and programmatic difficulties Somali settlement posed for her department. Although I did not broach the sensitive subject of Mayor Raymond's letter, I concluded from her statements that she subscribed to the understanding that informed Raymond's interpretation of Somali settlement – that it did have significant fiscal, practical, and emotional costs for the city of Lewiston. Early in the post-film discussion Ms. Smith suggested that Lewiston was nothing like Jasper and that there were "real

[2] A pseudonym.

issues" (as opposed to racism) associated with Somali settlement. She was quickly rebuffed by both program participants and leadership who pointed out that the fear and discomfort that kept people segregated in Jasper was at the root of the murder and inequality in the town. Only by considering Somalis less worthy or less-than-equal members of Lewiston was it possible to see Somali newcomers as outsiders not worthy of support. To ignore the racism causing all the trouble in Lewiston, one project participant claimed, was racist.

As the discussion progressed, I noted a change in Ms. Smith's demeanor. She stopped participating and appeared sullen and subdued. She believed that she carried a heavy burden in managing the fiscal and programmatic aspects of Somali settlement in Lewiston. She had acquired that responsibility, not because she had particular skills, interest, or expertise when it came to immigrant settlement, but because there were very limited immigrant services in town and she administered the city department that picked up the slack. It seemed to me that, just as she dismissed the reality of racism as a practical concern, in the perspective emerging as dominant in the program, her concerns were dismissed as masked expressions of racism that were best addressed with a change in perspective. The racism-focused orientation of the training project placed her in the same category as the three white supremacists who murdered a man by dragging him behind a pickup truck. It made the distinction between the city she had lived in her entire life and segregated Jasper, Texas, into a difference only of degree.

The "Two Towns of Jasper Project" offered a remedy for the stymied development of an open, inclusive Lewiston. It was a treatment derived from a particular diagnosis of the situation in the town, one in which racism breeds segregation and fear that produce conflict and inequality. In other words, the project provided an account of the epistemological roots of the narratives discussed in Chapter 2. Diversity-affirming narratives embraced the presence of Somali newcomers, and narratives of diversity troubles interpreted community tensions and failures of incorporation as the result of inexperience, exploitation, ignorance, and racism. Within this web of meanings in which problems of Somali incorporation were generally tied to problematic non-Somali individuals, people like Ms. Smith, who experienced Somali settlement as a challenge to city budgets, prior procedural norms, and community practices, struggled to express their views and develop institutional responses that demonstrated the speaker's position within the moral boundaries of belonging set up by these common narratives.

"REALIZING" AN INCLUSIVE LEWISTON

With the specter of media scrutiny, public outrage, and white supremacist actions following the publication of Mayor Raymond's letter fresh in many minds, Lewiston's leaders were well aware of the risks associated with uncharacteristic responses to the community's visible heterogeneity. Defining Lewiston as an inclusive community elicited actions *recognizably* consistent with the deeply held values that constituted the moral and pragmatic boundaries of the community. Lewiston's inclusivity was reflected in the city's programs and institutions as well as its populace. Responding to the demand for sensitive programs, local administrators, service providers, and political figures turned outward, appropriating standardized narratives and widely accepted methods of engaging cultural heterogeneity, pursuing inclusivity, and dealing with difficulties. In this way, the emerging meanings of Somali settlement and the inclusive community not only drove interpretations of behavior and assessments of the worthiness of individual city residents but they were also implicated in institutional responses to Somali settlement – in Lewiston's approach to managing cultural diversity and immigrant incorporation.

Symbolic boundaries and abstract values that constitute the "we" of the civil sphere have material consequences. In this chapter, I consider the impact of shared symbolic systems on local practice. Lewiston's programmatic and administrative pursuit of immigrant incorporation and the inclusive community exposes the relationship between diversity-affirming and diversity-trouble narratives and community administration and management. Institutional responses to Somali settlement in the city took four forms: legal compliance in service provision; community dialogues; cultural assimilation of Somalis; and diversity education for non-Somalis. Local officials and service providers developed policies and programs that complied with legal mandates and standards for accessibility and equality. Additional programmatic efforts provided cultural competence training to Somali newcomers. Diversity education programs informed community service providers about aspects of Somali culture and guided laypeople in examining the impact that their biases have on their behavior. While in this chapter I consider all four forms of institutional response to Somali immigrant incorporation, I focus a greater analytical lens on diversity training, a site where the tacit theories and common methods of multicultural incorporation are brought into focus.

The imprint of deep values and multicultural discourse was evident in the many institutional responses to Somali settlement in Lewiston.

However, the particular meanings underlying incorporation came into sharpest relief in diversity education. Close scrutiny of the character and role of diversity training revealed the highly therapeutic and individual orientation of diversity training seminars and other intervention efforts in the city. Institutional responses to Somali settlement demonstrated the "responsibilisation" (Lemke 2001)[3] of intercultural living, a reorientation away from open discussion and management of the structural and political difficulties and challenges associated with new immigrant settlement in Lewiston and toward the management of Somali incorporation as a project accomplished through the transformation of individuals. As some programs offered in Lewiston sought to change immigrant newcomers through the establishment of resettlement assistance, additional interventions assisted non-Somali Lewistonians in undertaking individual psychological and emotional work required in overcoming intolerance.

Lewiston's administrative and programmatic responses to Somali settlement took shape in interaction with regional, national, and international contexts that assigned meanings to diversity and designated desirable strategies for managing a diverse community. Community leaders adopted the practices and assessments disseminated by national and international agencies and codified in federal legal mandates and policy preferences. In addition to their orientation to external standards and practices, Lewiston leaders hosted a variety of advisory bodies, diversity experts, and federal agencies interested in taking an active role in shaping the nature of immigrant incorporation in the city. Non-municipal experts provided crucial administrative and didactic expertise. Diversity consultants representing a variety of organizations and contracted out of other locations advised the city on its hiring practices, service plans, school organization, accessibility policies, and community-building efforts. Diversity trainers coming from locations as close as Portland, Maine, and as far as San Diego offered frequent seminars geared toward increasing participants' multicultural skill sets. Local emphasis on legal accountability and best practices demonstrates the close connection between local and extra-local contexts.

---

[3] "The strategy of rendering individual subjects 'responsible' (and also collectives, such as families, associations, etc.) entails shifting the responsibility for social risks such as illness, unemployment, poverty, etc. and for life in society into the domain for which the individual is responsible and transforming it into a problem of 'self-care'" (Lemke, Thomas. 2001. "The Birth of Bio-Piolitics: Michel Foucault's Lecture at the College de France on Neo-Liberal Governmentality." Economy & Society 30:190–207, p. 201.

The Letter of the Law

Legal mandates and the mutual impact that city organizations had on one another as they sought to bring their behavior in line with those mandates played a key role in Lewiston's diversity management. City officials were guided by other communities and institutions, observing their organizational responses to national laws and policies regarding accessibility of services and equal treatment, as they attempted to respond effectively to the growing diversity of Lewiston. The influence of law and policy is evident in the following quotation.

What we didn't even know about was that there were a couple of executive orders concerning requirements for federally funded, um, for federal agencies and their federally funded beneficiaries to deal with limited English proficiency.... We had been going along our merry way doing the best we could when the city of Lewiston sent over their plan so we sort of, "Hmm, how did we miss this?" (official in local office of federal agency, in interview)

In developing city policies and programs around immigration and diversity, Lewiston collaborated with other locales that had a significant Somali settlement. The city established networks to share expertise with public officials in Portland, Maine; Minneapolis; Columbus, Ohio; and Clarkson, Georgia (Nadeau 2003b).[4]

Working with other offices and creatively on their own, many of Lewiston's leaders applied great effort to the task of ensuring that their departments and offices were complying with legal requirements and standards. Their efforts were noted. While this research was under way, the U.S. Department of Justice cited the Lewiston Police Department for best practices in preparing for the World Church of the Creator rally

---

[4] It should come as no surprise that federal policies and programs and the approaches of other municipalities influenced Lewiston's programmatic and policy response to new, nonwhite immigrant settlement. Existing research documents the impact of legal and normative requirements for equal opportunity on increased workplace diversity (Hirsh, C. Elizabeth. 2009. "The Strength of Weak Enforcement: The Impact of Discrimination Charges, Legal Environments, and Organizational Conditions on Workplace Segregation." *American Sociological Review* 74:245–271; Skaggs, Sheryl. "Legal-Political Pressures and African American Access to Managerial Jobs." *American Sociological Review* 74:225–244). Anti-discrimination policies exert influence at least as much through their impact on normative practices and management strategies as through the threat of litigation (Hirsh, "The Strength of Weak Enforcement." 245–271). Governments are also influenced by emerging best practices and perspectives. In observing the international rise of multiculturalism, Kymlicka notes that accepted multicultural practices tend to exert a normative influence on nations (Kymlicka, Will. 2007. *Multicultural odysseys: Navigating the new international politics of diversity*. New York: Oxford University Press).

and for the reporting and investigation of potential hate crimes in the community. As previously discussed in Chapter 2, the community also received the 2007 All-America City award.

Referencing the public recognition of their successes during interviews with me, municipal employees, city officials, and local service providers frequently shared their pride that Lewiston, in a very short time, had moved from having little understanding of national standards for accessibility, equal opportunity, and procedures for dealing with infringements of the civil rights of its citizens to meeting or exceeding existing legal and administrative guidelines for diversity. The success of the city in acquiring competence supported claims that, with a little effort, the inexperience partially responsible for diversity troubles in the city was easily overcome. In the months of turmoil sandwiched between the publication of Mayor Raymond's letter and the WCOTC rally, Lewiston found itself under investigation for possible equal opportunity violations and facing a civil rights' lawsuit. Efforts at addressing shortcomings in legal compliance capitalized on the spotlight and yielded considerable payoff and prestige for the community.

Despite the outward-looking nature of the emphasis on legal compliance and implementation of best practices, in interviews, many local policy makers and service providers stressed the unique advantages that being in a small town in a less populous state brought to bear on diversity management. Lewiston's leaders also noted the limited impact of generalized attempts at inclusivity and their success in making pro-diversity policies work for Lewiston. When compared with the major metropolitan areas frequently hosting immigrants, Lewiston was able to be responsive to Somalis in particular instead of merely developing fair rules and equitable institutions. The proximity of administrative bodies to Lewiston residents and the state's relatively flat governmental structure were conducive to flexibility and responsiveness in the face of unusual circumstances.

After the Somalis began arriving, there was a death in the community. Now, it is Somali custom for the body to be prepared by family members – male family members if the deceased is a man and vice versa. Well, it so happens that, in Maine, hospitals are only able to release bodies to morgues or funeral homes. When they told the family members that, it did *not* go over so well. So, I get this call from the hospital and I say, "Uh-oh" because I know that if we don't handle this one right we'll be in trouble. So, I make a couple of calls and, the next thing I know, [the governor himself is aware of the situation]. He issued an order for the release of the body to the family. (city official, in interview)

Compliance with federal regulations pertaining explicitly to diversity operated as a benchmark of success and, correspondingly, indicated the community's openness to diversity. Still, my informants wore stories like the one shared above as badges of honor demonstrating commitment to the spirit over the letter of the law. That is to say, in responding quickly and creatively in instances when the needs of a diverse constituency – in this case, the Somalis – fell outside the codified rules of diversity management, the administrators in Lewiston showed that they erred on the side of inclusivity and respect.

If working toward legal compliance with federal laws and policies was the first step many took in responding to Lewiston's newest residents, this strategy also persisted as an effective way of managing diversity in the town well after Somali settlement in Lewiston became an everyday fact of life. In the years after the crisis brought on by the letter and the WCOTC rally, legal compliance with abstract requirements for service provision remained a primary measure of the adequacy of the city's performance in welcoming and incorporating Somali newcomers.

Cultural Assimilation

Lewiston leadership acted quickly and efficiently to make their programs and procedures compliant with federal mandates. As time wore on, however, the pragmatic difficulties of Somali incorporation revealed the limited scope and impact of national standards guiding local action. Observing high levels of unemployment and sluggish gains in literacy and the acquisition of spoken-English among Somali residents, city planners and service providers quickly recognized that their successful efforts at compliance were not sufficient to support the economic and political incorporation of newcomers. So writes Lewiston City Administrator Phil Nadeau:

Issues associated with the ongoing employment needs of a growing refugee population have posed challenges for the city and for the many refugee residents who remain unemployed.... [L]ocal officials have recognized the significant weaknesses of a federal refugee resettlement policy that has largely failed to provide low literate, limited- to non-English-speaking refugees the required amounts of education and training to gain employment. (Nadeau 2011, p. 53)[5]

---

[5] Bean and Stevens (Bean, Frank D. and Gillian Stevens. 2003. *America's newcomers and the dynamics of diversity*. New York: Russell Sage Foundation) find that the administrative and fiscal costs of immigration are felt primarily at the local level while the economic benefits of immigration are observed at the federal level.

Responding to the need for Somali employment, language, and medical assistance, the city of Lewiston, the state of Maine, area hospitals, the school department, a retail company that supplies jobs for much of western and central Maine, and a host of social service agencies developed an array of programs and requirements geared toward providing employment skills and cultural information to the community's Somali residents (Bennett and Nadeau 2002; Nadeau 2003b, 2007, 2011). With funding from the state, the city hired a full-time immigrant and refugee programs manager to coordinate resettlement services, seek funding, and administer city, school, and AmeriCorps/VISTA projects in Lewiston. The city also expanded its adult education program and implemented language education requirements for non-English speakers receiving general assistance. Area hospitals worked with the city and state to form a public health committee focused on immigrant health needs. Lewiston organizations developed an urban farming and farmers' market program, implemented summer programs instructing newly arrived Somali children in American classroom etiquette, and created employment skills training workshops in which participants learned, among other things, that they must be punctual, serious, and engage in culturally American displays of deference and respect (e.g., making eye contact and addressing people as Mr. and Ms.). These are just a few of the many programs designed to help Somali newcomers as they sought to make lives for themselves in Lewiston.

Unlike the emphasis on top-down procedural and legal compliance outlined in the previous section, these many programs emerged as organic and pragmatic responses to the immediate needs of Somali incorporation. They arose from a plethora of collaborations and drew upon a hodgepodge of funding sources. The existence of such programs implicitly acknowledged Ms. Smith's claim that successful Somali incorporation required more than an anti-racist paradigm. As a departure from the multicultural mode of inclusion emphasized in diversity-affirming narratives, cultural education programs were occasionally met with skepticism and criticism (e.g., Fahrenthold 2006). However, given pragmatic concerns of Somali and non-Somali residents of Lewiston alike, they continued.

The existence of cultural education programs offering language instruction, education, and job training to Somali newcomers also nods to the persistence of alternative notions of outsider incorporation into the civil sphere. Interventions of this sort drew upon assimilationist ideas. Either implicitly or explicitly, such training assumed that responsible individuals (i.e., those worthy of social support in the form of financial assistance) must shed aspects of their home culture. It was understood that the broader cultural environment would not change to accommodate the cultural practices of Somalis. Instead, Somali newcomers must learn what it takes to be successful within their new environment as it was.

One may make an interesting comparison between the work Somalis did within these cultural assimilation programs and diversity training seminars like the Two Towns of Jasper Project. Through their participation in cultural assimilation programs, Somalis increased their American cultural competence and ability to navigate life in Lewiston successfully. However, as will be evident in Chapter 5, despite the widespread embrace of cultural preservation within public talk, Somali diversity work required the relativization, adjustment, and in some cases abandonment of some traditional practices that conflicted with mainstream culture. In contrast to the programs for Somalis, programs offered to non-Somalis were geared toward encouraging participants to change their mind-sets instead of making cultural adjustments to bring their behavior in line with Somali cultural norms.

Community Dialogues

In addition to improving program provision and accessibility for the Somalis, Lewiston officials sought to limit tensions in the community by opening channels of communication between Somali and non-Somali residents of the city. Occurring both before the publication of Mayor Raymond's letter in the town hall meeting discussed in the opening of Chapter 2, and in the spring after the WCOTC and Many and One meetings, this intervention took the form of large, open-format meetings and small, extended intergroup dialogues. Interviews and encounters with service providers, public officials, and community residents who took part revealed almost universal disappointment with Lewiston's community dialogues. Community dialogues faded as a method of diversity management in Lewiston because they failed to produce the desired outcome –a new, multicultural subjectivity among participants. This subjectivity is characterized by responsibilisation (Lemke 2001) – the process of individuals seeing themselves, instead of government, as the site of the production and amelioration of social problems like poverty, racism and inequality.

Fresh from the WCOTC and Many and One meetings in January 2003, Lewiston officials returned to the facilitation of community dialogue. In a departure from the disastrous town meeting, this time the city

did not go it alone. The Community Relations Division of the United
States Department of Justice worked with the city to develop a community dialogue process intended to "increase civic discourse" (Nadeau
2003b) in the city. The project resulting from these endeavors, Lewiston
Leads: Community Dialogue for Change, was designed to

encourage the broadest possible citizen participation, and to promote open
and honest community discussion, interaction, and understanding so that
all community residents may ... directly participate in identifying issues and
developing strategies to address community concerns which may touch upon
such issues as ethnic diversity; religious diversity; area social services; law
enforcement best practices; public school programs and activities; city programs; and other matters of public concern. (Community Building Planning
Committee 2003)

Five groups of six to eight individuals met weekly for three weeks.[6] Led
by facilitators trained by the federal Department of Justice, the volunteer
participants considered questions such as "What are the barriers that can
make it difficult to relate to people who are different?" and "What needs
to happen for more people to have positive experiences with the changing
cultural and social environment in Lewiston?"

At the conclusion of the three-week endeavour, the facilitators of each
group submitted minutes of the sessions. Read and analyzed by Lewiston's
Community Building Planning Committee, the minutes were the core of
a report distributed to the mayor and city council and posted on the city
website (Nadeau 2003a). The report contained detailed recommendations based upon the suggestions that emerged from the groups:

City should increase art/culture opportunities for residents.
    City should expand efforts to communicate information to the hardest to reach
populations.
    City should create a permanent/body committee to oversee actions imple-
mented from ... "Lewiston Leads."
    City should work to understand why immigrant populations are reluctant to
participate publicly and explore ways to enhance public involvement of immigrant populations.
    City should pursue or enhance affordable housing initiatives.
    City should look to developing more events to provide for greater community
interaction, e.g., block parties, street fairs, kid activities, farmers' market, multicultural fairs, etc. (pp. 22–23).

[6] There was some disagreement in my interviews and reports of the program as to whether
or not there were four or five groups. The program summary and report contain minutes
from five sessions.

Program participants also reported skepticism that anything would come from the dialogue process and, as in the Two Towns of Jasper Project, expressed their disappointment in the lack of participation among the city's Somali and working-class populations.

In offering the report for public view, Lewiston officials lamented the difficulty they experienced drumming up and maintaining participation from a broad segment of the community in the series of meetings. "Efforts to recruit participation in this community dialogue involved the contacting of some seventy or more local organizations and churches in the area. The resulting number of people who participated in the five scheduled public meetings was relatively small in number [about 60] but the level of engagement and enthusiasm for the effort was high" (Nadeau 2003a, p. 4). Ultimately, little came of the suggestions and the dialogue process. Due to lack of widespread community involvement in Lewiston Leads, the committee concluded that the "observations and recommendations cannot be represented as the opinion of the general community given the small number of participants" (Nadeau 2003a, p. 7). After the dissemination of the report, plans for future community dialogues were eliminated and the Community Building Planning Committee was disbanded.

Consisting of community members brought together voluntarily to converse and share their different perspectives, Lewiston's community dialogues struggled to make a positive impact on diversity troubles and community cohesion. In one case, the groups met repeatedly, and in the other meeting, the May 2002 town meeting discussed in Chapter 2, occurred only once.[7] Lewiston Leads: Community Dialogue for Change failed in the eyes of those who wrote the final report because the program never developed the appropriate subjectivity among its participants. Previous research suggests that talk in civic intergroup dialogues alternates between emphasizing the importance of intergroup cohesiveness and the value of preserving and protecting distinct group identities and cultures (Walsh 2007). In Lewiston, however, groups focused on mutual

[7] Lewiston's community dialogues have only a limited resemblance to those Walsh observed in her study of intergroup dialogue programs (Walsh, Katherine Cramer. 2007. *Talking about race: Community dialogues and the politics of difference*. Chicago: University of Chicago Press). Walsh claims that "civic intergroup dialogue programs" are designed to offer difference-focused and participant-led dialogue (as opposed to discussion) in which participants share personal views and experiences around certain topics such as immigration policy. Through the program, participants should develop increased awareness, understanding, and acceptance of the experiences of others. Had I encountered such programs in Lewiston, I would consider them diversity training, as discussed later in the chapter.

problem solving and decision making for the community in terms of specific program development, not on sharing perspectives. The result of this orientation to the dialogue process was a significant emphasis on problem solving at the level of the Lewiston community as a whole and neglect of the personal, direct communication and interaction that the dialogues were intended to create – the emotional work, it was believed, would foster greater interpersonal understanding.

In reacting to the minutes of the dialogue sessions, the Community Building Planning Committee wrote,

Citizen over-reliance on city to respond to all social, economic, cultural and educational needs in the city is problematic.... A greater level of non-city staffed citizen participation ... is an important vehicle for strengthening a sense of community, civic involvement and responsibility for overall quality of life.

This reaction from the committee elucidates what they expected of the process: participants learning through dialogue how they have each contributed to the current problems in Lewiston, and what they, outside of city institutions, can do differently.

In the view of the Community Building Planning Committee, successful intergroup dialogue hinged upon the willingness among those taking part to engage the topic of intergroup differences and memberships as emotional topics that are best handled through personal growth instead of structural change – the therapeutic experience of healthy communication and the development of bonds of understanding with members of other groups discussed in Chapter 4. While taking seriously their role as advisors to the city on the matter of diversity-related programming, participants did not take seriously enough the sharing and soul-searching required to make the dialogues a success in the eyes of those who planned them. City leaders rebuffed the emphasis on institutional and structural change arising from an intervention intended to produce a change in the participants themselves. Thus, community dialogues failed as a method of moral reeducation, while diversity education rose to the fore.

Diversity Education

Lewiston's public officials, municipal employees and service providers touted their success in offering culturally sensitive programs and services to Lewiston's Somali residents. They further noted their unsuccessful attempts at fostering constructive dialogue among Lewiston's residents and their industriousness and creativity in giving the Somalis what they need to be successful in the United States. However, outside of assimilation-based programs for Somalis, some of the most widespread and consistent work toward making Lewiston a city open to diversity took the form of diversity education. During my fieldwork in Lewiston, I attended more than a dozen diversity education sessions. Heralded as multicultural training, diversity training, and cultural sensitivity and awareness seminars, these events shared a common preoccupation with increasing the skill with which longtime Lewiston residents, as well as city officials, municipal employees, area employers, and local and regional service providers, interacted with their new neighbors. Diversity education in the field consisted of cultural brokerage and diversity training.

Cultural Brokers

In the first and rarest form of diversity education, Somali cultural brokers discussed Somali cultural norms and offered techniques for working through cross-cultural issues. While conducting research in Lewiston, I attended four sessions operating on the cultural brokerage model. Cultural brokerage sessions operated in a manner similar to the cultural assimilation programs offered to Somali residents of Lewiston. In each case, an educator or expert operated as a one-way conduit of information. Yet cultural assimilation educational programs sought to help Somalis acquire the information they needed to work within American culture, while cultural brokerage sessions were more explicitly multicultural in their aims, attempting to make participants aware of differences, not eliminating them.

Cultural brokerage sessions typically targeted local employers and employees of area agencies serving diverse populations. Thus, select business owners, social service workers, and health professionals were the primary consumers of cultural brokerage sessions. Brokers did provide helpful insight. Participants took extensive notes when brokers discussed how Somalis felt when summoned by beckoning with a finger ("that is how you call a dog") and when they got a glimpse of the bottom of someone's foot or shoe when an individual crossed their legs (they informed those who potentially might sit in such a way that for Somalis "that means you think the person is worthless"). Brokers listed other common American behaviors that Somalis found troublesome and attendees listened attentively.

Although attendees clearly valued cultural brokerage sessions for the opportunity to learn about Somali culture and ask questions about cross-cultural conflicts in a safe space, individuals frequently expressed discomfort at walking, as one participant put it, "the fine line between facts and stereotypes." While the amateur Somali cultural brokers leading all but one[8] of the sessions I observed did act as a resource, they also contributed to discomfort by offering cultural generalizations and failing to provide guidance as attendees sought to manage intercultural difficulties. For example, in one instance an employer shared his uncertainty when it comes to sensitively addressing persistent tardiness among his Somali employees. The cultural broker laughed and shook her head. "Somalis are a late people," she replied. A few minutes later the same employer spoke again. His other employees were grumbling, he said, because he was more forgiving of tardiness among Somali employees. How can he be sensitive to cultural difference and treat his workers fairly? This time the cultural broker replied. "Just tell them they are in America now. They need to be on time or they will lose their jobs."

Another session included a panel of four Somalis, one man and three women. The man answered all the questions, including those directly related to the economic incorporation of Somali women. When the panel was asked about the special challenges for Somali women, he said, "In Somalia, most women are not interested in being educated. They choose to stay home and raise the family. It is unfortunate that here they are forced to study and work outside of the home. Somali women are not suited to it and should only be given jobs that do not interfere with their roles as wives and mothers." The Somali women wore wry smiles on their faces as he spoke. Then, the facilitator, a female professor from Bates College, asked each woman on the panel by name if she agreed with the statement or would like to add anything. The three women declined to comment (for more information on Somali gender relations as they pertain to the cultural pragmatics of incorporation, see Chapter 5).

In instances such as these, cultural brokerage sessions demonstrated one of the persistent dilemmas of multicultural incorporation: determining whether a cultural difference should be valued and accommodated as diversity or condemned and eradicated as "old world tradition." Was it unreasonable to censure tardiness, ignore traditional gender roles, or to ask that Somali employees pray during their designated breaks? If employers believed it was their duty to offer a prayer room, might they also see it as their responsibility to support tradition by segregating that

---

[8] A professional Somali law enforcement trainer spoke to the Lewiston Police Department about Somali cultural issues in the provision of public safety.

space by gender? What should a social worker do about public housing in the case of polygamy or instances of the arranged marriages of
young women?

In cultural brokerage sessions, confidential discussion of the pragmatic
difficulties of Somali reception and incorporation in Lewiston frequently
overshadowed demands for public emphasis on the benefits of Somali
settlement. While cultural brokerage sessions provided an opportunity
for participants to voice the struggles they encountered in working with
Somalis, the sessions imparted little guidance when it came to navigating thorny cultural conflicts. Furthermore, cultural brokerage sessions
were offered most frequently to Lewiston-area professionals with a
professional stake in Somali incorporation while other Lewiston residents lacked a safe forum to share cross-cultural difficulties. Yet another
form of diversity education, diversity training, targeted Lewiston's non-
Somali laypeople. As we will see, diversity training engaged Somali settlement at some distance removed from the complexities of intercultural
negotiation.

Diversity Training

Diversity training was a common approach to diversity education for the
general population in Lewiston.[9] During my time in the city I participated
in a host of diversity training sessions sometimes offered to and other
times mandated for the general public, city employees, hospital and social
service employees, and educators. Although the programs I have placed
under the rubric of diversity training were variously called diversity training, anti-racist training, intercultural training, or sensitivity training, I
refer to them all as diversity training if the training was oriented toward
furthering multicultural goals of inclusivity and recognition by changing
individual psychology and behavior (Hernandez and Field 2003 also take
this approach). Such training is based upon the assumption that agencies,

[9] Diversity training is ubiquitous in Western society and increasingly common outside
the West. In 2002 in the United States, nearly 40 percent of businesses large enough
to file equal employment opportunity reports had offered diversity training within the
past three years (Kalev, Alexandra, Erin Kelly, and Frank Dobbin. 2006. "Best Practices
or Best Guesses? Assessing the Efficacy of Corporate Affirmative Action and Diversity
Policies." *American Sociological Review* 71:589–617). In the United States in 2006,
more than 200,000 diversity professionals plied their trade (U.S. Department of Labor.
2006. *Occupational Employment and Wages, May 2006 13-1079 Human Resources,
Training, Labor Relations Specialists, All Other*. Edited by the Bureau of Labor Statistics.
Washington, DC: U.S. Department of Labor). They are joined by a host of individuals and
organizations seeking to foster multiculturalism around the world.

institutions, and communities are best reformed through the reform of their members (Pendry, Driscoll, and Field 2007). The training programs differed in their stated purpose, site of application, and goals of participants. I observed, however, that these various training approaches conveyed a similar facility with a shared vocabulary and common exercises to be discussed in Chapter 4.

Sometimes by design and at other times as a matter of course, Somali Lewistonians were wholly absent from diversity training seminars. Instead of imparting information about Somali culture, the common didactic method in cultural brokerage sessions, discussions, and activities in diversity training sessions focused upon encouraging participants to explore their biases and the areas in which they are not open to the racial, ethnic, religious, sexual, and sometimes physical and mental ability differences in their community. The following example of a training session in Lewiston reveals the typical content and common reception of anti-bias training. The account also includes an instance in which a training participant expressed practical intercultural difficulties and considers the manner in which such expressions were often managed within the diversity training sessions.

One of the diversity training sessions in which I participated was offered by the Department of Justice to public works employees in the city of Lewiston. The manager of Lewiston's Refugee and Immigrant Programs informed me that the city's human resources department was requiring diversity training for all city staff. I contacted the director of human resources and asked if I could participate in subsequent sessions. He granted tentative permission, pending approval of the trainer and the regional office of the Department of Justice.

I arrived early at city hall, just to make sure that everything went smoothly. After checking in at the office of human resources and introducing myself to the diversity trainer, a mid-level official in the U.S. Department of Justice, I took my seat in the meeting room, the first to arrive. I sat with my notebook, jotting down first impressions as the other diversity trainees entered the room. The circle of seats was soon full, populated by myself and sixteen men, likely between thirty and fifty years old. It was a workday for them, and their attendance was mandatory. Most were wearing jeans and flannel shirts or sweatshirts. There were two police officers in uniform. A couple of others were wearing painting clothes and another was in a blue workman's uniform with his name on a patch on the breast pocket. The men were clearly acquainted and conversed easily, glancing occasionally in my direction and the direction of the trainer. I met their glances with a smile and packed away my notebook.

The trainer, Frank, called the session to order and introduced himself as a Maine native who had spent much of his life in Portland where he worked as a police officer. He was now living in Boston and working for the U.S. Department of Justice. He paused, seeking to make eye contact with the people seated in front of him. Most of the men were looking away, at their feet or hands. I glanced around the room. I sensed defiance and avoidance in the crowd.

Frank pressed on. Moving on to the details of the three-hour diversity training session, Frank highlighted the need for diversity training in light of Lewiston's growing Somali population, the first substantial non-white community in the city's history and the first immigrant newcomers in more than fifty years. He alluded briefly to troubles experienced in Lewiston the year before, when former mayor Larry Raymond published his letter informing the city's Somali residents that the city could not accommodate further relocation to the city by Somalis. He praised the work of the Lewiston Police Department in dealing with the subsequent rallies. Since that time, things had been pretty quiet in Lewiston, he maintained. But all the same, it was necessary to make sure that city employees, people representing the city, were up to speed with the legal and civil requirements for behavior.

He paused again and introduced the first task for the trainees, introductions. Nothing fancy, he said, just your name and your division. So around the circle we went and I learned that I was surrounded by the folks who kept Lewiston running: police officers, garbage collectors, street sweepers and snowplow drivers, folks from the department of sewers, groundskeepers, and custodians as well as master electricians, plumbers, and other tradespeople.

Frank covered a great deal of material that morning. He spent much of the first two hours talking about legal requirements for equal opportunity in hiring and promotion, on protected classes, and on the right to be free from hostility and harassment in the workplace. He requested very little in the way of audience participation and continued largely without interruption. Turning to the subject of racial jokes and friendly ribbing about race, sexual orientation, and religion at work, however, he stepped away from his flipchart and faced us. "What's wrong with a racist joke here and there?" he asked, trying, I suspected, to play his own devil's advocate. In response to the silence he went on. "If the joke doesn't pertain to anyone in the room or if it's directed at a friend, what's the big deal?" Silence.

Frank moved on to talk about the value of diversity, the fact that most of us are members of groups that are easily attacked and that even if we learn to laugh off jokes at our expense, those jokes perpetuate stereotypes. Furthermore, he continued, we don't know everything about the people surrounding us. We may make a joke about a racial group and learn later that one of our co-workers is married to someone or has an adopted child of that race. In general, he concluded, our behavior needs to demonstrate our respect for difference even if we feel that we don't like other groups.

At this point in the diversity training session, one of the participants, Dave, raised his hand. Frank stopped speaking and called on him. Dave spoke with an intensity that I interpreted to indicate both the emotional nature of his comment and, perhaps, his feeling of vulnerability at sharing in a group that had thus far been unyielding in their lack of participation. Prefacing his main point by highlighting his belief that recent immigrants should have the same chance to "make it" in this country that past generations were given, he went on, "You know, it's a two way street. I have some Somalians living right next door. It's not that I don't like them. They don't like us. I saw [female Somali neighbor] on the sidewalk and said hello but she just ignored me. I didn't do anything for her to treat me like that, did I? What about my respect? What about being a good neighbor?"

Frank thanked Dave for his comment. He validated Dave's bruised feelings but pointed out that Dave should not generalize from the behavior of his neighbor to all Somalis. Furthermore, Dave did not know why his neighbor ignored him. Perhaps she was having a bad day. Perhaps she did not hear Dave's greeting. Furthermore, even if his Somali neighbor was not being neighborly, Frank continued, Dave should appreciate the good things that Somalis bring to the community like opportunities to try new foods, learn about new customs, and hear a new language. Dave offered no response; so Frank moved on to discuss procedures for reporting harassment in the workplace.

Dave expressed hurt and resentment in the face of what he experienced as hostility and rejection. Within the anti-bias education session he learned that he should bury his bruised and negative feelings toward his Somali neighbor underneath an abstract appreciation for the diversity of Somalis. Frank's response lacked any mention of possible cultural factors that might account for the exclusion Dave felt – Somali Muslim prohibitions on contact between women and men that are not family, for example. As a participant in diversity training sessions in Lewiston, I encountered people like Dave time and again. Initially, I thought that the disjuncture between the content of the training and the cultural misconnections shared by training participants was due to the limitations of the diversity trainers. Perhaps they did not know enough about Islam and Somali culture to understand the issues adequately. Over time, however, I began to suspect that, in such instances, trainers like Frank were not just avoiding or inadequate to the task of mediating Somali and mainstream Lewiston cultures. On the contrary, in those moments trainers failed to recognize the challenging intercultural work required if trainees like Dave and Somali newcomers in Lewiston were to understand and embrace the strangers living next door.[10]

While cultural brokerage sessions focused on Somali cultural practices and could become mired in the details, complexities, and dilemmas of intercultural life, diversity training engaged the Somali presence as "diversity" at a level of abstraction that precluded emphasis on the complexity of intercultural exchange and instead reproduced the dominant discourse. Instead of fostering active engagement with and mutual understanding between Somali newcomers and other Lewiston residents, diversity training was oriented to the epistemological perspective encapsulated

---

[10] Despite the prevalence of diversity training, existing research offers scant evidence of its positive influence. Training sessions often elicit emotional responses from participants (Lasch-Quinn, Elisabeth. 2001. *Race experts: How racial etiquette, sensitivity training, and new age therapy hijacked the civil rights revolution.* New York: Norton; Pendry, Louise F., Denise M. Driscoll, and Susannah C. T. Field. 2007. "Diversity Training: Putting Theory into Practice." *Journal of Occupational and Organizational Psychology* 80:27–50). However, short-term emotional impact is not automatically parlayed into long-term psychological and behavioral change. Pre- and post-tests of participants in diversity training demonstrate that, on average, training does improve participants' attitudes toward other groups (Hill, Miriam E. and Martha Augoustinos. 2001. "Stereotype Change and Prejudice Reduction: Short- and Long-Term Evaluation of a Cross-Cultural Awareness Programme." *Journal of Community and Applied Social Psychology* 11:243–262) but does not increase the comfort with which individuals interact with members of different groups or exert reliable and lasting influence on the behavior of training participants (Paluck, Elizabeth Levy. 2006. "Diversity Action and Intergroup Contact: A Call to Action Research." *Journal of Social Issues* 62:577–595). Lacking demonstrable success in bringing about individual psychological and behavioral change, diversity training apparently also fails to exercise significant influence on social structure. Analyses employing longitudinal data from American corporations reveal that a corporation's diversity training has no impact on the racial and gender composition of middle management (Kalev, Alexandra, Erin Kelly, and Frank Dobbin. 2006. "Best Practices or Best Guesses? Assessing the Efficacy of Corporate Affirmtive Action and Diversity Policies." *American Sociological Review* 71:589–617).

in the diversity-affirming and diversity-trouble narratives ubiquitous in town – Somali diversity enriched the city and diversity troubles were the result of inexperience, ignorance, exploitation, and racism. This perspective offered little comfort to Dave, who experienced the cultural and linguistic differences between himself and his Somali neighbor as a painful and puzzling rejection. As expressed in the "Two Towns of Jasper Project," this perspective also provided little assistance to Ms. Smith, an individual shouldering significant responsibility for Somali incorporation in Lewiston and wrestling with the assertion that her difficulties stemmed from her own biases. As I will argue in Chapter 5, the intellectual and emotional appreciation of Somali diversity both enabled and constrained Somali inclusion in the Lewiston community.

Denied access to open acknowledgment of and problem solving around the complexity of intercultural living, both eager and hostile attendees in diversity training sessions often resisted the educational process. Some participants in these sessions had another venue, cultural brokerage sessions, where they could safely acknowledge intercultural difficulties. In other cases, diversity trainees were lower-class downtown residents who were simultaneously the most likely to be accused of racism and the people with the most unmitigated exposure to cultural difference because of their residential and social proximity to Somali Lewistonians. While the employers and service providers meeting with cultural brokers were additionally aided in their encounters with Somalis by the structure of a client/provider interaction, Somali and non-Somali neighbors navigated the waters of cultural distance in shared schools, shops, parks, and apartment blocs lacking such formal external controls. Training participants often expressed difficulties and asked for useful information. Never did I attend a diversity training session in which a comment like Dave's was met with information that might be of assistance to the individual seeking guidance. Diversity trainers either lacked information about Somali culture or proved unwilling to share that information in the training session. With their questions unanswered, training participants chose between assuming the "biased" label applied to them due to their discomfort or dismissing the diversity training process entirely.

THE RECOGNIZABLY INCLUSIVE COMMUNITY

The incorporation of Somali newcomers in Lewiston occurred through the moral construction of the Lewiston community as a place populated by kind, caring, and inclusive people open to the enriching diversity brought by Somali settlement. The meanings of the inclusive community and Somali settlement found their expression in everyday talk as well as in high moments and ritual. The moral boundaries of belonging erected through the assertion of deep values were implicated in the membership status of Lewiston residents like Brent Matthews, whose assault on the mosque extracted significant personal costs. This chapter has shown that institutional responses to Somali settlement also echoed the meanings underwriting Somali incorporation. Diversity-affirming and diversity-trouble narratives moved beyond the world of abstract representation in which it was enough to state that Lewiston was a welcoming community, enriched by Somali presence and in which intolerant people do not belong. Ascendant meanings and emergent understandings became reified in Lewiston's institutions as city leaders ensured that policy and programmatic efforts were recognizably consistent with the view that the city was an inclusive community and Somali settlement was an unqualified good.

Inscribing the meaning of multicultural incorporation in Lewiston's response to Somali settlement, those designing the city's policies, programs, and practices disseminated a de-institutionalized view of diversity troubles and community diversity that recast the work of immigrant incorporation as something achieved through the creation of moral, reasonable Lewistonians. City leaders complied with both the letter and the spirit of federal mandates and standards for equal opportunity and accessibility, thereby relegating the problem of community integration and Somali incorporation from the structure of social institutions to the disciplining (Foucault 1977) of city residents. Recognizing that abstract national policies were not sufficient to take community particulars into account and proved inadequate when it came to assisting Somali economic and educational integration, Lewiston's leadership worked to come up with creative solutions to help Somalis develop competence in mainstream society, not to incorporate Somali practices into the way things got done in Lewiston. In cultural brokerage sessions, off-the-record acknowledgment of cultural conflicts and rupture exposed street-level difficulties in deciding which differences are cultural differences to be preserved and which were obstacles to incorporation. In diversity training sessions, individuals expressed pain and confusion in the face of cross-cultural misunderstandings. All the same, procedural and policy approaches and even diversity trainers failed to engage the complicated task of bridging cultures, leaving Lewiston residents and service providers to navigate the challenges of intercultural living alone.

From Morality to Power

Institutional responses to Somali settlement provided for the cultural reeducation of Somalis and the moral reeducation of non-Somali residents of Lewiston. In orienting the management of Lewiston's diversity around Somali cultural adaptations and the moral reeducation of biased individuals, those developing the city's response to Somali settlement pursued the work of incorporation in a manner consistent with multicultural discourse – diversity-affirming and diversity-trouble narratives. An inclusive Lewiston was achieved through a change in Lewiston's people as both Somalis and non-Somalis learned how to see the world, conceive of their relationships with other people and behave in a manner that signaled their correct orientation.

The Structure of Exclusion

It wasn't just the occasional participant in diversity training sessions who balked at the emphasis on unchecked bias as the root of diversity trouble and psychological reform as the solution. The emphasis on creating more inclusive people in Lewiston rang hollow for some newcomers who encountered structural and material barriers to full participation in economic and community life. In the following account from the field, a focus group participant boldly pointed out that recognizing the needs of newcomers was not the same as meeting them and identifying the biases inscribed in policies and programs was not the same as eliminating inequality.

One February afternoon I was conducting a focus group with eighteen newcomers to Lewiston. I made contact with the participants, who were all women, through my relationship with one of the private social service agencies offering adult education and resettlement services in town. The focus group was quite diverse, consisting of people from locations as proximate as Boston and as far-flung as China, Brazil, and the Sudan in addition to Somalia. The level of education of participants ranged from no formal schooling to undergraduate degrees obtained at foreign universities. Most of the women spoke only limited English. Peer-translators facilitated their participation in the group. The participants had been in Lewiston for three to thirteen months. It was the first U.S. residence for only three of the eighteen. The rest had lived in at least one other American location, most having lived in two other towns or cities. I began the discussion by asking what helped or hindered them in feeling "at home" in Lewiston. Over the course of our ninety-minute session we discussed their experiences in Lewiston, the benefits and challenges of life in the community, their future aspirations for themselves and their families, and the perceived obstacles to success.

I experienced the discussion as constructive and largely positive. The general consensus of the group was that despite structural limitations (inadequate public transportation, public nuisances and safety hazards resulting from the large number of bars and heavy downtown traffic, the outdated and Spartan adult educational and vocational training, the difficulties in locating part-time work and child care, a lack of year-round community space, and difficulty communicating with neighbors), life in Lewiston was safer, easier, and more amenable to improvement than the other places they had lived both domestically and abroad. They felt that they could influence the nature of the community if and when they were willing to work for change. In the final moments of the meeting, I offered my optimistic impression of the talk and asked if my understanding seemed accurate.

At this point one individual, Antoinette, an African American woman who had participated only sporadically in the conversation up to that point, spoke up. Antoinette had earlier acknowledged a long history of social service participation. She recently moved to Lewiston from her hometown of Boston under the advisement of a social welfare agency that told her the wait for a subsidized, portable (section 8) housing voucher was much shorter in Lewiston. The social service agency paid her bus fare to Lewiston and encouraged her to return to Boston once she had received her housing voucher.

"You know," Antoinette said, nodding her head toward me as she addressed the other focus group participants, "she ain't going to change shit. She's just here for herself. You all are new here so let me tell you how it works. These white people come and ask questions and pretend to care and then they go away and nothing changes." Then she turned and addressed me directly, "These things we need, can you get them for us? Can you do anything? What will you do?"

I was unprepared for this unexpected and powerful challenge and acknowledged the truth behind it. With the heat of a blush burning my cheeks I admitted that I was not in a position to augment child care, English-language education, computer and job training, bus service, and public safety in Lewiston. Furthermore, it was also true that even in the long term, my research would have little direct impact on what services were available in the community. It wasn't that I thought those things were not important, I added defensively, but just that I was exploring the assumptions and ideas about diversity that structured the understandings about how newcomers became community members.

"See," my interlocutor snorted, "She thinks white people just need different ideas. She ain't going to change shit."

Antoinette challenged my focus on the role that ideas played in the nature of multicultural incorporation by naming a different kind of racism. Whatever claims to goodwill and inclusivity I might offer rang hollow in the face of Antoinette's pragmatic focus on racial and cultural privilege that was not a matter of outlook but, instead, an element of structural impediments to economic security and full community participation. Looking back over my notes later that day, I recognized that the positive tone I imputed to the meeting derived from the fact that focus group participants identified things that could be done to make Lewiston a more equal and inclusive community. I encountered such pragmatic specifics as a refreshing departure from the focus, as it often emerged in my research, on reforming biased individuals. Nonetheless these specific needs and recommendations were not small and insignificant changes. Instead, they would require significant funding and a dramatic change in the relationship between the community and those in need of financial, educational, and employment assistance. Antoinette challenged me to acknowledge that my own perspective, although thinking critically about the way meanings influenced the situations of Lewiston's newcomers, nonetheless hinged upon an epistemological insider's assumption about the importance of ideas. True, it was promising that the women I spoke with envisioned ways around the difficulties they encountered, but it would be even better if such practical and material difficulties were the explicit focus of intervention and reform.

Deep Values, Epistemology, and Praxis

In her criticism of me and the detached, hermeneutic stance I took on diversity troubles in Lewiston, Antoinette redefined racism as structural exclusion, inequality, and the inaction of those, like myself, with the good fortune of being freed from immediate material need. In addition to situating me squarely within the racist camp, Antoinette's undisciplined understanding of racism stood in direct conflict with the epistemology and praxis characteristic of the demonstration of inclusivity in Lewiston.

As detailed in Chapter 2, Alexander's work on the fusion of the civil sphere provides the baseline understanding of the cultural meanings crucial to incorporation. Alexander maintains that deep values and the social divisions they evoke are implicated in the outcomes of social processes at the highest moments and suggests that these values are a naturally emerging expression of interior beliefs and meanings. The observations I share in this chapter demonstrate, however, that the fundamental values associated with the moral boundaries of belonging were reified in praxis: practices, orientations, and approaches. There was no naturally emerging expression of inclusivity and moral worth in Lewiston. Instead the practical response to Somali settlement derived from the presumed and generally unquestioned association between deep values and a praxis of diversity consisting of institutionalized practices, manners of speech, and modes of expression – the emphasis on legal compliance, the provision of cultural assistance education for the Somalis, the establishment of community dialogues and diversity education for non-Somali residents of Lewiston. We will learn more about this praxis and its epistemological roots in the next chapter.

4

Disciplined to Diversity

When I attended my first diversity training, the "Two Towns of Jasper Project," I observed uncomfortable group dynamics resulting from the perspective that emerged in the group discussions – the view that the struggles of Somali incorporation in Lewiston resulted from the "fences" in people's hearts and minds. Participating in the frequent diversity training sessions offered in Lewiston, I noted a similar perspective emerging in a host of curricula developed by the various local, regional, national, and international organizations offering diversity training in the city. I began calling the psychological and anti-racist orientation characteristic of the method "confronting your inner racist" because of the emphasis placed upon participants coming, through the training process, to a greater understanding of their individual biases, the origins of these biases, and the impact they have on participants' lives and communities.

The focus on racially biased, bigoted, or otherwise immoral people and the adoption of abstract guidelines and programs as the panacea for the difficulties of immigrant incorporation and multicultural community building in Lewiston left me puzzled. My sociological predisposition to believe that culture and structure were important elements of both racism and multicultural incorporation was not reflected in the psychological orientation of the narratives and institutional strategies characterizing the response to Somali settlement. Likewise, programs and policies in Lewiston did not generally reflect my assumptions regarding the strain that cross-cultural contact can place on intergroup relations.[1] Where

[1] Establishing bonds of community in the face of diversity is difficult work. While much of the literature in the area of intercultural communication (e.g., Barna, LaRay M. 1998.

I perceived the need for deep and specific information about different cultures and careful anticipation of and strategizing around likely cross-cultural conflicts, I witnessed the adoption of culture-blind standards and the development of educational opportunities that focused on the psychology of individuals instead of structural limitations. Attending a number of diversity training sessions, cultural festivals, and community discussions, I increasingly felt that my observations in these settings shed little light on the pragmatics of Somali incorporation. Puzzling over what I experienced as a disjuncture, I realized that instead of concluding that the abstract, psychological, and individual pursuit of incorporation did not make sense, I ought to try to understand what sense my observations made. In other words, I needed to uncover the epistemology and praxis guiding institutional responses to Somali settlement. As it turned out, diversity training offered a route to the understanding I sought.

TRAIN-THE-TRAINER

As my first diversity training session – "The Two Towns of Jasper Project" – neared completion, the training leader took some time to discuss an additional educational opportunity that she intermittently described as a "train-the-trainer" conference, a term unknown to me. She distributed an informational pamphlet containing a program overview and registration form. The Building Bridges Leadership Training was a three-day workshop offered by the same organization. Participation in the leadership training cost $400. As described in the promotional pamphlet, the training, which would also take place in Lewiston, was

an experiential, highly participatory workshop that will present state-of-the-art techniques for managing diversity and becoming constructive advocates on behalf of other groups.

"Stumbling Blocks in Intercultural Communication." Pp. 173–189 in *Basic concepts of intercultural communication*, edited by M. J. Bennett. Yarmouth, ME: Intercultural Press; Bennett, Janet M. 1998. "Transition Shock: Putting Culture Shock into Perspective." Pp. 215–224 in *Basic concepts of intercultural communication*, edited by M. J. Bennett. Yarmouth, ME: Intercultural Press) focuses on individual psychological impacts, Putnam (Putnam, Robert D. 2007. "E Pluribus Unum: Diversity and Community in the Twenty-first Century – The 2006 Johan Skytte Prize Lecture." *Scandinavian Political Studies* 30:137–174) finds that social trust is adversely affected by ethnic diversity. Gathering survey data in a variety of American communities, including Lewiston, Putnam finds that people in diverse places have less trust in others, and less faith in the unselfish assistance and cooperation of their neighbors and their government. Community diversity is correlated with having fewer friends and being less happy and engaged in one's neighborhood.

These replicable techniques, which use "emotional healing" to resolve inter-group tensions, will be demonstrated in the large group and practiced in small groups. Participants will be given the opportunity to try these techniques and receive constructive feedback.

The anti-racist organization's informational literature further claimed that the training would provide the "foundational theory and concrete skills" necessary for coalition building in the face of "the historic divisions of race, class, gender, religion, sexual orientation, and other group identities." The Building Bridges Leadership Training, depicted as the next logical step on the path to building an inclusive Lewiston, piqued my interest.

As most of the diversity training programs I attended in Lewiston neared their completion, diversity trainers encouraged participants to pursue further training in sessions like the Building Bridges Leadership Training.[2] Train-the-trainer experiences were billed as a venue where participants could continue the important and deep personal work they began in diversity training, efforts that would impart skills desperately needed in Lewiston. Discussing the superiority of their particular diversity training approach (e.g., a focus on community building, proven success in creating race activists, a global leader when it comes to building productive professional-client relations), diversity-training leaders suggested to diversity training participants that they had what it takes to be advocates for diversity and allies in the fight against hate. Participation in their organization's diversity train-the-trainer program would provide the knowledge that trainees needed to harness their desire for justice and help bring about a more inclusive Lewiston. In addition to furthering their own emotional healing, participants in further training would acquire the tools and credentials they needed to become diversity professionals and activists who could contribute to the emotional healing of others.

Diversity train-the-trainer seminars provided the opportunity to shift focus from training participants' oft-neglected concerns with the everyday details of Somali incorporation and step into a setting in which the epistemology and praxis of diversity, described in the Building Bridges training materials as "foundational theory and concrete skills," was created and disseminated. Although to my knowledge no one else in Lewiston intended to seek further training, I observed that the city, state, and area agencies and businesses sought the knowledge and expertise

[2] Of all the training sessions I observed, only the U.S. Department of Justice training did not advertise future training opportunities.

of people holding diversity credentials acquired through such train-the-trainer programs.

BUILDING BRIDGES BETWEEN THE LOCAL
AND THE MACROCULTURAL

Local understandings of diversity troubles and immigrant incorporation found expression in rote meanings, practices, and dispositions that were recognizably consistent with the multicultural embrace of Somali immigration and the fact of an inclusive Lewiston. Although I traveled to Lewiston to uncover the cultural and everyday pragmatics of Somali immigrant incorporation, I concluded that the approach to Somali settlement that I observed in the town was not an exclusively local product.[3] To be sure, the mayor's letter prompted the mobilization of local pro-diversity and anti-immigration activists, but it also elicited the intervention of anti-racist and racist groups operating at the national and international levels. In developing their diversity management strategies, Lewiston leaders sought to be responsive to emergent community needs and issues, but they also oriented their interventions toward legal requirements and policy norms formulated elsewhere. Somalis and non-Somalis participating in diversity and cultural assimilation programs learned how to improve their community and their access to its resources, but they also acquired generalized skills intended to increase their ability to be good workers in and residents of any community. How could I account for the influence of extralocal contexts on tacit meanings and common elements of Somali incorporation in Lewiston?

As an extension of the training sessions that were an element of Lewiston's institutional responses to diversity troubles, and as the credentialing experience for many of the diversity professionals advising municipal, state, and federal bodies creating and implementing diversity policies in the community, train-the-trainer seminars were empirically linked to happenings in Lewiston. Common activities and approaches

---

[3] "In any particular location certain practices, anxieties, and ambivalences are present as specific responses to the intimate functioning of nonlocal agencies and causes.... What ethnographers .... want from subjects is not so much local knowledge as an articulation of the forms of anxiety that are generated by the awareness of being affected by what is elsewhere without knowing what the particular connections to that elsewhere might be.... In effect, subjects are participating in discourses that are thoroughly localized but that are not their own" (Marcus, George E. 1998. *Ethnography through thick and thin.* Princeton, NJ: Princeton University Press).

characterized the training sessions I attended in the city. As an ongoing participant in diversity training sessions offered as a mode of intervention in Lewiston, I determined that such training sessions were one of the sites in which local, individual, and particular contexts of meaning encountered macrocultural practices and perspectives.

In extending my research to diversity training, I engaged in Duneier's (2001) extended place method, broadening my focus on the local to include middle- and macrolevel contexts that impinged upon lived reality in Lewiston. A departure from my original research plan, my participation in train-the-trainer seminars was not guided by prior theoretical or institutional interests but instead arose from my experiences as an ethnographer in Lewiston. My attendance at many of the diversity training sessions offered in the community – exercises geared toward Lewiston's established majority, frequently led by trainers unfamiliar with the community and Somali culture, and typically encouraging participants to become better (anti-racist, white) people – led me to conclude that an adequate understanding of local life required a detailed look at macrocultural meanings and practices influencing the context Somali newcomer reception in Lewiston.

I sought opportunities to participate in "train-the-trainer" seminars. My diversity training experience in Lewiston supplied a springboard for determining which training organizations to approach. I began by researching the organizations represented by diversity trainers in the city. I also investigated the common diversity products and programs used in corporate, educational, and community settings. The two diversity train-the-trainer programs I eventually selected controlled a substantial share of the diversity training market in the United States. I enrolled in a high-profile corporate diversity train-the-trainer series offered by Corporate Org, one of the United States' largest professional development organizations and staffed by representatives of an agency known as a global leader in diversity consulting. In addition, I trained as a diversity trainer with well-established Rights Org, an international civil rights organization conducting a widely used school- and community-based diversity program. I selected these organizations for their impact within the field of diversity training, but also because their advertised approach and training curricula were consonant with most of the diversity training sessions I observed in Lewiston, even though these organizations were not the only agencies that had credentialed diversity trainers working in the city.

I contacted each organization and explained my status as a researcher seeking to learn more about the theory and methods shaping immigrant incorporation in Lewiston, Maine. Corporate Org was happy to offer the training to anyone willing to pay the registration fee and made no objections to the presence of a participant-researcher. Rights Org, however, offered the training at no charge to select individuals. I was required to apply for inclusion by expressing my commitment to anti-racist action and agreeing to be an active training participant, maintain the confidentiality of other participants, and protect copyrighted training materials. In light of these commitments, I have eliminated or altered information that might reveal the identity of the diversity organizations and training participants. I have also protected copyrighted material.

Rights Org and Corporate Org train-the-trainer programs lasted five days and took place in summer 2007, encompassing about forty work hours in addition to shared morning and optional midday meals. Corporate Org train-the-trainer sessions were held in the conference room of a business hotel in a major city on the East Coast of the United States. As Corporate Org trainees came from cities around the United States, Western Europe, South Asia, and the Caribbean, the majority of trainees resided in the hotel during the training. Rights Org training was held in the teachers' lounge of a suburban high school outside of a major city in the midwestern United States. The majority of training participants lived within a forty-five-minute drive of the site. Six individuals traveled farther, at most 1,000 miles, and were transported and housed by Rights Org. Corporate Org awarded a training credential and certificate to successful participants. Rights Org added successful participants to their pool of paid in-house diversity trainers.

Two trainers led each program. The program leaders had extensive backgrounds as diversity professionals and traveled significant distances to offer the training. They all reported previous experience in train-the-trainer programs, as well as employment as outside diversity consultants both in the United States and abroad, frontline diversity trainers, expert commentators on diversity issues, and members of various multicultural boards and diversity committees. The professionals offering the corporate diversity training operated a diversity-consulting firm with consulting contracts around the world. Rights Org training leaders held additional but related jobs and worked for Rights Org as a second career. All four program leaders were women. The corporate trainers were white women in their fifties or sixties while the civil rights trainers were women of color, one African American and the other Asian American, in their thirties or forties.

The characteristics of program participants varied within and between the sessions. Training participants were most often women. Only three men participated in Rights Org's training, reflecting, in part, gender differences in those who work in primary and secondary education – the field from which many participants were recruited. Twenty out of forty-four corporate trainees were men. Both groups of trainees contained participants from many racial, ethnic, nativity, and religious groups and different sexual orientations. Participants' ages varied. Rights Org training participants manifested the largest spread in ages, ranging from the mid-twenties to the late sixties. Corporate trainees were closer in age, generally falling between forty and fifty-five years of age, although the group did contain some younger individuals – recent college graduates with one or two years' professional experience. Many participants in the Corporate Org session held or sought employment as diversity professionals, either as in-house diversity and human resource staff or as private diversity trainers and consultants. Still others maintained upper-level corporate and public sector positions that included responsibility for organizational diversity and compliance with equal employment opportunity requirements. The majority of Rights Org diversity train-the-trainer participants worked as educators or in some other capacity within nearby primary and secondary educational institutions in such positions as school librarians, nurses, speech pathologists, and special education coordinators. A few retirees, social workers, and community organizers rounded out the crowd.

Foundational Theory and Concrete Skills

Diversity train-the-trainer seminars provided crucial insight into the happenings in Lewiston, Maine. By examining the training of diversity professionals, I gained perspective on the epistemology and praxis characterizing the culture of incorporation – the techniques and methods of intervention structuring the city's response to immigration, as well as the assumed truths attached to intercultural life. Through the moral reeducation of people and the designation of diversity professionals in possession of both credentials and legitimated techniques for managing diversity troubles, the seminars produced and disseminated a particular multicultural subjectivity, accepted practices, and unquestioned meanings underwriting the idea and characterizing the demonstration of an inclusive Lewiston and the value of Somali settlement.

Alexander's work on the fusion of the civil sphere through the application of abstract moral values provided the baseline understanding of the meaning of Somali settlement and the boundaries of belonging discussed in Chapter 2. In Chapter 3, I demonstrated that in Lewiston the narratives associated with these fundamental values were assumed to inhere in recognizably legitimate practices, manners of speech, and modes of expression. In this chapter I show that individual diversity trainers-in-training were disciplined to the external power of the cultural structures and, further, that multicultural incorporation consisted of both a praxis and an epistemology that provided a particular understanding of life in a diverse community.

Diversity trainers-in-training were disciplined by receiving implicit and explicit instruction in the correct praxis – the vocabulary, and style of communication associated with moral worth in an inclusive community (Voyer 2011a, 2011b). The internationalization of these lessons reinforced the dominant epistemology – particular notions of community, diversity, and modern, moral personhood. In Lewiston and in diversity train-the-trainer seminars, those to be incorporated were molded into cultural subjects worthy of inclusion, isolated as individuals singularly responsible for their own failures to conform, and distributed and ranked within a hierarchical space of those who may or may not belong with certainty to the community in which they reside (Foucault 1977).

In interrogating the dominant epistemology, it is helpful to first consider praxis, the "concrete skills" designed to produce "emotional healing" in diversity train-the-trainer program participants. After observing the way in which modern, multicultural individuals were created through the praxis disseminated within diversity train-the-trainer seminars, I consider the epistemological "foundational theory" emerging in the training setting – a particular view of what diversity is and how intercultural life should be managed. In concluding, I trace the missionary zeal with which diversity practitioners carried this praxis and epistemology back to places like Lewiston, Maine.

EMOTIONAL HEALING

The diversity training I observed in Lewiston and the train-the-trainer programs I attended differed in their stated purpose, sites of application, and the goals of participants. However, these various training approaches produced trainers who were similar in their facility with a shared vocabulary and common exercises. Focusing on exposing and challenging individual bias, the training was therapeutic in orientation and operated on the assumption that change in the culture and climate of an agency, institution, or community follows the psychological change of its members.[4] A perusal of flyers and quotations collected in Lewiston demonstrates that diversity train-the-trainer seminars generally claimed that successful participants would develop a variety of skills – "undoing" and "unlearning" their own stereotypes, "confronting" and "removing" their own lingering "hurt" and "misinformation," "healing [their own] guilt" and enabling their "courage," "power," and "leadership" in order to create "constructive" and "principled" "allies." A brief overview of the rise of diversity training shows that the psychological orientation I observed in diversity training, public talk, and program construction in Lewiston is consistent with developments in the meanings attached to discrimination, inequality, and intergroup conflict.

Alexander (2003) describes the process by which the Nazis' "final solution" to the "Jewish question" comes to represent the Holocaust as it is widely understood today: the ultimate evil, a horror still looming at the forefront of our collective consciousness as an irreversible past that may be repeated all too easily by any people in any society. According to Alexander, the Holocaust provides the cultural context in which contemporary injustices are defined.

It became a bridging metaphor that social groups of uneven power and legitimacy applied to parse ongoing events as good and evil in real historical time. What the "Holocaust" named as the most fundamental evil was the intentional, systematic and organized employment of violence against members of a stigmatized collective. (Alexander 2003, p. 67)

As the ultimate evil, the Holocaust also served the purpose of elucidating and creating a desire for the good and for inspiring a collective trauma in which identification with the victims of the atrocities leads to the universalizing perspectives on morality and rights and greater inclusivity in who is perceived to be a member of society (Alexander 2003). Applied to the case of Somali immigrant incorporation in Lewiston, the Holocaust operated as the archetypical instance of the profane in the sacred-profane dichotomy upon which conceptions of an inclusive community took shape. The host of behaviors, social relationships, and institutional characteristics associated with Nazi Germany had its counterpoint in a series

---

[4] These similarities are the focus of this research. When relevant, the following discussion includes differences between the programs, but comparative research on corporate versus activist diversity training is outside the purview of the present work.

of qualities characterizing the good, the moral, and the deserving people and society.

Alexander correctly identifies the centrality of the representation of the Holocaust in the rise of multiculturalism. I connect this rise to the nature of immigrant incorporation in Lewiston. The postwar era saw the precipitous decline of Social Darwinist theories of racial superiority and the eugenics movement that represented mainstream and even liberal progressive views in the United States prior to World War II (Paul 1998).[5] These earlier meanings and practices characterizing prewar U.S. diversity-management were reinterpreted through their association with the Nazism and the Holocaust. In 1952, the U.S. Congress eliminated the long-standing requirement that only white immigrants were eligible for naturalized citizenship (Takaki 1993). This move foreshadowed civil rights era immigration reform that lifted xenophobic immigration quotas codified in 1924 to preserve the cultural and ethnic character of the nation by severely limiting non-European immigration. The era also witnessed the rise of the civil rights movement and successful judicial and legislative attacks on laws and policies explicitly maintaining racial segregation, discrimination, and inequality. In addition to these major changes in the political and institutional character of American society, this period saw the rise of the view that discrimination and intergroup conflict, despite their long-standing existence, were unnatural psychoses – the product of individual fears that produce prejudice and discrimination (Lasch-Quinn 2001).

Lasch-Quinn (2001) documents the rise of therapeutic interpretations of and approaches to managing racial conflict. In the immediate postwar era, growing suburban white communities experiencing hostility between resident whites and incoming African Americans and Jews received a new kind of intervention. While such conflicts were not new to the American landscape, what was new was the idea that racial segregation and interracial hostility were unacceptable problems that should be addressed. The therapy group or T-group operated upon the assumption that community tensions were diversity troubles arising from the attitudes of community residents. T-groups focused upon bringing diverse neighbors together in the interests of changing attitudes. By the late 1960s this intervention became known as interracial encounter groups and later, ethnotherapy

---

[5] Wilde and Dianielsen (Wilde, Melissa J. and Sabrina Danielsen. 2011. "Creating Heaven on Earth: Birth Control, Eugenics and Belief in the Social Gospel." Paper presented at the Yale University Center for Cultural Sociology, April 1, 2011) demonstrate that the most left-leaning U.S. religious denominations embraced eugenics prior to World War II.

and racial confrontation groups. These groups were increasingly led by credentialed diversity professionals and characterized by emotional volatility and the requirement that white participants disclose their racist inclinations (Lasch-Quinn 2001).

T-groups initially emphasized discussion among diverse group members. Over time, however, the method became one largely designed for and offered by white people (Lasch-Quinn 2001; Thompson 2001). In the waning years of the civil rights movement, calls for equal rights increasingly gave way to calls for equal recognition and representation on the part of groups seeking the opportunity to participate in the political process without adopting majority culture. Radical and revolutionary groups such as the Red and Black Power Movements made bold demands for freedom, recognition, restitution, and redistribution (Nagel 1996; Takaki 1993). Stokely Carmichael and the Student Nonviolent Coordinating Committee (SNCC) turned away from the race-integrated quest for equality that marked social action up to that time (Takaki 1993; Umoja 1999). Under Carmichael's leadership, SNCC worked toward new goals, downplaying the involvement of white activists and supplanting the call for nonviolence with calls for armed self-defense among blacks (Umoja 1999). SNCC's changed approach heralded the beginning of a new stage in the fight against discrimination as activists sought liberation and separatism as opposed to integration and assimilation. In light of these changes, whites who had been a part of the civil rights movement struggled to find ways to continue their activism outside of the work done in the Black Power and related movements (Thompson 2001). While they formerly worked in race-integrated settings, white race activists now found themselves organizing in majority white areas and organizations and shifting their focus from racial justice to poverty, education, and class inequality. The growth in the therapeutic treatment of racial conflict came at an auspicious time for many white anti-racists who found an outlet for their activism as anti-racist educators and diversity trainers (Thompson 2001).

Although the geography and demography of Lewiston left the city outside the more contentious aspects of postwar multiculturalism, as widespread condemnation of Mayor Raymond's letter makes clear, the town and its people were accountable to the cultural prescriptions developed in the postwar and civil rights eras. In the wake of Somali settlement, the city required diversity training of its employees and hired an out-of-state, trained diversity professional to coordinate the city's response to Somali settlement. Diversity professionals brought an accepted multicultural outlook and practices to the community. In most cases, these individuals had acquired many of their credentials and tools in diversity train-the-trainer programs.

Just Tell Me How to Talk

The diversity train-the-trainer seminars I attended instilled in trainees a particular manner of speaking about diversity. Prescriptions around talk in diversity training was more than just a speech genre (Bakhtin, Holquist, and Emerson 1986) or specialized language for use in particular situations. As evidenced by the impact that diversity professionals had on public talk and program development in Lewiston, this particular praxis acquired moral status as behavior that is free from bias and privilege and should be used in all circumstances. The diversity train-the-trainer curriculum contained many language exercises in which participants learned how to talk sensitively about differences and how to employ the right words and techniques when confronting the biased language and behavior of others. The following field accounts show that diversity train-the-trainer program participants received both implicit and explicit language instruction.

D-I-V-E-R-S-I-T-Y

In this field note, a trainer-in-training used a word that was considered taboo. Training leaders explained the true meaning of her talk and the importance of inappropriate talk in perpetuating discrimination and inequality.

On the first day of Rights Org diversity training, trainees worked as a group to come up with ground rules for the workshop. Moving letter by letter, group members offered rules beginning with D-I-V-E-R-S-I-T-Y. One of the trainers recorded the words on the flip chart at the front of the room.

"Discuss" said one participant.

"Say more" the trainer responded.

"Discuss your feelings and interpretations with other people, especially if someone says something that upsets you. You may not hear what they are trying to say or they may not understand how their words can hurt."

"Very good." And so it went until the letter T.

"Truthful." "Tenacious." "Trusting and trustworthy." After brief explanations the words went up on the list.

"Tolerance" stated one participant.

"Okaaaaaaay ...." the trainer began slowly, her marker suspended over the overflowing page of the flip chart. "What do you mean by that word?"

"I mean we need to be tolerant of people who have different opinions. We need to tolerate people doing things differently."

The training leader turned from the chart to address the group. She suggested that perhaps we needed to come up with a new word for what the participant is trying to express. Tolerant, she claimed, is a potentially loaded word that "sticks in the craw" because it suggests that the one doing the tolerating holds the power and begrudgingly makes space for others. Our trainer counseled that tolerance was one of many "tricky words" and went on to state that we will develop a shared vocabulary over the course of the week. The offending trainee rephrased her ground rule as "respect," a word that already appeared further up the list under the letter R. We moved on to letter Y.

Diversity trainers-in-training learned from the discussion of the word tolerance that not all words would be tolerated within training sessions. Words had meaning outside of the explicit intentions of the speaker and yet the speaker was responsible for the implications of her talk in systems of domination and exclusion. The group also had a glimpse of what many participants hoped to acquire along with the training credential: a superior level of knowledge and expertise in the expression of multicultural notions of inclusion and equality.

"An Ouch for an Ouch"

The following account demonstrates that in addition to acquiring the correct vocabulary, diversity trainers-in-training learned that the ability to use the appropriate discourse could be thwarted by psychological and emotional scars and injuries that limited one's capacity to take an unprejudiced perspective. Attribution of bias to psychological injury was one way in which diversity training made the multicultural vocabulary introduced earlier appear organic to individuals. Instead of seeing acceptable talk as a language produced and employed in a social setting where it derives meaning, the implication was that the correct vocabulary should flow naturally from an undamaged individual.

Later in the first day of training, Rights Org trainers distributed index cards. Each card contained either a word or a definition. The task was to find the person with the matching word or definition. My word was "prejudice" and I easily found my match. While it initially appeared that the activity would be brief, the exercise soon felt interminable. Its endlessness was due largely to the emergence of what one of our trainers referred to as "teachable moments" – instances in which a member of the group violates the discursive rules of the sessions.

In discussing her experiences as the victim of nationalism, one trainee made an off-hand comment that could be interpreted as sexist. Describing the shortsightedness of a work-group of male and immigrant educators who discounted her contributions to a diverse classroom because of her white American perspective and background, the trainee alluded to her value within the group by stating that as a woman, at least she was able to see to it that the group ate well. I glanced at my fellow trainees, curious to see whether others had noticed the stereotype underlying her comment, that is, of women as nurturing through providing food. I wondered whether or not anyone would point it out. Earlier that morning the group leaders charged each of us with the task of addressing our own biases and prejudicial actions. They also encouraged us to share our reactions to biased words and actions expressed by others in the group. Such action on our part, they instructed, formed a crucial part of the therapeutic process by simultaneously forcing participants to confront their own biases while also empowering individuals to stand in the face of discriminatory behavior.

As if to buy time so one of us might muster enough courage to point out sexism in our midst, one of the group leaders looked at each of us in turn. "Okaaaaaay …. anyone have anything they want to say in response to that comment?"

Silence. While the trainer who solicited a response to the biased comment seemed ready to follow our lead and continue the exercise, the other trainer stopped the activity by suggesting that a comment requiring a response had just been made. She repeated the statement, labeled it sexist, and asked the group how the comment might be rephrased as a non-sexist expression of pain at being the victim of prejudice. Despite this explicit intervention the offending trainee apparently did not see that our mandated discussion of the remark was one in which she, not the educators who played the antagonists in her story, was at fault. Her problematic comment was tangential to the activity, pairing words and definitions, and yet she kept returning to her experience as if she hadn't made a coherent case for prejudice based upon national origin. Our trainers eventually decided that it was time to move on and suggested that we were witnessing "an ouch for an ouch." Consistent with the assumption that hateful and hurtful statements are borne out of pain, our leader told us that the trainee was apparently responding to the hurt that she experienced by lashing out at men and stereotyping women. The trainee appeared confused by the continued attention while the rest of us took note of her apparent incapacity to recognize and rein in her prejudice.

"The Politically Correct Way ...."

Schooled in the importance of using the correct vocabulary and aware that discursive failures indicate psychological scars and faulty vision, would-be diversity trainers also learned to model commitment to ideals of inclusivity and equality. Challenging talk that did not conform to discursive standards proved to be a crucial element of group praxis.

The matching exercise moved on to the topic of "ableism." The group became stymied in confusion and blunders once again. The trainees with the word and definition did not grasp that ableism is supposed to be undesirable (akin to racism) and that the definition of the term (prejudice or discrimination based upon differences in physical or mental ability) was intended to encompass disability as well. As the discussion of ableism continued, our trainers and many trainees winced as the term, disabled, was used again and again.

Intervening at last, one trainer pointed out the problems with the term, disabled. "It suggests that an individual is limited and incapable. It groups all differences in ability together without acknowledging variations in what people can do and in their experiences." In response to continued confusion, the trainer stated that disabled is a problematic word and that we should avoid using it. One trainee then asked if we should refer to disability as ableism instead.

In the growing frustration one participant, Anna, pleaded, "I don't understand what's going on here. Just tell me what the politically correct way to talk about disability is and that's what I'll do."

Another uncomfortable pause followed this plea. Then, Jane, a trainee and a longtime volunteer with Rights Org broke the silence. "I get very angry when I hear people talking about political correctness," stated Jane, her voice shaking with emotion. "This is about people not politics. We need to understand diversity at a deeper level. We should be thinking about real people and their experiences and how to make their lives better, not about what we need to say to keep from getting into trouble."

Anna appeared to be hurt by Jane's rebuke, fighting back tears as she looked down at her hands. One of the trainers spoke in support of Jane. "Jane is right. It is about people, so the best way to deal with these situations is to ask the individuals how they identify themselves."

Jane's validated reprimand of her fellow trainer-in-training was the first time in which a group member challenged the flawed vision, as instantiated in talk, of another training participant. Training leaders saw the confrontation of bias as an important practice in which all participants were expected to develop facility. While, despite the leaders' encouragement, no one was willing to challenge the gender stereotypic statement discussed earlier, only a few minutes later Jane confronted what she labeled as a superficial approach to diversity. Jane's comment also supported the idea of the organic nature of correct talk. Genuine multicultural expressions were not tied to politics or rules of conversation. Instead, inherently ameliorative talk flowed freely from people oriented toward diversity and social justice "at a deeper level."

"The Right Way to Say Whatever"

The preceding events illuminate the manner in which diversity trainers-in-training learned about the praxis of inclusion, came to understand misspeech as evidence of psychological trouble, and see correct talk as proof of multicultural vision. Participants in train-the-trainer seminars demonstrated their internal clarity and commitment to multicultural incorporation by policing the expressions of their peers. Adoption of the offered perspective and vocabulary did encounter obstacles, however.

Trainees were not merely docile in their acceptance of diversity talk as it emerged in the training seminars. Participants in the diversity train-the-trainer program initially challenged the terms set by program leaders. In particular, trainees reacted with suspicion to the emphasis on word choice, especially when that emphasis was denied and paired with the refusal to share the correct vocabulary.

During a group discussion of language, the group only tentatively accepted the training leaders' assertions that it was best to follow the lead of individuals when it came to describing differences. Several members of the group remained unsatisfied. What about situations in which you don't have the opportunity to learn how someone identifies himself or herself? What do you do when you are speaking of a group of people comprised of individuals who identify differently?

While the group asked for guidance in using language, one participant spoke up. "Please, if you could, just tell us the best way to say whatever characteristic it might be," one trainee, Sahra, requested.

The trainers rebuffed the plea by stating that we needed to be "sensitive to the individuality of any word and ask the individual." Not to be deterred, Sahra reworded her appeal. "Then could you tell us what each group wants to be called?"

"There is no right answer to that question," the trainer asserted. "It depends on the individual."

Sahra, her frustration clearly mounting, would not rest. "Please. I want to be proper. I am an immigrant from [nation in South East Asia]. Even though I am a citizen of this country, English is not my first language and I work very hard to talk like an American. I think it is very important that I use the right words when I speak so I am asking you to tell me what I need to know to talk about these subjects."

The trainers remained stalwart. "There is no answer," one of them stated definitively. "If you cannot talk to individuals you just pick what you're comfortable with and with what you think is most appropriate for our society. The words you will use will change depending upon the community you are working with."

Trainees resisted because training leaders' claims stood in conflict with the reality of the sessions and the world in which diversity trainers-in-training would eventually work – a world in which correct word choice mattered greatly. Trainees had already seen that word choice had the power to perpetuate inequality and discrimination. Furthermore, participants were judged by their ability to choose their words correctly. Trainees felt themselves at risk, in a situation where they hoped to demonstrate that they were good people with the correct orientation to diversity, and where they observed that their speech had the power to demonstrate them as otherwise. In group and one-on-one conversations, many trainees expressed a fear of being judged and felt as though they were going to "get jumped on" for making statements that did not meet "invisible" standards. They shared frustration that their true natures as caring and sensitive people were obscured by the emphasis on moments in which they offered poorly considered and glib statements. They sought the knowledge they needed in order to appear open to diversity even though most already felt that they were open to diversity. After all, a commitment to and interest in the pursuit of equality and social justice prompted many trainees' participation in the training seminars.

From Novice to Acolyte

Trainers-in-training first challenged the method and vocabulary of the programs. However, by the beginning of the third day opposition was minimal and the sessions progressed more smoothly as participants developed the skills necessary to perform successfully. Trainees quickly picked up and utilized specialized terms (e.g., ally, viewpoint, diversity, and bridging), the use of which indicated that one knew how to speak about diversity. They learned how to avoid other words, such as tolerance and disabled, that were tinged with power and considered inappropriate for truly inclusive actors. Trainees developed a sanitized and dependable style of communication. Trainees also grew more comfortable and skilled when it came to the recognition and confrontation of problematic statements by others. In addition, both training sessions spent considerable time explicitly schooling participants in particular strategies for discussing diversity and confronting prejudice. Those strategies were made plain in the following accounts from the field.

Oops and Ouch

The first activity in both diversity train-the-trainer programs was covering the ground rules. In each case the group developed participation policies. The trainers supplemented the groups' rules with additional requirements. Adherence to these further guidelines proved crucial for appropriate comportment within the train-the-trainer setting.

Corporate Org ground rules included a host of basic items such as silencing cell phones and avoiding side conversations. In addition to those constructed by the group, our trainers stated that we were to

1. Presume goodwill.
2. Speak for ourselves and from our own experience.
3. Be open.
4. Pay attention to our reactions.
5. When something rubs us the wrong way say, "Ouch" so we can talk about it.

With similar goals for individual participation, Rights Org trainers described particular desirable behaviors. In order to ground trainees in their own experience, trainers required that contributions to group discussion begin with "I statements" such as "I feel that ...." and "I don't understand ...." In the same vein, all comments and insights should come from personal stories, not assumed facts. Furthermore, trainees should use "person first language" when speaking of someone's group memberships, for example, person of color, person of Jewish faith, person with a difference in physical ability. Just as in Corporate Org training, trainees were asked to say "ouch" when another person's words were harmful and, further, should offer "oops" when the trainee expected that something he or she said might be injurious to others.

Over the course of the sessions, trainees became adept at speaking in such a way that their statements were unabashedly particular to themselves, offering no hypotheses extending personal experiences to broader assumptions about how the world might work. When speaking of others, trainees placed characteristics that might be associated with their diversity in the predicate position, minimizing the appearance that they were attaching their assessments to those characteristics and, correspondingly, avoiding endorsement of any kind of group stereotypes. When a trainee failed in these endeavors, other members of the group learned to say "ouch" and express distaste for problematic statements as personally offensive and emotionally injurious. In addition, while early on those who were called out frequently failed to understand or accept objections to their statements, by the latter stages of training participants rapidly comprehended the ouches of peers and accepted corrections without resistance. The following example demonstrates the skill trainees developed in talking about diversity, challenging others and accepting criticism.

The Way to Do Politics

On the third day of training we engaged in an activity designed to expose our lack of awareness when it comes to diversity and the lack of diversity in the public sphere. In the exercise, the trainer named a public position or occupation (e.g., newscasters, actors) and a different dimension of diversity (e.g., blind, African American). They asked that we name as many individuals as we could think of who fit both categories. We passed through several iterations of this exercise including listing Asian Americans involved in politics. In the post-activity wrap-up, one participant, Ellen, a school nurse in her late fifties or early sixties, commented that she had been unable to name even a single person who fit into these categories. "I had a very tough time with this one," she stated correctly beginning with an I-statement. "It's hard to name five Asian Americans because they are quiet when it comes to politics. I'm Jewish and we Jews are loud because we've learned that you need to be loud to get anything done."

"Ouch," Jane, the white women who rebuked Anna on Day One, responded immediately. Gone were the uncertain pauses marking the first day of training. "I heard you say that Asian Americans are quiet in politics. This statement bothers me because I feel like it endorses the stereotype that Asian American individuals are quiet."

Ellen responded quickly, "I am sorry. I didn't mean to say anything discriminatory against Asian Americans. It's just that growing up my family was very political – a lot of Jewish families were and we made a lot of progress."

At this point, one of our leaders, a woman who had already told the group that she is Asian American, spoke up, "I also experienced your statement as an ouch. For me, it feels you're saying that there is a right way of doing politics. To me that feels like a value judgment because there may be other ways of being politically active and getting things done."

With additional explication of what was troublesome about her statement, Ellen again apologized for her comment.

Disciplined to Discourse

Participants in diversity train-the-trainer seminars acquired the vocabulary, outlook, and style of communication required of those who would be identified as open and deeply multicultural individuals. The evidence presented in this chapter makes visible the focus upon specific word use and the belief that words have contingent and multiple meanings, implicit intentions, and directionality that are beyond the control of the speaker but that also indicate his or her inner state. Seemingly incongruous with an emphasis on the wrong words, leaders also claimed that there was no required vocabulary in the abstract. The refusal to acknowledge that there is, as one trainee suggested, "the best way to say whatever" flew in the face of the drive toward language conformity experienced in the training sessions.

Discursive failures on the part of trainees led to the assertion that the offending individual was psychologically damaged and lacked the perspective and deep understanding required of true advocates of diversity. With some early resistance, diversity train-the-trainer program participants successfully adjusted to the diversity training sessions. Trainees adopted the expected manner of speaking and responding to the speech of others and endorsed the notion that missteps should be attributed to internal deficiencies on the part of the speaker. When accused of demonstrating bias, trainees learned to respond with modesty and acceptance. In acquiring competence within the training setting, participants demonstrated their own correct orientation to difference, their emotional health, and their status as allies in the fight against bigotry and discrimination.

The rise of the perspective that Somali settlement was beneficial instead of problematic for Lewiston was tied to foundational definitions of community and the moral criteria for membership. Public talk and ritual celebrated a citizenry that was committed to the community, and welcoming, accepting, and caring of others. But how does one recognize the good people of Lewiston? Despite the preoccupation with the moral basis of membership, I observed the emergence of a stereotyped view of the problematic people in Lewiston – a caricature built upon accents and vocabulary. As a participant researcher in diversity train-the-trainer sessions, I observed the counterpart to the racist stereotype – the performance of moral correctness through the successful enactment of legitimated praxis. In diversity train-the-trainer sessions, people who considered themselves truly pluralistic *before* their participation in the training attained the "concrete skills" and "state of the art techniques" they needed in order to be the people they believed that they were. Disciplined to the praxis of multicultural inclusion, unbiased individuals were made through their performances. In addition to disseminating a particular praxis, diversity train-the-trainer programs also promulgated an associated truth, to which we now turn.

FOUNDATIONAL THEORY

Diversity trainers and training seminars played a role in maintaining and disseminating the epistemology and praxis of incorporation in Lewiston. While their explicit goals ranged from helping individuals confront their biases and discriminatory behaviors to extinguishing flare-ups of intergroup hostility and helping institutions and businesses avoid legal trouble, trainers implicitly ensured the doctrinal status of a particular epistemological and behavioral approach to incorporation by enforcing speech norms and recruiting new individuals into the fold. In becoming disciplined to and ultimately promoting a particular interpretation of multicultural life in Lewiston, diversity trainers influenced what counted as diversity, diagnosed intercultural problems, and assessed the merit of the talk and behavior of others. For these reasons, diversity training provided insight into the mainstream epistemological orientation assigning meaning to Somali immigrant incorporation and underwriting the creation of multicultural Lewistonians. In diversity train-the-trainer seminars, the complexity of intercultural communication was subjected to the strictures of a particular foundational theory – a way of seeing and understanding diversity.

The Nature of Prejudice

The methods of diversity training were grounded in a particular view of what diversity is, why diversity troubles arise, and what the quest for inclusivity and harmony entails. Through this typically uninterrogated web of meanings, diversity was defined as enriching, the battle lines in the fight against bigotry were narrated, and the threat posed by prejudiced people was exposed. This epistemology of diversity, the view to which the heterogeneity of everyday intercultural relations in Lewiston was subjected, becomes visible through analysis of the meaning diversity training assigns to intercultural relations.

The epistemological orientation of diversity training was revealed in the structure of activities, the focus of interventions, and the avoidance of particular subjects. As was the case in most diversity training sessions I attended in Lewiston, both Rights Org and Corporate Org training sessions took the diversity within the group and the psychological states of trainees as the material for the sessions. This was the typical approach to diversity training, even in cases where the group lacked significant visible diversity. The diversity "in the room" became the subject of a host of activities designed to variously reveal the "hidden" diversity of the group and the rifts that intragroup differences create.

Valuing Diversity

In this field note, training participants learned that diversity was ubiquitous, often surprising and a wonderful asset to group life – an interpretation that reprises the diversity-affirming narratives discussed in Chapter 2.

On the second day of Rights Org diversity training, I arrived with a large object, a red and orange lobster buoy collected from the shoreline in my hometown, in a canvas bag. After a brief call to order and distribution of the day's schedule, our trainers announced that it was time for us to reveal the "personal artifact" that we had brought with us. In showing the item, we were to describe what it was and what it said about us. We should then pass it around the room. It was a lengthy and good-natured exercise. Some members of the group brought items and shared personal stories of pain and loss or triumph in the face of adversity that brought tears to the eyes of many. Others shared items that symbolized their hopes and successes. Still others, like me, brought artifacts that tied them to far-flung homes, family roots, and pivotal historical moments.

At the conclusion of this exercise, the group shared responses and impressions. Trainees expressed their empathy and sympathy. They remarked that they appreciated the deep information that personal artifacts imparted. "I feel lucky to work with such a diverse group of people," one of the trainers stated in drawing the exercise to its conclusion. "Thank you for being willing to share a little bit about who you are with us. I feel that it is so important to remember that people have so much more to them than what you see at any given moment."

Many of the participants in the train-the-trainer programs attended on the basis of their personal or occupational interest in gender, race, sexual, or ethnic discrimination and inequality. Through "personal artifacts" and other related exercises, the group learned that diversity included much more than the typical litany of race, color, religion, sex, national origin, age, and disability, the "classes" protected by federal equal employment opportunity laws. Trainers in the corporate session referred to these different ways of understanding difference as "Big D," legally recognized, and "little d," complete diversity. In both train-the-trainer series, trainees were asked to dispense with our preoccupation with Big D diversity and to understand that diversity work was much more than advocating and keeping track of Big D diversity. True diversity, the trainers instructed, derives from the many identities we each claim – family histories and personal geographies, and the experiences and cultural immersion that influence how people see themselves and how they are seen.

By encouraging training participants to avoid the propensity to reduce the complexity of diversity to checkboxes on application forms, diversity train-the-trainer leaders demonstrated that diversity is everywhere, a necessary and wonderful element of each individual and a valuable aspect of the relationships between people.

Feeling Hostility

While the previous exercise emphasized the diversity of the group in such a way that trainees developed greater awareness of the nature and scope of diversity and experienced the group's diversity as an asset, the training sessions moved quickly into activities that exposed the fissures that can occur when diversity encounters bias. In the following account from another exercise, aspiring diversity professionals learned, as the trainers instructed, that any difference that may attributable to diversity could become a dividing line, acting to polarize groups.

In the early afternoon on our second day of Rights Org training, the trainers looked around the circle of chairs, smiling, "Time to rise! Let's do an activity that gets us out of these chairs."

Everyone rose and for a moment people were busy pushing the chairs against the wall and standing, as instructed, in a line in the center of the room.

"This is a game called Beliefs and Opinions. Individuals' beliefs and opinions are derived in large part from their culture and upbringing. People generally hold their own views and ways of doing things in high esteem. I am going to name two views and assign one of these views to each side of the room. Please go to the side of the room that matches your beliefs. If you have no opinion, stay in the center. By participating in this activity, we are going to see how our views differ from the views of others and how we respond to people who do not share our beliefs and opinions."

"Direct control versus negotiation" was the first binary choice. I was a bit puzzled as I had expected more provocative choices – for example, suburbs versus urban or liberal versus conservative. All the same, I moved with some others over to the wall for negotiation. A number of trainees stood on the other side of the room, and a great many people chose not to take sides and remained standing in the center. The group passed through several iterations of the exercise, often stopping to share thoughts about the merits of holding one preference over the other. What began as good-natured ribbing, for example, for people who chose climbing the corporate ladder over putting the family first (e.g., "Hey, you can't take it with you, you know! Put your effort into the gene pool!") grew more serious as a trainee who valued competition over cooperation stated that people who cooperate are "really collaborators" with a mediocre system while competitors perform a service for society by pushing everyone to achieve to their fullest potential. Although the trainers briefly reminded everyone that comments should not denigrate other groups but instead should provide a rationale for why the chosen group was worthy of selection, the point was easily driven home: it is very easy to feel superior in the face of difference. Furthermore, when differences are brought to the forefront, even if they are abstract and unrelated to the situation at hand, they can lead quickly to hostility.

"Beliefs and opinions" provided a foundational understanding of diversity troubles. Through their participation in "cultural artifacts," trainees learned that diversity was multifaceted, highly individual, and a product of one's "cultural programming," as it was called by the Corporate Org trainers. From "beliefs and opinions" it became apparent that intergroup hostilities arose almost automatically when people came into contact with those who do not appear to share their values. These tensions arose from individuals' unexamined high regard for their own views and way of life.

The hostilities emerging in "beliefs and opinions" were associated with abstract values upon which people could disagree but which were also not easily related to specific practices or situations (for example, in negotiating culturally distinct gender relationships or religious practices). Instead of residing within situations or relationships, the tensions emerging in the exercise were depicted as the result of individual interpretations, histories, and predilections instead of cross-cultural negotiation. The meaning assigned to diversity troubles was similarly abstract.

Escalation of Hate

Through participation in activities such as those just described, diversity trainers-in-training gleaned early insight into the value of diversity and the dynamics that create group boundaries and tension. Trainees also learned that when it comes to bias, there is no such thing as unremarkable or insignificant behavior. Instead, unchecked bias was depicted as dangerous and the root of all diversity troubles. Both training sessions used activities designed to uncover the value judgments that tend to coincide with exposure to differences. Training leaders used these activities to segue to discussion of a causal chain that began with bias – the escalation of hate.

The escalation of hate provided the foundational rationale for the individual and psychological focus of diversity work. As Corporate and Rights Org trainers presented it, the escalation of hate began with avoidance and other small acts of bias such as failing to use inclusive language and unquestioningly accepting stereotype-consistent information. The second level of escalation consisted of prejudice and bigotry: the use of slurs and biased jokes, name-calling, and scapegoating. Open discrimination, harassment, and social exclusion indicated level three. Violence and attack characterized level four while genocide, the apex, was level five. Corporate and Rights Org attached different names to the escalation of hate. Despite the different terms offered in the sessions, each training organization offered an understanding of prejudice drawn with limited elaboration and rewording from the same source, Gordon Allport's *The Nature of Prejudice*.[6]

In 1954, psychologist Gordon Allport published his foundational text, *The Nature of Prejudice*, a voluminous account of the workings of prejudice from the formation of in-groups to the development and dissemination of stereotypes to intergroup conflict and bias. Like many notable scholars of his time (e.g., Asch 1955; Milgram 1974), Allport's work displays a preoccupation with the Holocaust, the German Nazi extermination of 6 million Jews, and a desire to understand how average German citizens could participate in or at least remain silent in the face of the genocidal project unfolding in their midst.

Allport identifies prejudice and the preferential thinking at its base as creating the conditions for genocidal acts. The text contains a five-point scale of behavioral manifestations of prejudice. This scale maps on to the escalation of hate.

1. *Antilocution.* Most people who have prejudices talk about them. With like-minded friends, occasionally with strangers, they may express their antagonism freely.
2. *Avoidance.* If the prejudice is more intense, it leads the individual to avoid members of the disliked group.
3. *Discrimination.* Here the prejudiced person makes detrimental distinctions of an active sort. He undertakes to exclude all members of the group in questions from certain types of employment, from residential housing, political rights, educational or recreational opportunities .... or from some other social privileges.
4. *Physical attack.* Under conditions of heightened emotion prejudice may lead to acts of violence or semi-violence.
5. *Extermination.* Lynchings, pogroms, massacres, and the Hitlerian program of genocide mark the ultimate degree of the violent expression of prejudice. (Allport 1954, pp. 14–15)

Notably, Allport claims that the prejudices of individuals are the building blocks of the behaviors higher on the scale.

Activity on one level makes transition to a more intense level easier. It was Hitler's antilocution that led Germans to avoid their Jewish neighbors and erstwhile friends. This preparation made it easier to enact the Nurnberg [sic] laws of discrimination which, in turn, made the subsequent burning of synagogues and

---

[6] Corporate Org cited Allport's seminal work while Rights Org offered no citation or credit for the concept.

street attacks upon Jews seem natural. The final step in the macabre progression was the ovens at Auschwitz. (Allport 1954, p. 15)

In presenting the escalation, Corporate and Rights Org trainers provided a pivotal element of the epistemology of diversity: there are no excusable or benign behavioral manifestations of bias and prejudice. As expressed in the Rights Org training, even something as seemingly insignificant as name-calling paves the way for acts of bigotry, discrimination, violence, and, ultimately, genocide. "Genocide has its roots," a Rights Org trainer recited; "it started as a small seed of bias that went unnoticed or unchecked."

The "escalation of hate" legitimated the individual, therapeutic orientation of diversity training by providing for the seamless transition from individual psychology to violence and exclusion at the societal level. Given this epistemological orientation, even institutionalized discrimination was attributable to individual expressions of bias that created the context for the rise of increasingly wide-reaching and violent expressions of bigotry.

Perpetrator, Victim, Ally, Accomplice

Armed with the escalation of hate as the model of diversity troubles, participants in train-the-trainer seminars were encouraged to develop self-understandings that assumed the ongoing struggle against bias. As the following account from the field demonstrated, the escalation of hate was depicted as a perpetual and all-encompassing aspect of existence, the backdrop of every experience and encounter.

After learning about the escalation of hate, Rights Org training participants took a worksheet, "The Four Roles" home from the session – homework for the evening in addition to the required reading and journaling. The single sheet of paper contained a 2x2 grid. Each of the squares contained a different word: Victim; Perpetrator; Accomplice; Ally. Individuals were to recount incidents in which they acted in each of those roles. Trainees did not discuss the worksheet until after lunch the next day. Participants began by separating into small groups to share their worksheets and then returned to the larger group to share any impressions taken from the exercise. There were three other people in my small group, all white women in their twenties. One was a school social worker and the other two were elementary teachers. Most of us found it difficult to come up with examples of ourselves in each role.

The nature of subsequent large-group discussion made it clear that the trainers expected that most people would find themselves unable to fill in the worksheet. As trainees shared the difficulty they experienced in attempting to recall situations relevant to the exercise, the trainers nodded sympathetically. "It is a new way to look at things. Victim or perpetrator. Accomplice or ally. We are always in one of these roles when bias is happening aren't we?" a trainer commented. They then challenged the group to dig a little deeper in thinking about typical responses when confronted with fear and uncertainty in interactions with diverse others. They suggested that most people had heard friends and family telling racist or homophobic jokes. Had we responded to their behavior or laughed away our discomfort? The trainers assured us that the decision to leave biased behavior unchallenged is taken by the perpetrator as a sign of agreement, inviting that person to continue and perhaps even intensify his or her prejudicial acts.

In the Corporate Org train-the-trainer series, trainees completed a similar worksheet and shared their responses in groups of two and three. Following the small group session, the entire group engaged in a discussion of the "reality of stereotypes." The trainers pointed out that stereotypes are nonrational, based upon limited knowledge and/or experience of other groups, and come to be self-fulfilling prophecies. Furthermore, stereotypes are a "two-sided coin" in that in their existence, there is always a victim and a perpetrator. As demonstrated through the "4 roles" and "reality of stereotypes" the epistemology of diversity situated all individuals in the ongoing continuation or the eradication of prejudicial behavior through their choices to confront bias or be silently complicit in its operation. There was no neutral territory for those who felt they had confronted their own inner racist. They must also challenge bias in others.

Common Ground

Established as the truth of diversity, the "escalation of hate" underwrote strategies for intervention and repair in situations where diversity led to tension and conflict. Rights and Corporate Org training sessions focused on eliminating and confronting expressions of bias as they offered an understanding of the actions that would remedy group conflict and limit the intensification of prejudicial acts. In the following accounts from the field, diversity trainers-in-training learned that locating shared traits or values would challenge stereotypes. Thus, co-identification was the solution to diversity troubles, be they intergroup tensions on the assembly line, bullying on the school grounds, discriminatory policies, or confronting bigoted behavior.

In the wake of the group discussion of prejudice, a trainee in the Corporate Org session, a West Indian religious leader of African descent raised his hand. "I feel myself in a bit of a bind," he began carefully. "What do you do when diversity challenges a basic philosophy? I hold personal and religious beliefs that homosexuality is wrong and I feel those beliefs conflict with my desire to value diversity."

"That's easy," one of the trainers responded. "No one is asking people to give up their beliefs, or buy into other people's lifestyles or beliefs but we need to be able to respect others as fellow human beings. We need to find common ground."

"Look, we all hold stereotypes and we all know how it feels acting on stereotypes, being stereotyped and seeing it happen to someone else," the other trainer added, moving from the prejudice of the participant who raised the question to the more abstract world of the people we would be training.[7] "But if we can get our clients to know one another – to know even one personal fact about someone that they think they can't get along with, we can put an end to the escalation of hate."

Working from the Personal
The train-the-trainer curricula reflected this emphasis on personal connections as the remedy for intergroup conflict. As such, diversity trainers in training participated in and learned to deliver exercises intended to foster relationships among trainees.

In the interests of establishing common ground among participants, the training experience maximized interpersonal contact and communication. Most of the exercises comprising the curriculum of the training provided opportunities for sharing personal information, often in pairs or in small groups. The trainers frequently insisted upon mixing the trainees by asking that participants share with someone new, and by using varying techniques to divide into small groups. In addition, trainees were expected to spend significant time with their peers outside of the sessions. Upon arriving in the morning, training participants sat together for breakfast. Corporate Org provided lunch in a small dining room adjoining the training room. The trainers joined trainees at the small tables provided next to the buffet. While not expressly required, attendance at meals was clearly an important part of the training. Although Rights Org

---

[7] I suspect that the adept trainer knew that to suggest and focus upon the work the trainee has to do as a result of harboring prejudice against homosexuals would likely result in defensiveness on his part, making it more likely that her message would not be heard and accepted.

did not provide on-site lunch, trainees still took their meals together and organized group lunches on two of five days. Both trainers and trainees referenced lunchtime discussions in training lectures and group discussion, and even expressed "ouches" that had occurred over lunch and other breaks and required explication and redress.

In the following account from the field, training leaders demonstrated the centrality of personal engagement when they paused the training to reprimand trainees for their failure to engage the diversity training process as individuals in need of emotional healing through their sharing instead of as workers seeking expertise and a professional credential.

Upon returning from lunch on the second day of Rights Org training, training participants found their trainers sitting grimly in their seats. The agency's regional director, who had been in and out of the sessions up to that time and who was to play a key role in deciding trainees' suitability for diversity training position within Rights Org, sat beside them.

"We're going to be departing from the agenda for a bit," the director announced, "We need to process."

One of the trainers continued, "We are finding that as a group we keep working from the professional and we need to be working from the personal. We need to be experiencing things as individuals."

I was confused. From the quizzical looks on the faces of other trainees and the questions that arose subsequently, I surmised that I was not alone in my bewilderment that, apparently, we had been doing the training incorrectly.[8]

One of the trainees suggested that we were eager to be trainers ourselves and so we often sought to discuss the training material as opposed to the substance of the training.

The regional director responded with some annoyance that we were not trainers yet. "You need to bring your participation back to 'I' statements," she stated, "You need to be participants in full before you can be trainers in full."

At this point a white male elementary teacher who, I observed over the course of the training, excelled at being a peacemaker, suggested that we were hiding our personal reactions to the training behind our professional concerns.

[8] Discussion with several trainees at the end of the day confirmed this suspicion. Just prior to lunch we had been discussing appropriate responses to incidents of bullying and name-calling on the playground. We had departed from the practice of speaking from our own experience. After all, many of us had not experienced such an incident on a playground as a victim or perpetrator since our own elementary school days.

Another trainee, Mike, an older man who self-identified as Jewish and reported significant community organizing experience, began to expound upon the tight connection between his personal and professional selves. However, Mike continuously neglected to use "I" statements. The director repeatedly interrupted him with the interjection, "I!" Mike responded patiently, attempting each time to reword his sentence appropriately. As the resulting contribution was largely incomprehensible he soon abandoned the enterprise and sat quietly.

One of our trainers stepped forward. "I think that these training sessions can be difficult and emotional. I think maybe you all are not comfortable going there and confronting your own biases so you are moving over to the professional."

Perhaps in an effort to save face in light of the suggestion that we were uncomfortable confronting our inner racists, a member of the group[9] stated that many of the training participants had significant experience with diversity training and that meant the group experienced the sessions as "less raw."

"Well what are we here for, anyway?" the other trainer rejoined impatiently. "We're here first to explore our biases and prejudice and to unlearn what we can."

This comment incited a bit of a mutiny on the part of the group. Several people voiced frustration that trainees had not been given many opportunities to share deeply and that the reading assignment from the night before, a short article on white privilege, was a good one and yet the schedule had not provided time to discuss it. The trainers consulted briefly and then announced that they would throw out the schedule in favor of small group sharing time.

In addition to providing a further example of how trainees are disciplined, these events demonstrated the fundamental belief that diversity work consists of, first and foremost, honest self-exploration and establishing personal relationships based upon sharing deep feelings and critical experiences. Successful diversity training, even for trainers-in-training, depended upon trainees' authentic participation: dispensing with roles that provide distance from the material and fellow trainees; leaving unsaid ideas that don't draw directly from highly personal and emotional experiences; and taking one's own shortcomings when it comes to bias and prejudice as the object of reform and subject of discussion. When criticized for not engaging the emotional work the training

---

[9] I failed to include the identity of this person in my notes.

required, diversity trainers-in-training did not challenge the terms set by training leaders. Instead, they complained that they had not been given sufficient opportunity to undertake those crucial aspects of the training experience.

Coming Together through Diversity

Establishing close personal contact with fellow trainees and sharing deep and personal information about themselves with others was viewed as a necessary aspect of the training process. The two activities described next demonstrate that diversity training promoted such sharing with the expectation that it would lead to the recognition of common ground. Common ground was not a natural outgrowth of interaction, however. It was constructed carefully through the identification of abstract commonalities and the attentive management of the differences that might be brought to the surface.

The training curricula sought to bridge the gaps people felt between themselves and those with whom they assumed they had little in common. In addition to fostering meaningful personal contact between training participants, training exercises often encouraged trainees to identify with the others in order to find their "match." These activities were dubbed "bridging" exercises because they elicited information helpful in establishing common ground. Bridging activities included the formation of an enclosed human chain by trainees clasping with one hand someone with whom individuals shared a visible characteristic and, with the other hand, someone with whom they shared an invisible trait or belief. Two bridging activities discussed below clearly demonstrated the notion that diversity troubles are addressed through contact and common ground that was carefully constructed within the training setting.

"Norms and values" was the last exercise late in the afternoon on the first day of Corporate Org training. Trainees began their participation individually, filling out a worksheet in which each person identified eight important sources of his or her own cultural programming (e.g., parents, neighborhood, religion). Individuals then identified at least two norms, rules, or values derived from each source. After completing the worksheet, trainees formed small groups in order to discuss the worksheet. Armed with a flip chart, each small group listed the norms, rules, and values that emerged in the group. They designated a spokesperson to share that list with the rest of the room. The trainer had a flip chart of her own to further aggregate all the lists.

My small group noted that despite the variety of sources of cultural programming members listed and the different norms and rules they identified, the values people reported evinced significant overlap. Nearly universally shared values included family, freedom, independence, social responsibility, education, and economic stability. Upon discussion in the larger group, one trainee observed that many of the norms and rules she had identified could really be understood as having at root values she shared with the larger group.

Wrapping up the exercise, the trainer stated, "When you really consider your own internal diversity you find out that you have a lot more in common with other people than you think and you also find out that can have just as much internal conflict as cross-cultural conflict with other folks."

"Norms and values" established common ground by abstracting from varying personal histories and cultural practices to the principles people believed motivated their behavior, forging commonalities between individuals on the basis of endorsement of unquestioned and universalizing deep values like family and freedom. An additional activity worked in the opposite direction by encouraging individuals to forge connections on the basis of seemingly trivial details. The instruction trainees received in the use of the activity "Matchmaker" demonstrates that the common ground identified in diversity training was not a natural subject, but instead, one that was created to obscure material conflicts and constraints.

Early on the second day of corporate training trainees engaged in a "warm-up" exercise in which each individual received a worksheet requiring a list of details such as month of birth, favorite ethnic food, length of commute to work, number of siblings/children, and kind of car. After filling out the form, trainees walked around the room, seeking individuals who had given the same answers. The group recognized this exercise as an "ice-breaker" designed to get people interacting and comfortable with one another. In the post activity wrap-up, the trainer discussed the merits of the exercise. "Not only is this a good ice-breaker," she said. "It is also a great introduction to the idea that people have more in common than they think."

"That's right," added the other trainer, "however there are some adaptations you might want to consider depending on your audience. If you have a lot of levels of the organization represented in the room, you want to make sure that you take off anything that can play upon tensions that might already be there. For example, it's probably not a good idea to talk about what kind of car you drive, what languages you speak, or your favorite travel destination when you have upper- and middle-level managers in a session with folks who are working on the assembly line. You might find you're working at cross purposes."

"If I've got a session like that, with a lot of layers of employees in the room," rejoined the first trainer, "I wouldn't even use this. I would use something less risky."

In this telling recommendation, the trainer made it clear that the acknowledged "diversity in the room" should include only those differences that might be addressed by the focus on bias and prejudice. The training exercises were not designed to build bridges spanning material differences in status and wealth. Instead, diversity trainers were to provide exercises that took the economic inequality in the room as the status quo, a background condition sidestepped by discussions of mundane interests and universal principles. The emphasis on the "take away" values of Matchmaker and other exercises demonstrates the tight connection between the epistemology espoused within the sessions and the tools that diversity trainers would use to interpret and remedy diversity troubles in places like Lewiston.

Constructing a Problem, Seeing the Solution

Diversity train-the-trainer seminars offered diversity itself as the solution to the ailment of bias and prejudice. Training sessions emphasized establishing personal connections between trainees and fostering a sense of commonality among participants. Carefully controlled interactions elicited information on the varied cultural backgrounds, personal experiences, and everyday interests of trainees. Training activities provided opportunities for structured sharing that led program participants to recognize in their fellows their own tastes, values, and personal history. Trainees acquired a nuanced set of tools that would allow them to avoid exposing intractable and material elements of the divisions between people, characterized by trainers as "levels of the organization," that endangered the good-natured common ground sought by diversity trainers.

Talk, activities, and information making up the content of diversity train-the-trainer sessions espoused a particular view of the dynamics of difference and the reality of intercultural relations. According to this epistemology of diversity, differences reside within individuals as a product of their cultural background writ large. Bias arises from unexamined preferential and superior opinions of one's own culture. While initially an individual characteristic, bias easily finds expression in individual behaviors that pave the way for increasingly repressive and widely dispersed acts of discrimination. No one may claim that he or she is not implicated in this system or is neutral as regards the operation of prejudice. Bias is ameliorated and the progression of hateful acts halted through challenge and through shared exegesis of intrapersonal diversity. The epistemology of diversity that emerged in diversity train-the-trainer seminars was neither made explicit to trainers nor was it offered for assessment and reevaluation.

MULTICULTURAL TRUTHS AND MULTICULTURAL SELVES

Diversity training sessions provided methods used in the discursive construction of multicultural individuals who were familiar with the meaning of diversity troubles underwriting the training curricula. These meanings and practices constituted the epistemology and praxis of incorporation. Skill building focused on the emotional healing of training participants as they increased their awareness of their biases, their ability to relativize and minimize their negative reactions to difference, and the comfort and skill with which they challenged the prejudice of others. The training approach equated diversity with carefully censured interpersonal differences; demonstrated the propensity for in-group bias to form; asserted that such bias was the foundation of overt discrimination and intergroup conflict; and touted interpersonal contact and the establishment of common ground as the remedy for prejudicial thoughts, discriminatory acts, and even mass violence and exclusion.

In addition to the empirical linkages between diversity train-the-trainer programs and the diversity training sessions and diversity professionals in Lewiston, diversity training sessions offer insight in to the epistemology, praxis, and discipline characteristic of immigrant incorporation in the city. The meanings of Somali settlement and the Lewiston community shared many similarities with the epistemology of diversity. Individuals in Lewiston touted Somali settlement for its economic benefits. Diversity train-the-trainer participants learned how to "lead the strategic charge" in making the "business case" for diversity – greater diversity within the organization would lead to increased return on investments, improved employee recruitment and retention, greater innovation, increased flexibility of the workforce, and increased access to and success in submarkets. Public talk in Lewiston emphasized the role of Somali settlement in increasing the cultural richness of the community. In diversity training seminars, diversity was also depicted as an enriching, invaluable, and unavoidable aspect of interpersonal relationships. For example, the "personal artifacts" exercise described earlier reinforced the diversity-affirming view that difference is a pleasurable and enriching aspect of group relationships as well as reinforcing the view, reflected in an emphasis on the global ties derived from Somali settlement in Lewiston, that encounters with diverse others increase the connections between individuals and other times and places.

Diversity-trouble narratives proved similarly consistent with the epistemology of diversity. Inexperience, resource limitations, exploitation, and racism played a key role in accounts of diversity troubles in the city. Three of these preoccupations were reflected in the diversity train-the-trainer curricula. Lewiston's diversity troubles were interpreted to be rooted in simple inexperience or problematic attitudes and behaviors instead of in the structure of society or the material negotiation of cultural difference. The trainings represented diversity work as the ongoing knowledge and skill acquisition that would inevitably occur as individuals continued the honest and authentic exploration their own biases and sharing with diverse others. This emphasis mirrored the focus in Lewiston on skill building and meeting standards in the management of community diversity. The narrative emphasis on biased and selfish individuals as the cause of diversity troubles in Lewiston was consistent with the escalation of hate described within diversity training. In Lewiston and in diversity train-the-trainer seminars, psychological limitations, bias, and problematic people emerged as a primary site of intervention when it comes to addressing intergroup tensions and discrimination.

Just as this epistemology was evident in both Lewiston and diversity train-the-trainer seminars, so, too, were individuals in both settings disciplined to the cultural pragmatics of incorporation. Through their attempts at realizing an inclusive community (e.g., attendance in diversity training sessions and adherence to standards and best practices) Lewistonians acquired strategies for indicating their status as a moral community of moral, healthy individuals who ought to be considered allies in the fight against hate. Participants in diversity train-the-trainer seminars developed proficiency in particular discursive techniques. In Lewiston, discursive performances could be constructed against a foil – the local racist persona developed in public talk. According to the dominant epistemology and praxis, Lewiston residents like Mayor Raymond, Brent Matthews, Dave, and Ms. Smith revealed their psychological limitations when they sought to offer an account of discrimination that spoke to differences in lifeways and material circumstances instead of bias.

THE CULTURE OF INCORPORATION

The epistemology and praxis of incorporation constructed diversity in such a way that institutionalized discrimination and many of the meaningful and material differences between groups were effectively erased from consideration. Although in the diversity train-the-trainer series, trainers acknowledged that diversity makes communication and understanding more difficult while making conflict more likely, skill building in the sessions focused almost exclusively on increasing the individual's ability to relativize and minimize his or her negative reactions to difference instead of communicating across difficult cultural barriers. This approach obscured accounts, experiences, and differences that did not fit the methods and epistemology of the sessions.

In the case of Somali incorporation in Lewiston, it could be suggested that the means justify the ends – that the epistemology and praxis of multicultural incorporation made it possible for Lewiston to overcome resistance to the settlement of a racially, ethnically, and religiously distinct group. While a disciplined Lewiston is certainly more inclusive of newcomers and accepting of cultural difference in the abstract, the next chapter demonstrates that the payoff of Somali inclusion may fall short of the promise of Somali belonging. Ironically, of all the actors, narratives, and institutions structuring Somali settlement in Lewiston, it is the Somalis and Somali settlement services that were least reflected in the epistemology and praxis of diversity train-the-trainer sessions. Of the diversity-trouble narratives identified in Chapter 2, only the attention to limited resources for managing diversity troubles in Lewiston was not reflected in the epistemology of diversity. This attention to resources was inconsistent with the epistemology of multiculturalism because it drew notions of incorporation that depicted Somali cultural traits as an obstacle to community life instead of welcomed diversity. Of the institutional approaches to Somali incorporation described in Chapter 3, only the cultural assimilation programs for Somalis were not reflected in the way that diversity trainees were disciplined to the cultural prescriptions. The nature and substance of Somali settlement services was inconsistent with the abstract and psychological emphasis of the epistemology and praxis laid out in the previous chapter. For this reason cultural education programs for Somalis drew intermittent criticism despite the fact that both Somalis and non-Somalis in the city acknowledged their practical necessity.

The lack of fit between the epistemology and praxis of multiculturalism reflects the inescapable facts of material and cultural distance – the limited interaction between non-Somalis and Somalis, language barriers, desire among many Somalis to limit their social interactions to their own enclave, and the existence of significant differences in practices around child-rearing, gender relations, economic transactions, and the relationship between religion and public life. It is these distances, so carefully left out of the constructions of the "diversity in the room" that proved of utmost significance to many Lewiston residents, particularly Somalis. In the next chapter I demonstrate that the culture of incorporation does enable Somali incorporation, but the position of Somali newcomers remains partial and contingent. Lewiston Somalis must do significant work to construct a diversity deemed worthy of inclusion.

5

Familiar Strangers

On Friday, January 6, 2006, the full-color front page of the *Lewiston Sun Journal* boasted a photograph unrelated to any story headlining that day. "A Smile Is Her Umbrella," read the title of an image of a laughing African woman who had just slipped in the falling snow. The pink umbrella she had been carrying rested, up-ended, beside her. Her arms, face, and boots were covered in fresh, white snow. The caption read:

Oops! Haba Adbelmalik[1] wipes snow off her face as she and her son Hamud have a laugh after she fell down the icy hill ... during Thursday's snowstorm. She has been in Maine for less than a month and is still getting used to the snow and ice. (Dillingham 2006, p. A1)

On most days, Lewiston's daily newspaper featured a color front-page photograph of people and places in the community. Somali residents of the city often appeared center stage in these photographs, taking a place within the paper's parade of snowdrifts, senior citizens playing bingo, rainbows, icicles, puppies, children eating ice cream and running through sprinklers, dew-covered spider webs, and high school students heading out to a prom. In celebration of St. Patrick's Day 2007, the *Sun Journal* featured a photograph of a young Somali girl at her school's celebration of the holiday wearing "an Irish wristband to go with her green hijab" (Van Reeth 2007, p. A1). Other photographs depicted Somali women

---

[1] The names of individuals depicted in photographs are changed. The names of those submitting letters to the editor or making other explicitly on-the-record contributions to the public sphere are retained.

happily harvesting produce from their garden plots to take the famers' market and tending their children at the playground. The paper presented images of graduating high school seniors wearing their mortar boards over their hijabs while awaiting their diplomas and Somali youth sitting alongside their classmates as they made care packages for members of the armed forces deployed in Iraq. Photographs captured Somali children as they enjoyed cotton candy, played basketball and soccer, and mimicked the facial expressions of their favorite wrestlers while waiting in line for admission to the professional wrestling event being held in the Lewiston Collisée.

The snapshots of community presented in the *Sun Journal* offered a brightly optimistic view of life in the town, confirming the diversity-affirming emphasis on appreciation of cultural heterogeneity as a "splash of color" bringing increased vitality to community life. These images also showcased Lewiston's inclusive character by sharing the perceived joy, beauty, and comfort experienced by Somali newcomers and emphasizing the welcoming and successful integration of Somalis in the town. For many non-Somali residents of Lewiston, especially those living and working outside of the downtown area where most Somalis resided, *Sun Journal* photographs of the Somalis in their midst and the corresponding text acted as the primary authority in defining the character of Lewiston Somalis and the nature of their relationship to the broader community.

Somali incorporation in Lewiston might have appeared assured by the new faces in familiar scenes featured in the local newspaper. Lewiston life was not significantly changed: the scenes were familiar, only enriched by the arrival of newcomers taking part in community life. These were images derived from the multicultural epistemology laid out earlier – the view that recognition of common ground and fundamental similarity circumvented diversity troubles. However, other moments exposed the precarious nature of Somali belonging. Sometimes Somali residents of Lewiston appeared to fall short of the expectations of their neighbors. When Somali newcomers in Lewiston did not seem to offer smiling faces in response to the hardships of relocation, cultural adaptation, and conflict, the shaky foundations of the welcoming community and the more intractable elements of Somali alterity were exposed.

The previous chapters have sketched the cultural pragmatics of incorporation that provided the context for Somali inclusion in Lewiston. This chapter considers the impact that this cultural context had on Somali settlement. I demonstrate that the meaning of Somali-ness took a form consistent with the position of Somalis as objects of multicultural desire embraced when they presented a Somali-ness that was constructed in such a manner that it fit the dominant epistemology. Somali Lewistonians were also disciplined to mainstream praxis. They performed their own multi-cultural orientations as individuals, but they also performed as a group.

Lewiston's Somali community, far from being characterized by una-nimity and cultural consensus, reflected significant internal variations in cultural, subcultural, and religious practice. Furthermore, group mem-bers held a diversity of perspectives on the manner and outcome of Somali assimilation. The acceptance, incorporation, and accommodation of diversity characterized in Chapter 2 fostered an emphasis on Somali group identification and recognition. This context of reception created incentives for the emergence of a single Somali leadership and the exag-geration of the solidarity of Lewiston's Somali population. The multicul-tural incorporation of Somalis in Lewiston was therefore not simply a vehicle for the inclusion of a preexisting ethno-national group. Instead, Somali incorporation depended on the creation and maintenance of a group image that was acceptable to non-Somali Lewiston.

The construction and negotiation of the cultural position of Somalis was visible in common narratives woven through accounts I collected and events I observed. In analyzing these field data, I identified two con-trasting and contradictory but tightly interwoven narratives of alterity and likeness constructing Somalis as "familiar strangers." These narra-tives imbued Somalis with value derived from their ethno-cultural dis-tinctiveness but also made that distinctiveness benign because, at root, Somalis were depicted as being just like everyone else.[2]

The narratives of alterity and likeness emerging in Lewiston influ-enced not just the public perception of Somalis but also the character of the community's Somali organizations and the display of Somali-ness. Observing the rise and fall of various Somali community organizations and the negotiation of Somali culture and identity as it was displayed and celebrated in an annual Somali cultural festival demonstrates the mate-rial consequences of the cultural position of Somali newcomers in the city. Exoticized as Lewiston's "diversity," Somalis were recognized and

---

[2] According to Barth, ethnic groups are created through processes of inclusion and exclu-sion that occur, not within isolated groups, but through the interaction and acceptance of different groups co-existing within a single social system. The maintenance of ethnic boundaries within a system requires the construction of a located identity that can be rec-ognizably performed and which carries with it widely recognized understandings of the values held by those who identified with that identity (Barth, Fredrik. 1969. *Ethnic groups and boundaries. The social organization of culture difference.* Bergen: Allen & Unwin).

engaged as a bounded and cohesive group despite increasing awareness of the limits of such an approach for service provision and for understanding intra-Somali community dynamics. In the face of increasing settlement by other immigrant groups, Somalis struggled to maintain a separate cultural and political identity.

A Fragile Inclusion

Social psychologists use the term "familiar stranger" to designate individual people one encounters on a regular basis but with whom one does not interact (Milgram 1972). Milgram's familiar stranger is someone with whom, based upon shared routines and locations, one assumes commonality. Somalis' status as familiar strangers did not rely on the interpersonal familiarity gained when individuals encounter the same faces at the supermarket, on the bus, and at the city park. Instead, both the assumption of belonging and the recognition of cultural distinctiveness pertained to Somalis as a group generally – adhering to generalized characteristics instead of specific individuals. The belonging of individual Somalis in Lewiston was closely intertwined with the successful projection of a Somali group identity that was acceptable to the broader Lewiston community. As detailed in this chapter, tensions and misunderstandings punctuated the process of establishing Somali-ness, and by extension Somali individuals, as a legitimately incorporable element of Lewiston's diversity.

Narratives of likeness and alterity found expression in the media accounts, official documents, and the public talk of Somali and non-Somali Lewiston residents. I will briefly compare these narratives by placing them in contrasting pairs. While I conducted my field research I observed that likeness and alterity accounts were less closely correlated with particular types of individuals or groups and instead arose when they made the most sense. Sometimes public discussion emphasized alterity, at other times likeness and, sometimes, the two narratives appeared side by side, spoken by the same individual and in the same conversation. Alterity narratives focused on Somalis as others – a group with the right to be left alone to pursue their own interests and whose distinctiveness must be recognized and preserved. Alterity narratives circulated widely in Lewiston; at the same time, likeness narratives emphasizing Somalis' shared values and experiences with fellow community residents were also espoused widely. Taken together, these seemingly contradictory narratives were consistent with the epistemology laid out in the previous chapter.

Commonality identified through particularity legitimated Somali belonging, respect, and inclusion, casting Somalis as familiar strangers imbued with value as cultural outsiders at the same time that those differences that made them other appeared as consistent with the core values of the mainstream.

Likeness narratives identified Somalis as immigrants, particularly drawing on the idea that the United States is a "country of immigrants," as people of faith trying to live a righteous life through good deeds, attendance at weekly services, and studying the holy word, and living as parents, homeowners, workers, and neighbors contributing to the life and well-being of Lewiston. Alterity narratives, on the other hand, emphasized the otherness of Somalis by highlighting their refugee status, adherence to Islam, Somali identity, and position as newcomers to and, in some cases, transitory residents of Lewiston. Contrasting related aspects of these narratives elucidates the complicated meaning of Somali Americanness in Lewiston.

Refugees, Immigrants

Over the course of nearly three decades of refugee settlement, the Somali population of the United States grew substantially. While many Somalis newcomers did arrive in this country as refugees, others have come through family reunification programs. Still others immigrated in the years before Somalia's chaos. Many Somali residents of the United States are American-born, members of the growing second generation (see Goza 2007 for a demographic analysis of the Somali population of the United States). Although not all Somalis were refugees, within the narrative of stranger-ness, Somali residents of Lewiston were described as refugees forced from their homes and unable to return, as in the following quotation:

We came to this country with nothing. We came leaving family behind to die and to starve. We wait but still we cannot go home. (Somali informant, in focus group)

In their letter of response to Mayor Raymond's letter, the Somali elders highlighted their position as refugees and asked that, on the basis of their plight as people without a country, the people of Lewiston treat them with patience and hospitality (Elders of the Somali Community 2002b). Similarly, when Brent Matthews rolled a frozen pig's head down the center aisle of the Lewiston-Auburn Islamic Center during Friday prayers, the community reacted vociferously. Accounts of the Somalis' status as refugees, the difficult conditions under which they were forced from their homeland, and the continuing impact that disorder in Somalia had on the well-being of Somalis in Lewiston provided a moral grounding for the airing of distaste for Matthew's behavior and the Somalis' need for respect and kindness at the hands of their fellow community members.

The story of the reluctant resident, the refugee, stood in sharp contrast to accounts of Somali residents of Lewiston as familiar immigrants who, like the immigrants coming to Lewiston before them, were realizing a dream with their immigration. As demonstrated by the following quotation, immigrant narratives emphasized freedom and choice.

I am happy to be here. Right here! This is where I will be forever! ... We could be anywhere. We choose to be here. (Jawab Aden as quoted by Taylor, 2006b, p. A1)

As immigrants, Somalis sought to make a better life for themselves and their families by taking advantage of the opportunities available in the United States. Allusion to the United States as a country of immigrants frequently punctuated optimistic accounts of the prospects for Somali incorporation in Lewiston. A local Somali organization, the African Immigrants' Association, made explicit use of the immigrant status of the Somalis in calling for the need for child care, tutoring, translation, and employment services for the Somali community.

Muslims, People of Faith
The familiar stranger status of Somalis in Lewiston was also visible in the contrast between public talk emphasizing the status of Somalis as Muslim strangers, and talk focusing on Somalis as decent, god-fearing people of faith.[3] For example, there was no controversy surrounding the opening of an Islamic community center and mosque on downtown Lewiston's Lisbon Street despite the fact that disputes over the placement of Islamic houses of worship were surfacing elsewhere (Goodstein 2010). The *Sun Journal* added the Islamic center to the list of "Churches and Religious Services" it ran in the paper each Saturday. Religious prohibitions against borrowing with interest that required a special

[3] Research shows that Americans typically hold nonreligous people and atheists in low regard, considering them outside of the moral pale. Widespread aversion to atheists is greater than public distrust of commonly maligned ethnic, racial, religious, and lifestyle groups (Edgell, Peggy, Joseph Gerteis, and Douglas Hartmann, 2006. "Atheists as "Other": Moral Boundaries and Cultural Membership in American Society." *American Sociological Review* 71 (April): 211–234).

financial arrangement for the property also proved unremarkable (Price and Talbot 2006). Instead it was considered only natural that Somalis, like other city residents, were familiar people of faith in need of a place to worship.

At times, however, public narratives emphasized the alterity of Islam in citing the need for cultural accommodation and separation. When some Somali members of the community sought city funds to purchase land for a cemetery, they were initially rebuffed on the grounds that there were insufficient funds to be purchasing burial grounds for every religious group in Lewiston. Later attempts at securing aid were successful in developing an area for burial on the basis of the distinctiveness of Muslim beliefs and practices concerning the dead and, in a nod to refugee status, the need for Lewiston's Somali community, whose dead were so far removed from their homeland, to have a resting place that might restore some of what is missing to those who die in exile.

Newcomers, Parents, Homeowners, and Workers

Narrative emphasis on newcomer status also emphasized the alterity of Somalis. Alluding to a lack of familiarity with mainstream American cultural mores as well as inexperience in practical matters such as dealing with municipal services, law enforcement, educational institutions, and the medical establishment, the newcomer narrative made a case for increased accessibility in the form of translators, immigrant-adjustment services, and cultural competence in service provision. In newcomer accounts, the people of Lewiston were hosts to Somali guests whose presence, however temporary, demanded welcome. The recent and noncommittal nature of Somali settlement in the community was underscored in comments like the following:

Author: So, now that you've settled here, what do you think your life in Lewiston will look like in five or ten years?
   Female Somali Informant: (laughing) Five or ten years? I followed my people here. I'm here for now and I'll stay until it's time to go.

As discussed in the following discussion of emerging Somali American identity in Lewiston, the alterity narrative also insulated many Somali cultural practices from criticism. Whether it was native language use or even more controversial practices such as female circumcision/female genital mutilation and the requirement that women wear the veil, the outsider position conferred by newcomer status precluded debate on the merits of what are otherwise widely debated topics.

The likeness counterpart to the distinct and different newcomer is that of a common and committed community member. This narrative is evident in the following quote:

We are homeowners, our children are citizens, and we are the future workforce of the Lewiston community. (Somali elder speaking at public rally)

In this likeness narrative, Somali residents of Lewiston had recognized ties with others in the city who would seek to have their children in successful schools, desired the opportunity to make a living, and hoped to eventually purchase a home for their family. As familiar community members, Somalis in Lewiston were attempting to live the American dream – an opportunity lacking in Somalia, in the Kenyan refugee camps where they awaited the opportunity to settle in the United States or Europe, and in struggling areas of greater Atlanta in which many Somali residents of the city made their first contact with the United States.

Neighbor and Constituent

Identified and engaged as a distinct community, Somali residents of Lewiston encountered a social, cultural, and political context primed to recognize group leaders and develop group-specific programs and interventions. Not all Somali residents of Lewiston sought representation and support through the Somali community, however. Imagining extensive involvement and full incorporation, some Somali residents of the city offered an alternative conception of the meaning of Somali-ness and the underlying distance between Somali-Lewistonians and other city residents.

In terms of understanding community and action, many of Lewiston's Somali residents looked beyond the borders of the enclave. In focus groups, formal interviews, and casual conversations, Somali residents of Lewiston emphasized the need for broader community engagement and civic involvement among Somalis living in the city. "On the Somali community side we need to do more," said one Somali city resident who had been living in the city for five years and was completing a bachelor's degree in nursing. "Somalis need to become more involved," he said. "People should run for office and engage in other civic matters." As members of a focus group took stock of all the services, institutions, and resources they felt should be made available to all Lewiston residents, a newly arrived Somali woman spoke through a friend who could translate, "We also have to work for Lewiston. Not just asking. Say hi to our neighbors even if we don't know each other. Talk to the teachers and the [police] officers so they think about your children." Although this woman felt her own ties to the community were limited, she hoped that her children would consider Lewiston home and intended to do her best to create inclusive community boundaries.

Such inclusive visions did not always go unchecked, however. In January 2007, incoming Lewiston mayor Larry Gilbert appointed individuals to the citizens' advisory committee for city planning. Mayor Gilbert, sympathetic to the goals of the Visible Community, a downtown grassroots organization consisting of both Somali and non-Somali Lewistonians fighting urban renewal projects that would demolish a significant share of the residential property in the city center, appointed many members of the group to the committee. Among Gilbert's appointees was Ismail Ahmed, a Somali man active in the organization, employed by Lewiston public schools, and founder of the international student association at the University of Southern Maine, Lewiston-Auburn. Following Mayor Gilbert's announcement, the Lewiston city council became embroiled in contentious debate over Ahmed's appointment. A rift developed in the six-seat council between those who believed that only registered voters, who were necessarily U.S. citizens, should serve on city panels and those council members who believed that noncitizens should have a voice outside the city's dealings with immigrant organizations and agencies. Ultimately Mayor Gilbert made use of an abstention and his tie-breaking authority to push the issue ahead. In the face of the mayor's decision to circumvent a full council discussion of noncitizen involvement, one councilor left the meeting in anger while others declared their intentions to step down at the end of their term.

At the center of the controversy, Ahmed remained silent. He did not speak on behalf of the overwhelmingly unnaturalized Somali community but instead allowed others to point to his record as an active contributor to the life of the community. In light of his upstanding service, on what grounds could the city council deny him a voice? Despite the contentious city council meeting, objections to the mayor's handling of the situation focused on procedure (the mayor's strategic use of his right to vote), not Ahmed's candidacy. Further, the ire was largely confined to city hall. Despite newspaper coverage, many Lewiston residents, both Somali and non-Somali were not aware of the situation. Although dissension hinged upon Ahmed's immigrant status, his successful nomination was settled as an issue of including one of Lewiston's own, an upstanding member of the community, Somali or not, citizen or not.

Incorporated as Other

The meaning of Somalis as familiar strangers whose local belonging could be contingent and challenged is more than a symbolic construction mobilized in public talk and the imagery presented in the local newspaper. Somali residents' positions as incorporated others in Lewiston influenced the relationship between the wider community and their Somali neighbors and shaped the public construction and display of Somali culture. In other words, the construction of the meaning of Somali-ness set the terms for Somali political and social integration and provided the context in which Somali American culture emerged in the city. Examination of the struggles and conflicts in Somali community representation and organization and the evolving nature of Somali cultural celebrations highlights the material ramifications of the cultural position of Lewiston Somalis.

BEING THE SOMALI COMMUNITY

Early Somalis settling in Lewiston encountered a city lacking specialized refugee and immigrant resettlement services. As discussed in Chapter 3, the growing Somali immigrant population prompted those responsible for administering relevant social support programs to turn to nearby Portland's experienced refugee support organization and to partner with federal and state organizations with expertise in immigrant settlement (Nadeau 2007). In terms of meeting the special needs of Somali newcomers, Lewiston sought to conduct assessments and offer services to Somali residents of Lewiston through "Somali representatives" (Nadeau 2011) – individuals and organizations representing the Somali "community." Shortly after initial Somali settlement in Lewiston, a select few Somali community organizations and spokespersons emerged as the recognized voices of and conduit for financial assistance and social services directed toward the city's Somali population. Several Somali Lewistonians acquired employment as case managers and community specialists in the city's schools, hospitals, and social services agencies. A relatively stable cadre of individuals and groups also stood behind publicly recognized campaigns to acquire fiscal resources and social support that would foster the success of Somalis in Lewiston as they sought employment and education and developed cultural programs. This same collection of individuals and groups was routinely consulted by the city and other organizations developing and expanding social services and responding to community tensions arising from increased diversity in Lewiston.

In late 2003, the Lewiston-Auburn Islamic Center, Somali Community Services of Maine, and the women's organizations, United Somali Women of Maine and Daryeeelka, were recognized within Lewiston as representing the Somali community. During interviews, city officials named the leaders of these organizations as well as a small group of Somali individuals employed by the city, the public schools, hospitals, and local social service organizations as the Somalis to whom they turned with questions and queries about how to best serve the city's Somali residents.

This emphasis on identifying and working through Somali organizations and spokespeople depended upon the belief that Lewiston's Somali residents were a unified community, able to speak and be spoken to as a cohesive whole. In the early stages of fieldwork, I asked a long-time Lewiston resident who was employed in the city planning department to share her general impressions of Lewiston's increasing diversity. She replied:

In Lewiston so much has happened around the Somalis. We have always been a diverse city with the Francos and the Hispanics coming in seasonally or working at [the egg factory]. But the Somalis have made themselves a presence. I think they are savvy about how to speak in a unified voice. They get Somali workers in agencies, and were more organized from the beginning. They are getting a lot done quickly.

The assumption of Somali unity characterized the relationship between the city of Lewiston and its newcomers from the start. Indeed, Mayor Raymond addressed his inflammatory letter to "the Elders of the Somali community." He received in reply a letter penned by individuals identified as those elders.

The assumption of a Somali group-ness influenced the behavior of many Somali and non-Somali Lewistonians. The idea of unity motivated the nature of Somali incorporation and led to the careful construction of a public Somali-ness that exaggerated the unanimity and uniformity of Lewiston's Somali residents.[4] There was tremendous

---

[4] It may be tempting to attribute this emphasis on a cohesive Somali community to methodological nationalism in which a national identity is mistaken for an ethnic identity (Chernilo, Daniel. 2008. "Methodological Nationalism: Theory and History." In *Annual Conference of the International Association of Critical Realism*. London: King's College; Wimmer, Andreas and Nina Glick Schiller. 2002. "Methodological National and Beyond: Nation-State Building, Migration and the Social Sciences." *Global Networks* 2, 4: 301–334). However, with the possible exception of Somali Bantus, Somalis do consider themselves a single ethnic group and the nation of Somali was considered an ethno-national project. For these reasons, the problems of group representation are not a methodological problem but instead, a philosophical and practical problem – the assumption that Somali

fluidity in the Somali population of Lewiston. Although estimates suggest that the number of Somali residents had hovered between 2,000 and 4,000 since 2003 and the time of this writing, the city provided services to new arrivals in the community each month I was present in the city. Ongoing settlement in the town was matched by the departures of others who moved to reunite with family or follow news of work in other communities. Furthermore, some Somalis in Lewiston reported associating only with members of their own clan and shopping only at stores affiliated with their clan (Huisman, Hough, Langellier, and Toner 2011). Therefore, at any given time, many of the Somalis in Lewiston were new arrivals unacquainted with most other Somalis in town. This continuously shifting population, the lack of a large public meeting space, and the realities of diffuse familial and clan networks render problematic the notion that Somali residents of the city kept in touch and coordinated their efforts at becoming settled in Lewiston. Prior research has established that Somalis in the diaspora tend to be well connected with friends and family around the world through telephone communication and the internet. While these ties are important sources of information, emotional support, and financial assistance, Somalis may settle in areas inhabited by few other members of their support networks (Bjork 2007). However, despite its logical and practical limitations, the notion that there was a coherent Lewiston Somali community governed public perception and policy responses to the city's Somali newcomers.

Demonstrating Unity

My discussions with the local Somalis seen as community representatives as well as with other Somali residents of Lewiston led me to conclude that most Somalis considered the establishment of Somali organizations an important step in becoming settled in the city.[5] The quest for specifically Somali social service and civic organizations represented a desire for

---

group identity implies cohesiveness and common interests (Kivisto, Peter and Thomas Faist. 2007. *Citizenship: Discourse, theory, and transnational prospects.* Malden, MA: Blackwell).

[5] This finding supports Ford's observation that Somalis in the United States see the development of Somali organizations and institutions as the key to the group's success in their new country (Ford, Richard. 2004. "Somali Pastoralists in Lewiston, Maine: Searching with Participatory Tools for a New Life." Pp. 59–77 in *Somalia: Diaspora and state reconstitution in the Horn of Africa,* edited by A. O. Farah, M. Muchie, and J. Gundel. London: Adonis & Abbey).

self-sufficiency among Somalis. Seeking to establish cultural competence in service provision, the city embraced the rise of Somali organizations and services. Such organizations fell comfortably within a long history of immigrant organizations and community centers and also corresponded to the idea that Somalis are familiar strangers in Lewiston who should be incorporated into the social order without requiring their assimilation into the larger collectivity.

Unfortunately, even bracketing the aforementioned population flux, the perception of Somali unity and the notion of Somali representation through established Somali community services often proved problematic in the eyes of many Lewiston residents. In his analysis of Somali leadership in the city, Lewiston resident, community leader, and researcher Ahmed (2011) noted that early Somali leadership in Lewiston closely resembled traditional Somali leadership – linking status with age, propping up the traditional exclusion of women from public life, and maintaining religious conservatism and tribalism:

Upon arrival in Lewiston, for example, Somalis had several meetings to address issues that affected the community. Most of these meetings were held behind closed doors, and they involved an element of deception, such as pre-selecting participants and convening before sunrise or late at night in the mosque.... Deliberations are ad hoc, and councils are summoned by mutual agreement as need arises, depending upon the mood and self-interest of the most charismatic leader. (Ahmed 2011, p. 85)

Ahmed's quote speaks to a concern increasingly common among Somali residents of Lewiston and non-Somali city leaders working with Somali newcomers – the lack of democratic process and transparency in selection of community leaders and in decision making. As city leaders shared in interviews, the problems of identifying Somali leadership were compounded by the increasingly apparent failure of some identified leaders to represent the entire Somali community of Lewiston. Problems of Somali cohesion and leadership grew visible as Lewiston's early dependence upon Somali organizations for service provision increasingly appeared to benefit only some community residents. Some of the difficulties in service provision laid bare tensions and divisions imported from Somalia. Take as evidence the letter of complaint and call to unity that Lewiston resident Abshir Boore submitted to the local daily newspaper, the *Lewiston Sun Journal*. Boore wrote:

I was born in Mogadishu and am currently attending Lewiston High School.... In Lewiston, I have found that our Somali community is divided into factions and clans. I thought we left that problem back home, but unfortunately we are still divided into clans even though we live in a free country.

I have experienced this personally and honestly. A friend has been denied help because he belonged to the wrong clan.

I would like to see all the Somali communities become one. I hope we can, as young people, follow the ideas of truth, liberty and justice for all.

I hope to see the government of Lewiston open more dialogue and understand how different clans in the Somali community treat each other.... The government should also be careful to track where all its aid money goes to make sure it isn't misused by some for its own interest....

We are asking the government to help us stop corruption and discrimination in the name of building the Somali Community. (Boore 2004, p. A6)

In interviews, local public officials and community leaders increasingly echoed Boore's view of divisions within the Somali community. These individuals discussed the difficulties in navigating the complexities of Somali intragroup relations and coming to understand that not all Somalis in Lewiston are acquainted, have similar interests, or even understand the dialects of Somali spoken by one another.[6] One city official shared with significant consternation his interactions with several people who presented themselves as Somali elders and religious leaders who should be consulted by the city. Attempting to verify these claims was difficult. He resorted to inquiring about those individuals when meeting with Somalis he dealt with in his work. In most cases, those he asked did not offer consensus on the authority of those in question. "Unfortunately," he told me, "we just end up working with people who speak the best English and hope that they are doing what they say they are going do."

Whatever the relationship between Somali community organizations and a desire for self-sufficiency on the part of Somalis who call for such organizations, my observations in Lewiston and the research of others suggests that Somali ethnic and clan divisions rendered problematic the tying of social service provision and civic engagement exclusively to Somali organizations (Ahmed 2011; Hopkins 2006; Kusow and Bjork 2007; Mott 2009). Mott (2009) interviewed Somalis in Columbus, Ohio, who complained about corruption, false representation, and clan favoritism among people in position in Somali organizations. Hopkins's research points to the significance of clans in understanding Somali social

---

[6] Language difficulties are most likely due to the increased settlement of Bantus who have their own language and make up an ethnic underclass in Somalia. Research suggests that Bantu ethnic identity has been constructed in part through the encounter with Western humanitarian and racial discourses (Besteman, Catherine. 2012. "Translating Race across Time and Space: The Creation of Somali Bantu Ethnicity." *Identities* 19:285–302).

organization in the diaspora.[7] Clan affiliation formed a backdrop for much of the political history of the Somali nation (Farah 2000; Lewis 2002; Luling 2006). While in Lewiston and the United States generally there is considerable intermingling of Somali clan groups (Goza 2007) and ethnic minority Bantus from Somalia (who were not considered Somali prior to emigration), evidence suggests that clan exerts an influence on the relationships between Somalis in the diaspora, playing a determining role in the distribution of social and economic support and kin and friendship networks (Bjork 2007; Hopkins 2006).

Just as in Lewiston, in London and Toronto Hopkins (2006) observed that the typical model of immigrant group recognition and service provision is through group-identified community-based organizations. These organizations represent the public face of the group. Hopkins suggested that Somali immigrants are not well served by this mode of public incorporation or social service. It hinders the development of political power, limits the visibility of Somalis as stakeholders in local governance, and deters Somali group mobilization. More specifically, in terms of Somali immigrants, ubiquitous community-based groups frequently fail to communicate with other groups, offering redundant services and competing for the same grants and other resources. Furthermore, clan divisions imported from Somalia mark the establishment and work of some Somali organizations. While the organizations may not intend to discriminate on the basis of clan affiliation, they are often founded by groups of clan or family members and they are viewed by others as being closed to outsiders (Hopkins 2006).

Ahmed (2011) hopefully noted the rise of new, younger leadership emerging in Lewiston. These new leaders sought greater collaboration with the city, greater membership with the broader community, and democratic participation across gender and clan lines. Boore's decision to write a letter to the editor exposing and criticizing divisions in the Somali community further suggests the declining influence of intra-Somali divisions among the next generation. As clan identity is often established through the recounting of one's lineage, it is significant that younger and second-generation Somalis in the diaspora are abandoning the practice (Luling 2006).

---

[7] I would have liked to discuss the issue of clan in more depth with Somalis in Lewiston. In my experience, however, the topic of clan was taboo among Somalis speaking to an outsider. I learned very quickly that inquiries into clan membership and clan dynamics would probably mean an end to an interview or discussion and, likely, cost whatever additional contacts I might have made. I quickly abandoned explicit discussion of the topic.

Struggling for Recognition

Despite increased evidence of problems associated with using Somali organizations to administer financial and social support to Somali residents of Lewiston, the underlying presumption that Somalis were a bounded and cohesive group of strangers best represented and served through their own organizations persisted. Instead of seeing the difficulties of community representation as challenging the wisdom of identifying and working through such representatives in providing assistance to Somali Lewistonians, public opinion and city officials embraced different criteria for establishing the legitimacy of Somali organizations and representatives. The following account demonstrates that claims to group representation on the basis of endorsement by other Somalis and English-speaking ability waned as the public legitimacy of Somali community representatives hinged increasingly and implicitly upon their ability to make themselves familiar by endorsing multicultural ideas of inclusivity, respect, and democracy. The interactions between and strategies of Somali organizations vying for recognition as representative of the city's Somali community reveal the compelled enactment of a secular, cultural authenticity.[8]

On December 14, 2003, the *Lewiston Sun Journal* published a story documenting a power struggle in Lewiston's organizational landscape.

Two groups ... are privately and politely jockeying to be leaders of the community.

Members of each group, the Somali Community Services and the newly formed African Immigrants' Association, say they want the same thing. They want to serve as a bridge between African immigrants and the local, state and federal agencies that help them. Both groups want to set up a multicultural center, both want to improve transportation, day-care and educational services for Somalis and both want to appoint a board of directors that would be identified as leaders of the community.

Despite these similar goals, an effort to join forces has failed. And, as each group moves forward with its plans, accusations are flying.

"They only want to help certain people who believe in certain things," Mohamed said, referring to the members of Somali Community Services as religious fanatics who only look out for people in their own families and clans. Mohamed accused Somali Community Services of receiving money to hire a tutor, then making the tutor available only to their children. Members of the new group also

---

[8] Fernando (Fernando, Mayanthi L. 2010. "Reconfiguring Freedom: Muslim Piety and the Limits of Secular Law and Public Discourse in France." *American Ethnologist* 37:19–35) demonstrates a similar and fraught drive to secularity among Muslims in France.

accused the existing group of taking donations from single mothers and other struggling Somalis, then using the money to buy a new mosque and open their own businesses....

Abdizirak Mahboub, the executive director of Somali Community Services, denied both allegations. The Lisbon Street mosque is run by a separate organization, called the Lewiston-Auburn Islamic Center, he said, and Somali Community Services doesn't cater to particular families.... Mahboub is opposed to having another Somali organization – not because he is worried about competing for grants and other money, he said, but because he believes it is unnecessary....

Although the situation in Lewiston resembles more of a political campaign than a war, its roots seem to be similar to those that have plagued Somali for decades....

More than two dozen African immigrants, including Somalis and a couple of local Togolese immigrants, are involved in the formation of African Immigrants Association....

[City administrator] Bennet has met with representatives from both Somali Community Services and African Immigrants Association.... Bennett has noted that those involved with Somali Community Services seem to be deeply rooted in traditional Muslim beliefs, while the others have adopted more Western ways. (Chmelecki 2003, p. A1)

In the wake of the article detailing the power struggle between Somali Community Services and the African Immigrants' Association, executive president of the association, Kadar Said, sent a letter to the editor of the *Sun Journal* in which he attempted to depict the issue, not as a power struggle between two organizations, but as a struggle between two styles of leadership. He wrote:

The article, "Jockeying for Power," was about the difficulties of Somali leadership.... The question behind the article was, are the Somalis moving out of the authoritarian leadership toward the democratic style?

Somali Community Services differentiates and provides no assistance other than to their own affiliates.... We should not forget the past abuse of tribal and religious wars in Somalia, and we should give full information to the local community about those who act as a smoke screen to perpetuate dictatorial style in Maine." (Said 2003, p. A6)

The newspaper article suggested that Somali Community Services was the culturally and religiously more conservative organization; however, there was no open condemnation of conservatism in the newspaper. Said, on the other hand, attempted to explicitly link Somali Community Services to problematic anti-civil characteristics only hinted at in the original article.

Hidden Voices

Multicultural incorporation in Lewiston was accomplished in part through Somali organizations that were recognizable to city officials and consonant with expectations that immigrant communities integrate while maintaining their distinctiveness. However, the legitimacy of Somali organizations in Lewiston required that they demonstrate a group distinctiveness that included endorsement of diversity. In the end Said's view did "stick" to Somali Community Services, leading the organization to fall out of favor in Lewiston as mounting evidence led to the perception that the organization's leaders were anti-democratic and intolerant.

In the illustrative incident discussed next, with its ties to the public condemnation of homosexuality, Somali Community Services demonstrated to the broader community that it was not a "multicultural" organization. As the events recounted make clear, in the case of Somali Community Services, suspected affiliation with the local mosque and appearance as culturally and religiously intolerant as compared to the African Immigrants' Association proved disastrous.

On April 5, 2004, social activist Faisal Alam spoke before a group of approximately forty individuals. His lecture, *Hidden Voices: The Lives of Queer Muslims,* was well attended on that cold April Monday evening. Bates college students and staff representing the school's Multicultural Center and GLBT student organization, members of Lewiston's multicultural Many and One organization, and several of Lewiston's Somali residents listened as Alam lectured on the nature of Islam, highlighting the faith's emphasis on peace and justice. Founder of the Al-Fatiha Foundation, an organization providing political and social support to gay Muslims and working toward religious inclusion of practicing homosexuals, Alam lived his early childhood in Pakistan before immigrating to the United States.[9] Beginning his talk by emphasizing the size and diversity of adherents to Islam in the United States and around the world, Alam turned to a discussion of the large number of homosexual individuals practicing Islam.

As Alam spoke, stacks of a photocopied handout passed down the aisle. A statement from the Lewiston-Auburn Islamic Center, the page contained a formal condemnation of homosexuality with supporting verses from the Qur'an. Dissemination of the statement disrupted the

---

[9] For more information on Faisal Alam and Al-Fatiha, see the Alam's website (http://www.faisalalam.com/).

crowd as people began talking among themselves and casting scornful looks about the room. Others refused the page with a shake of the head and turned their attention back to Alam.

While members of the audience reacted variously to the letter passing among them, its distribution and content were met with nearly universal disapproval. Alam paused to address the disruption. Asserting his role as the speaker, he decried the actions of representatives of the Islamic Center distributing the statement. "This is not a debate," he declared, "If you wish to make a statement, you can do it when I am done speaking." He went on with his lecture. However, as the tenor in the room changed so did Alam's presentation. He moved quickly from an emphasis on the existence of and need for recognition of the diversity within Islam to a discussion of the persecution of gay Muslims. He spoke of his own failed marital engagement and ensuing nervous breakdown, described how painful it was for him to live a dual life before he overcame tensions between homosexuality and Islam, and shared the stories of Muslim men and women around the world for whom homosexuality is a death sentence.

Motivated by a desire to counter the message that there is no inherent contradiction between being Muslim and being gay, representatives of the Lewiston-Auburn Islamic Center distributed a letter that they believed summarized the anti-homosexual character of Islam as reflected in the teachings of the prophet Mohammed. Discussion following Alam's lecture, media coverage of the presentation, and limited attention in the opinion pages, however, left the Islamic Center's doctrinal concerns unexamined. The real issue to be addressed in the eyes of many was the intolerance exhibited by mosque representatives attending Alam's presentation. One such individual quickly defended the actions of his group claiming that they had no desire to bring harm to Alam and were merely concerned with rectifying misrepresentations of Islam. Yet his words had little impact on public interpretation of the evening's events.

The editorial staff of the local paper articulated prevailing sentiments by alluding to the more infamous document written two years previously, the letter written by Mayor Larry Raymond in which the Somalis were blamed for causing Lewiston's financial hardship and asked to discourage further immigrant settlement in the city. The editorial analysis of Alam's talk criticizes both letters for their failures to display appreciation for diversity:

Intolerance takes many forms, some of them more insidious than others.

Two years ago Mayor Larry Raymond was admonished for a letter he sent to the Somali community in Lewiston....
At a lecture Tuesday [*sic*], intolerance again showed itself. But this time, it was from a segment of the Somali community.
Leaders from the Lewiston Auburn Islamic Center passed out a statement during a presentation at Bates College by Faisal Alam.... Alam spoke about the difficulty of being both Muslim and gay, and the anger and hate he and other homosexuals face. He got a taste of it again, right here." (Rhoades 2004, p. A6)

The distribution by leading members of the Lewiston Auburn Islamic Center of a letter offering a religious condemnation of homosexuality was interpreted by many as indicating intolerance and hate. Some of those distributing the letter on behalf of the mosque were also involved in Somali Community Services. Mosque representatives were not the only Somali voices heard in the wake of Alam's talk, however. A statement distributed at the conclusion of Alam's presentation by the African Immigrants' Association modeled a commitment to diversity. It read, "We commit ourselves to construction of a community free of hatred among or within us, where no one must live in fear and terror, where all live freely and equally."

While between the December newspaper article and the April lecture Lewiston heard little of the conflicts between Somali Community Services and the African Immigrants' Association, the latter organization entered the spotlight that evening. Only three days later, the *Sun Journal* featured a story recounting the organization's success in acquiring not-for-profit status and their frustrations in acquiring funding and establishing a center of operations.

When I first started interviewing city leadership in autumn of 2003, no one mentioned the African Immigrants' Association or its leadership as a group or individuals that were consulted on matters relevant to the city's Somali population while Somali Community Services was widely endorsed as the most influential Somali organization in the city. This trend continued throughout the winter of 2003. I began asking explicitly about the African Immigrants' Association and its relationship to the city. While city officials increasingly recognized potential problems of representativeness and conservatism associated with working through Somali Community Services in service provision, they had no reason to believe that the African Immigrants' Association would be a better partner or community representative. By the following summer, however, the African Immigrants' Association was increasingly recognized by the individuals with whom I spoke as the "go-to" organization. Somali Community

Services, on the other hand, was now characterized as a "special interest group" and an "inappropriate partner," as one city official put it, for Lewiston.

By the end of the calendar year, Somali Community Services operated at the periphery of Somali organizations, receiving little public support or media attention. While still offering tutoring and other programs, the organization increasingly drew funding from outside organizations, for example, contracting with a regional recipient of Homeland Security funds designated for providing summer bridge programs that integrate academic preparation and religious education for young Somali men at risk of being recruited by anti-American and extremist religious groups.

Meanwhile, the African Immigrants' Association became the acting political and cultural face of Lewiston's Somali community. The group continued to display an appreciation for and openness to all types of diversity. As a result of their success in this regard, the African Immigrants' Association's leadership had the ear of city officials and received funds and referrals in order to offer social services for immigrants in the city. The organization maintained a public role condemning intolerance when it was visible among Somalis in Lewiston and acted as representatives of the Somali community through involvement in local decision making and the establishment of an annual Somali cultural celebration.

THE SOMALIS, OF ALL PEOPLE …

The multicultural incorporation of Lewiston's Somali residents proved a precarious and coercive situation. Somali inclusion hinged upon the diverse status ascribed to Somali identity and the perception that Somali-ness was also accepting of the diversity of others. In contrast to the increasingly anti-civil reputation of Somali Community Services, the African Immigrants' Association provided a conception of Somali-ness that provided for the continued incorporation of Somalis in Lewiston.

The contingent nature of Somali incorporation was obvious in Lewiston. As we chatted over lunch at the counter of a downtown diner in the days after Alam's lecture, one non-Somali community member shared the surprise and disappointment she felt after reading about the Islamic Center's statement.

I was angry. When the Somalis first came to Lewiston, some of us worked very hard to show everyone in the community that diversity is a good thing. Since we welcomed their diversity, the Somalis, of all people, should accept the diversity of others.

Somali immigrants, my informant made clear, were accepted in Lewiston on the premise that diversity is a welcomed addition to the community. On the receiving end of the embrace of diversity themselves, Somalis in Lewiston must be fully aware that their inclusion, more so than for those who did not represent diversity, required their endorsement of all types of difference qualifying as diversity.

Just as the public legitimacy of Somali voices and organizations hinged upon their multicultural tone, the Somal American identity emerging in Lewiston reflected the position of Somalis as familiar strangers bringing valuable and benign diversity to the city. The following examination of emerging Somali American identity and culture in the city demonstrates the impact of the pressure to authenticate the public secularity and tolerance demanded of all would-be members of the Lewiston community.

DEFINING AND DISPLAYING SOMALI-NESS

Returning to Lewiston in 2005 after an absence of nearly a year, I noted a change in the community that had not been apparent from afar despite my continued contact with city residents and my subscription to the local newspaper. While, at the onset of Somali settlement in Lewiston in 2001 and 2002, the city lacked significant racial heterogeneity and had a very small immigrant population, by 2005 the situation was quite different. Diversity had come to Lewiston's diversity.

Lewiston's Kennedy Park offered a pleasant bit of green space in the city's downtown area. Bordered on one side by city hall, the public library, and the police department, on another side by the offices of the *Lewiston Sun Journal,* and on the two other sides by low-income tenement buildings interspersed with social service agencies, churches, and variety (i.e., convenience) stores, Kennedy Park boasted the traditional bandstand, a public pool, basketball courts, skate park, and numerous park benches. The smell of baking bread often greeted those entering the park, which stood kitty-corner from the factory of Country Kitchen and Barowsky Organic Bakery, a large bread company employing some residents of the downtown area.

During my time in the field, I often passed the time in Kennedy Park, jotting down field notes or preparing for upcoming meetings as I listened in on the conversations of others, watched the children playing, and took in the sun. When I first began my fieldwork, those with whom I shared the space appeared to be either white or Somali. However, when I returned to Lewiston for follow-up data collection in later years, I noted the dramatic increase in the heterogeneity of people using Kennedy Park. In addition to the expected cast of characters, I observed dark-skinned women with their children speaking languages other than Somali and not dressed in hijab. A group of people who spoke in the manner associated most commonly with African Americans in the United States sat on a bench not far from my own. As I glanced around and listened to the sounds of Kennedy Park, I felt that something had changed.

That afternoon I met with Ann, the director of a downtown social service agency that hosted some of my focus groups. Ann confirmed the increasing diversity of Lewiston's newcomers and reported that in the past three months her agency had served twenty new immigrant families and most were not Somali. Furthermore, in addition to immigrants she had a growing clientele of African Americans moving to Lewiston from Boston and New York on the advice of social service agencies in those locations who told them that Lewiston had "opened up" to outsiders. The next day I checked in on an acquaintance, Asad, a Somali man who had been in Lewiston for several years and worked as a case manager for recent arrivals. When I pointed out the number of non-Somali newcomers I observed in town, he nodded and discussed his growing clientele from Sudan, Togo, and the former Soviet Union, newcomers arriving both as refugees and as secondary migrants. "Of all these groups, Somalis are the largest group being resettled *and* the largest group of secondary migrants," Asad assured me.

Shortly after my discussion with Asad, I conducted two focus groups with women who had recently relocated to Lewiston and were being served by Ann's social service agency. Eighteen women participated in the discussions. Whereas in previous years the groups were almost exclusively Somali, this time only three participants were ethnic Somalis, three were Somali Bantu, and the rest of the group included Brazilian, Sudanese, Congolese, Chinese, Ecuadorian, Estonian, and African American women. Analyzing the U.S. Department of Immigration Statistics data on the immigrant population of Lewiston over the period of 2003–2008 confirms Asad's assertion that Lewiston's Somali population dwarfed all other immigrant groups.[10] Of the 1,235 green cards issued to Lewiston

---

[10] Independent analysis of Department of Immigration Statistics 2003–2008 Yearbooks of Immigration Statistics (http://www.dhs.gov/files/statistics/publications/yearbook.shtm).

residents over that period, nearly 1,000 went to people born in Somalia. However, other resident immigrants had come from more than fifty nations including Togo, China, India, and the Philippines.

Despite the increased presence of nonwhite newcomers who were not Somali, public discussion of Lewiston's diversity, newcomer settlement, and service provision for cultural minorities, were directed toward Somali arrivals and employed the term "Somali" as a catchall for all immigrant groups in the city. The centrality of Somalis as the face of diversity in Lewiston and the status of Somali service organizations and public employees as the vanguard in serving diverse newcomers derived from the status of the Somalis as diversity pioneers in Lewiston.

Diversity Pioneers Rewriting Race

As discussed in Chapter 1, Somali immigrants to the United States tend to reside in areas that are historically white, less urban, and further removed from substantial African American and immigrant populations (Goza 2007). For the most part, this trend is due to the intentional secondary migration of Somalis, not the capricious decisions of social service and resettlement agencies. Many of the early Somali newcomers in Lewiston moved from initial placements in majority African American neighborhoods in greater Atlanta and indicated a desire to settle where they might raise their children as Somali and free from the cultural pressures they experienced in the Atlanta area. One of the reasons that historically white areas are appealing is that as diversity pioneers, immigrants settling in such areas acquire greater freedom of identification and incorporation (Waters and Jimenez 2005). Opting out of places where the traditional and established ethnic political and community organizations would link Somali interests with the interests of African Americans, many Somalis settle in communities lacking significant racial diversity and typical levels of educational and residential segregation by race. Given the limited African American population of Lewiston and the history of the area as failing to recognize a strict racial boundary between whites and blacks, the city offered the potential to avoid "downward assimilation" (Portes and Rumbaut 2001) into a multiethnic minority underclass and instead develop a distinct Somali American identity.

With considerable freedom from racial identification, Somalis I encountered in Lewiston used a double lens in considering race and their relationship to it. Many identified the hostility and discrimination they experienced in Lewiston and observed in the nation generally as racism.

However, Somalis did not assert identities that have a place within the United States' black-white racial dichotomy. Writing a letter to the editor in support of presidential candidate Barack Obama, Hibo Omer simultaneously challenged the utility of racial labels and lamented the racial lens with which Americans viewed the future president. Omer wrote:

As an immigrant in this country, I don't understand why race is such a big issue in America.... Recently, Sen. Barack Obama announced his presidential candidacy. Since then, his background profile is on every news program. Why is it such a big issue? Just because he has a black father, does that make him incompetent to do the job? Then again, does presidential candidacy require a special prerequisite? ... Let us judge the man by his character and not the color of his skin.... The candidates who have the solution should be qualified for the job. (Omer 2007, p. A8)

The following provides a more explicit example of the way some Somalis in Lewiston established their unique identity while recognizing the racial myopia of American society at large. When asked in a cultural brokerage session if she felt any particular connection to the African American women she knew when she lived in Georgia, Khadija, a member of a regional Somali women's organization often called upon to represent and act as an intermediary for Lewiston Somalis, replied, "I made some good friends just as I have made good friends here. But I am Somali and Muslim. From Africa. I don't share the same culture or religion. We are not the same people." During the same session, Khadija acted as a translator for other Somali women taking questions. One member of the panel, an older Somali woman who had recently arrived in Lewiston and spoke no English, took the opportunity to respond to the question. "We are different but we are sisters. We share the same struggle," she said through Khadija who quickly added, "She means, we are all trying to make a better life and it is not always easy because of the color of our skin."

My observations in Lewiston confirm the work of others who find that Somali residents of the United States generally do not endorse American race categories, do not identify as African American, and tend to identify their race as Muslim and Somali (Huisman 2011; Kusow 2006; Roble and Rutledge 2008). Other self- and group-identities offered by Somalis in Lewiston included immigrant status, African, and clan affiliation. However, previous research has neglected to observe that some Somalis recognize a connection to African Americans, not through some natural affinity but through their ascribed status as black in a nation where blackness is associated with underclass status and the struggle against prejudice.

During my field research I witnessed many instances in which Somalis asserted racial and religious identities that set them outside of a binary American racial perspective, claiming to be, for example, Muslim-Somali-Americans. Ajroush and Kusow (2007) find that Muslim identity can act as a resource for Somali Americans negotiating the American racial order. The white Muslim immigrants from Lebanon with whom they spoke felt that their racial majority status was threatened when they made their religious affiliation visible. In order to assert their Somali-ness as opposed to belonging to some trans-ethnic racial category of "black-ness,"[11] Somali immigrants, on the other hand, accentuated their religious identity over and above their black racial identity and more so than they report doing in Somalia (Ajrouch and Kusow 2007).

Despite these aspects of self-identification, within the broader American context Somalis find themselves located on the black side of a black-white racial dichotomy that generally ignores religion and fails to attach significance to their African-ness or Somali ethnicity. Outside of Lewiston and similar sites that have seen significant Somali settlement and little other ethnic heterogeneity that would count as racial diversity, the category "Somali" has little public meaning, at least in the United States. This is not the case in Scandinavia, however, where definite stereotypes regarding the Somalis as "inassimilable" and "problem immigrants" have emerged (Fangen 2004, 2006; Kleist 2007). In the face of widespread negative group stereotypes, Fangen (2004) finds that the Somalis with whom she worked sought to distance themselves individually from the stereotype instead of critiquing negative assessments of Somalis as a group. Unlike the situation observed in Norway by Fangen, I observe the collective project to produce an acceptable, assimilable Somali-ness.

In Lewiston neither the development of entrenched negative stereotypes, the rise of the assumption that Somalis will be incorporated as African Americans, nor the failure to establish Somali-ness as a meaningful alternative category of identification occurred. In this town "Somali" acted as a shorthand descriptor of all notable cultural, racial, ethnic, and religious diversity as well as an indicator of newcomer and immigrant status. Unlike the situations documented by Fangen and Kleist, as the *Sun Journal*'s parade of happy Somali faces attested, in Lewiston Somali-ness held a different meaning. Somalis in Lewiston were familiar strangers

---

[11] In Somalia, Bantus are considered black while Somalis commonly believe that they have an Arab ancestry (Lewis, I. M. 2002. *A modern history of the Somali*. Athens: Ohio University Press).

visible in their diversity, part of a known and valuable segment of the community, and, as we shall soon see, in possession of an increasingly familiar culture and holding a continuously achieved status as one in a long line of immigrant groups seeking to realize the American dream in Lewiston, Maine.

EMERGING SOMALI AMERICAN-NESS

A multicultural emphasis on the unity, desirability, and inclusivity of Somali culture influenced the way that Somali-ness was defined and displayed in Lewiston and precipitated moments of contestation and negotiation in the meaning of Somali identity. Considering the typically inflammatory subjects of Islam and Somali gender relations and observing the developmental trajectory of the annual Somali cultural celebration reveals the dynamics of representation of Somali American-ness, the erasure of Islam as an everyday aspect of public Somali culture, and the contestation between Somali cultural identification and pressures toward a pan-African cultural identity in Lewiston.

Just after 6 P.M. on Friday July 2, 2004, I walked into the Lewiston High School gymnasium. A young Somali boy, probably around thirteen years old, greeted me at the door. He smiled, handed me a piece of colored paper, and suggested that I could take a seat in the stands. As I walked toward the bleachers, I glanced at the goldenrod yellow paper I held in my hands. It read:

> Well come celebration of culture and diversity in the Twin Cities
> Lewiston and Auburn
> Somali Culture Night & Community Celebration
> Prepared by African Immigrants Association

The announcement continued by listing the events of the next eight hours. The first thirty minutes of the evening, reception, would be followed by an introduction to the event and the African Immigrants' Association. Thereafter guests would be treated to Somali food and an hour of basketball compliments of the city's Somali youth basketball league. The African Immigrants' Association then would present honorary awards to city officials who had worked diligently on behalf of the Somali community. A brief history of the African Immigrants' Association prefaced the singing of the Somali and American national anthems and a presentation on the American Revolution offered by a Bates College professor. From 9 to 10 o'clock the audience was introduced to Somali culture and music and would observe traditional Somali dance. From 10 P.M. until 2 A.M. the gym would be transformed into a dance club, offering tunes spun by a prominent local disk jockey and performed by a regionally popular Somali singer.

Somali, Africana, Somali, Africana

Based upon attendance and the accounts of organizers, the first annual Somali Culture Night was a tentative success. On Saturday, the day after the festivities, the local newspaper printed a photograph of the event. The image depicted an unveiled Somali woman standing at the end of the buffet line serving a Somali dessert to one of the non-Somali attendees of the event. Indeed, organizers reported, if there were glitches in the evening, they surrounded the timing of the food and the late hours. A local note in the paper two weeks after the event acknowledged the difficulty around food:

A group of local Somalis had good intentions when they invited the general public to a big party to celebrate the anniversary of the day that north and south Somalia joined as one country. They invited the people of Lewiston-Auburn to come to the party on July 2 and learn about their culture. They planned eight hours of food, music and dancing.

Only not in that order, to the disappointment of some.

Many of the non-Somali guests showed up at 6 P.M., ready to fill their dinner plates. Since most Somalis don't eat their nighttime snack until 9 or 10 P.M., the buffet tables were empty.

Said Mohamud, one of the event's organizers, I was afraid things would get ugly.

"I could see it in their faces," he said. "People were hungry." (Chmelecki 2004)

In addition to the problem of different eating schedules, organizers found that the event continued much too late into the evening for most non-Somali guests. The event also ran more than an hour behind schedule. Thus, it was well after 9 P.M. when Lewiston's city officials were honored. By that late hour, none of those individuals remained to accept the certificates of appreciation that had been prepared for them. I was one of the few non-Somalis still present.

Preparation for the Somali Independence Day Party 2005 reflected lessons learned in 2004. The event sought to balance Somali cultural practices and the need to be responsive to the expectations of the non-Somali attendees looking for the opportunity to experience Somali culture – the food, music, and material artifacts touted in diversity-affirming narratives. The festival began at 6 P.M. and wrapped up at 11 P.M. Publicity for the event clearly stated that food would not be available before 7 P.M. Local officials, instead of coming as honored guests and in place of basketball, appeared as speakers on the program. Culinary options featured Somali dishes as well as food from other regions of Africa. Clothing and jewelry from Somali and other African nations were for sale. In addition to Somali folk music and dance, the event also included a Sudanese dance troupe and a pan-African drumming group based in nearby Portland.

Citing increased attendance between the first and second Somali Culture Night/Independence Day Celebration, in June 2006 the African Immigrants' Association announced plans for the third annual party, to be held July 1. However, an important detail of the event had changed. It was now called the Africana Festival. The African Immigrants' Association press release noted that the event would include crafts, food, music, and other cultural information from Sudan, Togo, Ethiopia, and other African nations in addition to Somalia. Furthermore, unlike past years, Maine governor John Baldacci was expected as a keynote speaker and the cities of Lewiston and Auburn assisted with sponsorship of the event.

In terms of attendance, the 2,000 individuals visiting the 2006 Africana festival made it the most successful annual event up to that point. While in past years, speakers at the festival focused upon the Somali community of Lewiston and Somali as well as U.S. history, the 2006 Africana festival made diversity the theme of the evening. Festival organizer, Omar Ahmed, said, "Diversity is not only found in the workplace, it is to be all one family. We have a great opportunity in Lewiston-Auburn to achieve a better society if we choose to embrace the diversity of the people who live here" (Sargent 2006). The director of the African Immigrants' Association highlighted the organizations' efforts to expand its membership among other groups beside Somalis. In a letter to the editor thanking the Lewiston community for making the Africana festival a success, Said Mohamud, president of the African Immigrants' Association, spoke a truism straight from multicultural epistemology. "Our main goal," he wrote, "is to gain greater understanding and cultural awareness among members of our community. We have learned that when diverse cultures meet and learn more about one another, better relationships are made and stereotypes are broken" (Mohamud 2006).

The early development of the annual cultural celebration in Lewiston reveals the influence of the desire on the part of festival attendees for consumable culture – exotic food, music, jewelry, and other artifacts over engagement with the everyday interests and activities of Somalis in Lewiston such as the youth basketball and soccer leagues. The transition from Somali Cultural Night to the Africana Festival also represents a shift in the public definition of Somali-ness – a movement from the centrality of Somali to African identity in Lewiston. However, the event the following summer offered a twist that makes both the assumption of a purely consumable Somali-ness and the development of simple pan-Africanism in Lewiston problematic. Somalis in Lewiston resisted both the superficial embrace of Somali-ness as diversity-affirming culture for mass consumption and incorporation under the banner of African identity.

As in previous years, the announcement for the 2007 festival came at the end of June. Again issued by the African Immigrants' Association, the press release gave the date and location of the fourth annual Somali Independence Day Celebration. With the exception of claims that African food and wares would be available for purchase, the press release mentioned nothing of the inclusion of other African nations or cultures in the event but instead offered a brief description of Somali independence from its colonizers. The event highlighted the meaningful and fundamental stranger-ness of Somalis instead of focusing on the group as familiar and consumable as diversity. Newspaper coverage of the event shared a similar focus on Somali-ness. The photograph associated with the story displayed several Somali girls holding the Somali flag. In a definite shift from the celebration of diversity marking the Africana festival, this Somali Independence Day Celebration highlighted the refugee experience of Somalis in Lewiston and a yearning for Somalia. Speakers at the event focused upon the importance of Somali culture and the need to remember those family and friends still residing in Somalia. Lewiston mayor Larry Gilbert began his remarks to the crowd with a few words spoken in Somali. The evening's entertainment focused upon local Somali youth as well as Somali performers from all over New England. The reemergence of the Somali cultural celebration did not mean the demise of the Africana Festival, however. On Saturday, September 1, the Africana Festival was reborn. Still sponsored by the African Immigrants' Association, the second "First Annual" Africana Festival in Lewiston was organized primarily by Ghanaian and Sudanese members of the organization.

As late as 2012, Lewiston's annual Somali Festival persisted and the publicity for and staging of the event continued to recognize the position of Somalis as familiar strangers in Lewiston struggling to balance offering cultural diversity that is consumable in the form of food, dance, and music, on the one hand, with, on the other, asserting a Somali cultural commonality and distinctiveness that is not for public consumption. In later years, the festivals sought to assert Somali distinctiveness to a greater degree. Initially the histories of the nation of Somalia and the United States were linked in an annual celebration of freedom and independence held in early July; beginning in 2009, however, the Somali celebration was moved to late June and no mention was made of American Independence Day. A *Sun Journal* article announcing the upcoming 2009 celebration underscores the emphasis on Somali alterity. It read:

Cultural music will be played as The Multi-Purpose Center on Birch Street welcomes the sixth annual Somali Independence Day Festival to Lewiston at 7 P.M. this Saturday.

Said Mohamud, founder and president of the African Immigrants Association, said he hoped the event would bring together Somalis, Americans and their friends from different cultures to promote diversity. "It's a better way for Somalis to intermingle with Americans; we hope to support Somali integration to the community without letting go of our language, identity and culture," he said.

According to Mohamud, the festivities will promote and celebrate the Somali population in Lewiston and the 15,000 African immigrants residing in central and southern Maine.

National African folk dancers and members of the community perform throughout the celebration. Food is also an essential ingredient to this year's festivities, with sweets provided to children, and somosas – a cultural recipe consisting of potatoes, beans, lean beef, herbs and vegetables – served to adult guests. (Huynh 2009, p. A4)

The form that Somali cultural expression took in Lewiston and the public meaning given to Somali culture depended in part on the way Somali-ness was represented at events like Somali Independence Day celebrations. The event showcased music, dance, crafts, and traditional Somali food. The recent history of these celebrations shows that Somali American identity in Lewiston was an identity and culture in transition.[12] Lewiston Somalis resisted pressures to place Somali-ness into a general category of African-ness. Although it continued to operate as a distinct identity in the community, Somali-ness in Lewiston was influenced by the cultural context of recognition and incorporation.

---

[12] It must also be noted that other non-Somali cultural celebrations in Lewiston changed significantly during my time in the field. The city's long-standing Festival de Joie marking the Franco heritage of many area residents struggled and was resurrected as a smaller festival, Festival FrancoFun (pun intended). The widely popular Greek festival sought to represent the diversity of the Greek Orthodox Church's membership by offering Ethiopian and Armenian food as well as the traditional Greek fare.

While Somali festivals provided a glimpse of public Somali-ness emerging in Lewiston, they also hinted at the erasure of other aspects of Somali culture: everyday adherence to Islam and rapidly changing gender relations. The article promoting the 2009 festival underscored the efforts on the part of the leadership of the African Immigrants' Association to navigate the complexities of representation and cultural preservation in instances in which typical Somali cultural practices could not be made consumable to other festival goers.

Although Mohamud hopes the event will promote community integration, he also hopes it will serve as a reminder to Somalis of the importance of balancing integration with the preservation of Somali culture. "Somalia, unlike other countries in Africa, is very homogeneous. We have one common language, religion and culture. It's something we're very proud of."
    An advantage to holding the Somali Independence Day celebration in the United States is that, "we're celebrating in a democratic country where women can celebrate and participate," Mohamud said. He added that because many immigrants are single mothers with children, once a year this event allows them the opportunity to get together and be present in the community. (Huynh 2009, p. A4)

In the preceding article the food, dance, and music offered at the festivals was touted as something that bridges cultural differences. On the other hand, Islam and the Somali language were not for mass consumption but, instead, elements of Somali identity in danger of being lost. Furthermore, Mohamud also indicated a potentially thorny cross-cultural issue – the position of women within traditional Somali society as compared with expectations equality characteristic of the United States. As we shall see, the position of Somalis as familiar strangers neutralized the negative impact that adherence to Islam and traditional Somali gender relations might have had on assessments of the assimilable character of Somali-ness.

The Wrong Kind of Diversity

The following account of public response to the death of a Somali resident of Lewiston demonstrates the selective recognition of the diversity and nature of the city's Somali residents – a recognition that extends to cuisine and clothing but not to conceptions of justice and redress. Allies who mobilized on behalf of Somali Lewistonians in the face of what they perceived as discrimination and hate did not mobilize alongside Somali residents of the city who understood the death of one of their own as suspicious and a communal harm that must be remedied. Alternative notions of responsibility and accountability held by Somali protestors did not resonate with a mainstream focus on racist intent.

On Sunday, May 28, 2006, at 6:45 in the evening, Lewiston police officers took forty-six-year-old Ahmed Samater into custody on the charge of disorderly conduct. A man with a known drinking problem, Samater had been previously detained and released on the condition that he abstain from alcohol. Therefore, the arresting officers also charged the visibly intoxicated Samater with violating the conditions of release. They placed Samater in an unoccupied cell in the Androscoggin County jail. Samater was found unconscious in his cell shortly before midnight and pronounced dead soon after (LaFlamme 2006).

Samater's death galvanized the Somali community of Lewiston in a way that Mayor Raymond's letter and Brent Matthews's attack on the mosque never had. While some Somali residents of Lewiston had reacted publicly to the letter and the pig's head incident, when it came to demonstrations and protests they were far outnumbered by non-Somali city residents. In the early days after Samater's death, however, the normally quiet Somali community sprang into action. Calling for an end to police brutality in Lewiston and an inquiry into the circumstances that led to Samater's death in police custody, nearly forty Somalis picketed the Lewiston Police Department. The chief of police expressed his regrets about the death and his surprise at the emotional response to it as Somalis from around the nation decried the death of one of their own and echoed calls for justice. When, some months later, the Maine State Office of the Chief Medical Examiner ruled that Samater died due to intoxication, the Minneapolis-based Somali Justice Advocacy Center requested that the Maine Civil Liberties Union initiate an independent investigation into the incident (Williams 2007).

Somali residents of Lewiston took Samatar's death as evidence of the excesses of violence and power, mistreatment and abuse at the hands of the police, and a loss of life that required redress. Drawing upon negative encounters with local law enforcement, a history of victimization through state-sanctioned violence, a culturally informed understanding of death as a loss to the family, and a conception of justice requiring that wrongful deaths result in the payment of blood debts by the perpetrators to the family and clan of the deceased (Lewis 2002), local Somali protesters called for justice in a recognizable form – the establishment of responsibility and retribution in the form of compensation for the death.

In the eyes of the broader public, however, Samater's death, although lamented, was understood as the unfortunate outcome of Samater's irresponsible behavior and did not rouse widespread protests or demonstrations by non-Somali residents of the city. Absent were the rallies designed to show support for the Somali community, calls for eradication of the scourge of racism in the community, criticisms of local law enforcement, and attempts at the widespread anti-racist education of Lewiston's white residents that characterized the public response to the publication of Raymond's letter and Brent Matthews's attack on the mosque. Such widespread mobilization did not materialize because it required recognition of Samater's death as evidence of the perpetration of unambiguously hateful or discriminatory acts directed toward innocent victims. In terms of the epistemology and praxis that mobilized support for Somali settlement, Samatar, an acknowledged alcoholic with prior encounters with the police, did not offer a diversity warranting a defense and his death was not recognized as an injustice worth organizing over.

With no comfortable place within legitimated understandings of group interests and culture, Samatar's death and the alternative understandings of justice that Somali protestors voiced in its wake were easily dismissed and quickly forgotten. The events rarely resurfaced in public talk and private conversations. When the attorney general's office absolved the police from any wrongdoing and confirmed the earlier finding that Samater died from intoxication, the story created little stir outside of tight-knit Somali circles. Similar silencing, erasures, and selective vision were visible in the public position of religion and traditional Somali gender relations.

Religion

Most Somali immigrants in Lewiston, and in the United States generally, are Sunni Muslim. Research shows that religious identity tends to be important to Somalis in the United States, often more than in Somalia where living in a Muslim society made Islam a taken-for-granted aspect of everyday life supported by social institutions and widespread cultural mores (Ajrouch and Kusow 2007; Berns McGown 1999). In the United States, however, Islam is far from an unremarkable pillar of community life. Somali immigrants are members of a religious minority in a society oriented around Judeo-Christian philosophical orientations, holidays, symbols, and cultural mores (Huntington 2004; Taylor 2007). In addition to its absence from the structure of social life, during the first decade of the twenty-first century, Islam was a faith held in some suspicion by the majority (Abdo 2006; Gottschalk and Greenberg 2008; Peek 2011; Polgreen 2010).

Far from being unique to Somali newcomers, increased religiosity is common among many immigrant groups in the United States as the expression of religious identity can work as an affirmation of cultural identity and provide a community of faith as the surrogate for extended family and community networks lost upon emigration (Kurien 1998). For immigrant groups settling in areas already home to those who share their religion, religiosity can also act as a catalyst for incorporation at the same time that it serves to shore up ethnic identity. For example, Shandy and Fennelly (2006) find that in one rural community, Christian immigrants from the Sudan who practiced at the local Lutheran church were incorporated into the community much more smoothly than Muslim Somali immigrants who found no preexisting community of faith in which to take part.

Many Somali Lewistonians were drawn to the city out of a desire to maintain their religion and culture. Unlike Somali clan identities, which appear to lose their salience among the youngest members of the Somali diaspora, religious identity remains exceedingly important to Somali youth, particularly after 9/11 (Berns-McGown 1999; Shepard 2005). In fact, research in the United States, Canada, and the United Kingdom has found that Somali youth identify themselves as Muslims first and Somalis second (Berns-McGown 1999; Shepard 2008). Despite the emphasis placed upon Muslim identities, young Somali immigrants negotiate the relationship between religious beliefs and everyday behaviors in various ways. Berns-McGown interviewed Somali youth in Toronto and London. Her young adult and adolescent interviewees attempted to balance their home culture and faith with the values of the society around them. In so doing, they individually established the limits of their conformity with mainstream behavior. For example, one young woman would go to parties but would not dance. Another would dance but would not date. Regardless of the balance they established, all of the young people with whom she spoke felt that they were limiting their behavior due to their religion, and nearly all experienced tensions with their parents when it came to the relationship between their behavior and Islam.[13]

In Lewiston, as elsewhere, many Somali parents reported the fear that Western sexual openness and use of alcohol, individualism, and materialism would degrade the chastity, sobriety, and collective and

---

[13] In many ways, this research is most interesting in that it establishes empirically for Somali youth what we take as given among young people generally: Somali Muslim youth are not automatons. They also rebel and determine their own balance between tradition and the present, parental guidance, and individuality, faith, and secularism.

familial orientation they sought to instill in their children. In her later work, Berns-McGown notes that, over ten years of observation, the Somali mothers in Toronto with whom she worked became increasingly accepting of and comfortable with their children's reinterpretation and varying adherence to Somali cultural and religious practices (Berns-McGown 2007).

Islam is an important aspect of identity and a cornerstone of social organization among many Somali residents in Lewiston. The Lewiston-Auburn Islamic Center was founded very early in the Somali settlement in Lewiston and, as already discussed, early social service provision through Somali Community Services also had strong ties to the mosque. Given these facts and the reality of a national preoccupation with "Islamic fundamentalism" in the years following the September 11 terrorist attacks, the very period considered in this research, I was surprised to note that the religiosity of most Lewiston Somalis had very little explicit negative impact on the public meaning of Somali-ness. Despite the centrality of Islam as an organizing feature of everyday life, religious adherence was largely erased from public presentations and perceptions of everyday Somali culture by Somali and non-Somali members of the community alike. Islam was instead relegated to high moments: births, funerals, and holidays such as Ramadan, and instances of drama and volatility such as Kadar Said's criticism of Somali Community Services or the decision by a local non-Somali man, Brent Matthews, to harass Somali residents of Lewiston. Instead, with the increasing dominance of the African Immigrants' Association over Somali Community Services, the emergence of a public Somali culture became marked not by the traditional Muslim views associated with Somali Community Services, but by the celebration of diversity and freedom that characterized smiling immigrant faces in the newspaper and Somali cultural celebrations.

Invisible Gender Inequality

One day in the field, I sat with a host of area social workers, adult education teachers, nurses and doctors, and employers in a cultural brokerage session – as described in Chapter 3, a meeting in which local public officials and service providers met with a panel of Somalis to receive relevant insight into Somali culture. The purpose of this session was to provide attendees the opportunity to talk over their questions and concerns with

a panel of female Somali individuals who could advise them on strategies for dealing sensitively with their Somali employees and clientele. The
panel was late and the session organizer, a social worker employed to
assist refugee resettlement in Lewiston and Portland, took the meeting
in hand. "Since our guests have not yet arrived, does anyone have any
questions that they would like to ask this group while we don't have any
Somalis present?"

After a short pause a woman sitting in the back of the room raised
her hand and then stood. "My name is Dr. Jones and I am working with
several Somali patients at [local hospital] as a primary care physician."
At this point she paused and took a deep breath. "I was surprised to
learn that many of my female Somali patients had been circumcised. I
have a deep respect for other cultures but I am finding it very difficult to
broach the subject of female circumcision with my clients because, even
if it is an element of Somali culture, medically it is a very troublesome
practice."

Following the concerned doctor's comment, silenced reigned for a time.
Then the session organizer spoke again, "Do any of the other doctors
have experience with this? If so, perhaps you can speak to Dr. Jones privately at the end of the session if you do not wish to speak now." Silence.
"I would like to say that female circumcision is a traditional Somali cultural practice that is dying out here in the United States and is declining
in Somalia, too. Any other questions or concerns?"

I sat, dumbfounded, by the matter-of-fact treatment of a topic I knew
to be highly contentious and emotional in other contexts. The United
Nations, African Congress, World Health Organization, and countless
other organizations and groups stand unified in their demands that the
practice of female circumcision (FC, more commonly known among its
opponents as Female Genital Mutilation or FGM) come to an end.[14]
How was it that the cultural brokerage session seemed so far removed
from that vitriolic discussion?

Limited freedom of association and community engagement among
Somali adolescent females, FC/FGM, arranged and early marriages,
polygamy, the veil – these elements of traditional Somali gender relations
may receive considerable negative attention elsewhere, but in Lewiston
they were discussed infrequently and then in the past tense as behavior

---

[14] For more information on the topic of FC/FGM, see the World Health Organization's
website: http://www.who.int/topics/female_genital_mutilation/en/index.html.

that existed in Somalia, or in the present tense as unremarkable and even amusing cultural differences. This is the case with a joke I heard one evening at the fast food chain Tim Hortons. "You know, the Somali guy next door came over and we were watching the game and talking about how it is different here from Somalia. He said, 'Women here are so bossy. They don't know their place.' I said, 'Listen, buddy, my wife knows her place and this is it so you better watch your step or we'll both end up missing the last quarter.'"

  Somali practices around gender change significantly and rapidly in the diaspora. Somali immigrants to the United States generally report significant change in the family relationship when it comes to gender dynamics. While there is not agreement among all Somalis regarding a division of household labor typical for life in Somalia, in general women were singularly responsible for day-to-day aspects of child rearing, cooking, and household maintenance. In the diaspora, women have become increasingly responsible for the economic well-being of the family by working outside the home alongside their spouses, if, as is not always the case, their spouses have managed to leave Somali with them (Taylor 2004). Furthermore, while children in Somalia were often raised within networks of extended family and neighbors who shared in the responsibilities of child rearing, in the United States these networks are significantly diminished in size and the ability to provide assistance. In these changing circumstances, Somali husbands and fathers increasingly report that they are taking on domestic duties such as cooking, cleaning, and changing diapers (Ford 2004; Koshen 2007; Kusow 2004; Somali Community Services of Maine Inc. 2003).

  Furthermore, as research on the Somali second generation demonstrates, there is tremendous heterogeneity in the extent to which young Somali women are limited in their activities and friendships as their mothers were. In Lewiston, use of the veil varied. In the early years of Somali settlement in the community, Somali women typically wore the veil; over time the city became home to more and more women wearing simple scarves and an increasing number of women who did not cover their heads at all.[15]

---

[15] Joppke (Joppke, Christian. 2009. *Veil: Mirror of identity.* Malden, MA: Polity) notes that while the veil has been the subject of controversy in Europe, in the United States, this has not been the case because of the seemingly contradictory fact that the United States is simultaneously an increasingly religious society with a strict separation between religious and political life. Joppke also points out that in the United States, Muslim identity is not stigmatized as a lower-class immigrant identity, as it is in much of Europe.

THE CUNNING OF INCORPORATION

The trajectory of the annual Somali festival and the public erasure of potentially controversial aspects of Somali culture[16] demonstrates the influence of the cultural pragmatics of incorporation on the character of Somali American identity emerging in Lewiston. The enthusiastic yet selective embrace of Somalis as familiar strangers who both embodied diversity and exemplified inclusion ensured that Somali residents of Lewiston retained group distinctiveness but also determined that their otherness was recognizable as fundamentally consistent with the values of the mainstream. In her critical liberal stance of the politics of recognition, Povinelli (2002) notes that multicultural requirements exercise a particular form of domination over indigenous and minority citizens. Observing the manner in which Australian indigenous people engage liberal multiculturalism, Povinelli concludes that those who would count as diverse are required to perform an acceptable diversity and yet to do it authentically. That is, to

desire and identify with their cultural traditions in a way that just so happens … to fit the national and legal imaginary of multiculturalism; that they at once orient their sensual, emotional, and corporeal identities toward the nation's and law's image of traditional cultural forms and national reconciliation and at the same time ghost this being for the nation so as not to have their desires for some economic certainty in their lives appear opportunistic. (Povinelli 2002, p. 55)

Somali residents of Lewiston experienced an equally difficult and coercive situation. They were expected to be and assert their place in Lewiston as newcomers taking their places as the workers, homeowners, and neighbors that made the community what it was. However, Somali efforts in this regard were not enough to determine their incorporation. They were also required to erect and enact a sanitized and consumable public Somali-ness in which significant elements of the organization of the everyday life of most Somalis – namely, adherence to Islam and gender relations that diverged from the mainstream – were relegated to oblivion as nonpublic, symbolic, and historical facts not worthy of consideration or attention when it came to understanding Somali-ness, the experience of Somalis, or best practices for meeting the needs of Somali residents of Lewiston.

---

[16] The heading of this section is adapted from the title of Povinelli's book on the recognition of Australian indigenous people (Povinelli, Elizabeth A. 2002. *The cunning of recognition: Indigenous alterities and the making of Australian multiculturalism*. Durham: Duke University Press).

Homeward?

Somali belonging in Lewiston was contingent and partial as Somalis maintained their position as the outsiders who have been allowed in because
of a constructed, even if genuine, performance of the desired subjectivity. On November 18, 2005, less than two months before Abdelmalik,
whose photo was discussed in the opening of this chapter, laughed at her
own fall in the snow, the *Lewiston Sun Journal* ran a picture of a Somali
woman carrying a box on her head and a baby on her back. The bare
late autumn trees and blue sky formed the backdrop of the image. The
woman was smiling as she looked beyond the camera at the distance she
had yet to travel. Her baby, wearing an uncertain pout and with the hood
of her jacket covering one eye, thoughtfully considered the camera with
the other eye. The caption read:

Homeward: Hamina Sabat walks through Lewiston's Kennedy Park on a sunny
but windy day ... with her family on her way home from the grocery store. She
carries a box of disposable diapers on her head and her 4-month-old daughter,
Tahabah, on her back. Sabat ... has lived in Maine for the last six years. (Leiva
2005, p. A2)

Smiling Somali faces represented the expected reaction to the hardships
of resettlement and cultural adaptation in a city where the climate was
sometimes inhospitable. Sabat's picture underscores an alterity more
intractable than the newcomer status to which the *Sun Journal* report
attributed Abdelmalik's tumble, but which is intended to endear it the
reader all the same. Extended tenure in the area notwithstanding, Sabat's
image speaks of differences, people, and ways of doing things that are out
of place and, for that reason, noteworthy and enjoyable as local "color."

The initial identification of Somali organizations in Lewiston derived
primarily from the multicultural embrace of Somalis as strangers to be
incorporated as colorful "others"; however, over time social inclusion
was extended to the strangers who most effectively appeared familiar. In
other words, the emphasis on engaging Somalis as a distinct and unified
community arose from their status as fetishized objects of multicultural
desire (diversity), but the increasing application of mainstream standards
for determining the legitimacy and success of claims to group representation demonstrates that Somalis were also subjects of the cultural pragmatics of incorporation.

The embrace of minority groups as legitimate and valuable participants in public life offers an avenue for the incorporation of immigrant
newcomers, but this does not mean that these groups are not reworked by

their encounter with the mainstream. Recognized group representatives, public identity, and celebrated culture are shaped by the normative and cultural context of reception that seeks particular forms of intragroup governance, cultural expression, and content. Somali, Muslim immigrant residents of Lewiston come to be represented by an organization that successfully appears secular, democratic, and inclusive as opposed to religious, authoritarian, and traditional. The organization held a position of authority in establishing a local public Somali-ness for a new cultural context. This organization influenced Somali-ness in Lewiston by putting on an annual cultural festival that made Somali culture palatable to and consumable for the broader Lewiston community. As a public Somali-ness worthy of incorporation emerged in Lewiston, potentially troubling elements of Somali distinctiveness were eliminated from view.

Somali newcomers in Lewiston were incorporated into the community in a manner consistent with the epistemology, praxis, and discipline characterizing the cultural pragmatics of incorporation. The diversity they brought to the community was the raw material from which common ground with other residents of the city could be constructed. In comparison with modes of immigrant inclusion requiring total cultural assimilation or *jus sanguinis* notions of local and national belonging that make incorporation impossible, the politics of recognition observed in Lewiston provides Somali newcomers greater welcome, support in maintaining some aspects of their culture and religion, and the opportunity to capitalize on opportunities for social support and economic and political integration. Despite its improvement over other models, the incorporation of Somali residents in Lewiston hardly constitutes a neutral welcome and full embrace. The moral "fitness" and social acceptance of Somali-ness and Somali organizations hinged upon their adoption of expected praxis – the deft performance of a modern, moral, and psychologically fit group-ness.

Conclusion

Cultural Scaffolding

The construction of the inclusive civic community and an incorporable public Somali-ness, the disciplining of Somali and non-Somali citizens to a particular mainstream praxis, and the development of programs and policies founded upon an epistemology that emphasized individual bigotry as the root of social ills – these things constitute the cultural pragmatics of newcomer incorporation in Lewiston, Maine.

Not all Lewiston residents were disciplined to the epistemology and praxis characterizing Somali immigrant incorporation. Not all Lewistonians either adopted a multicultural worldview as an article of faith or capitulated to instrumental motivations for acting disciplined. Nor did all individuals fit neatly and willingly into the categories created by the symbolic boundaries of belonging that arose in Lewiston. Not all the practices observable in the community derived from legitimated praxis and not all narrative frames proved consistent with the dominant epistemology. In addition to observing the emerging cultural and performative consensus in Lewiston, I also observed a tremendous heterogeneity of situations, speakers, and encounters. As with any study of social life, only a minute fraction of all that I observed and an even smaller share of all that was going on in Lewiston has appeared in this analysis.

However, while it has been important to identify agency and creativity in Lewiston as it appeared in the form of contestation and challenge, it is also crucial to recognize that conformity with the cultural structures of incorporation was not necessarily coerced, unwittingly adopted, or self-interestedly enacted. The people of Lewiston and participants in diversity training seminars were not generally cowed. Instead, they adopted the symbolic boundaries and related epistemology and praxis as the cultural scaffolding on which they could construct order, normalcy, greater certainty, and commonality in cooperation with their fellows. In adopting the perspective and practices presented in these pages, the people I observed reached a tentative collective agreement on the order of things. Just how tentative that collective agreement was cannot be understated.

A NEW MAYOR IN TOWN

On October 2, 2012, ten years to the day after Mayor Raymond published the letter with which this book began, another Lewiston mayor, Robert Macdonald, addressed a disgruntled crowd at a Lewiston city council meeting. Macdonald was attempting to diffuse public criticism resulting from a BBC piece on Somali settlement in Lewiston (BBC News Magazine 2012). During an interview featured in the BBC piece, Macdonald said, "You know what, when you come here you accept our culture, and you leave your culture at the door." The piece had created quite a stir in Lewiston.

In the days, and even the final televised moments, prior to offering a formal statement on his quotation, Macdonald noted that the slanted media "spin" and self-interested political adversaries had mischaracterized his comment (Taylor 2012; Thistle 2012b). At the city council meeting that evening, Macdonald read a prepared statement:

As Mayor of Lewiston I want to clarify the previous comment I made, "Leave your culture at the door." What I meant by that comment is that I believe when people come to the city of Lewiston from other countries they need to assimilate into the American culture. I did not mean that they have to abandon their religion, their traditions, their language, nor their style of dress. Lewiston has a long history of immigrants settling here, such as the French and the Irish. I fully recognize that as individuals we are all a product of our experiences and our cultures, which makes up the very fabric of who we are.

The many Somalis and other immigrants who have relocated here have enriched the diversity that Lewiston offers and that is a good thing. As Mayor, I value every person in the city of Lewiston. We are all people, period. From all different walks of life, but now one community.

Over the last year I have experienced very positive interaction with our new Mainers. They have treated me very well. Actually, they have treated me like family. I have been particularly impressed with the ability of many to speak multiple languages. Immigrants with multi-lingual skills will play a huge role within our continued economic resurgence. I am excited about the immigrant youth who are attending colleges, first-rate colleges I might add, and will be able to share with our community what they have learned. I am also proud of the businesses that have been established by our immigrant residents. It is also important to mention that over the last 10 years an increasing number of immigrant residents have obtained US citizenship and have become registered voters.

In closing, I did not intend for my previous comments to be hurtful or upsetting. Again, I was speaking of my desire for immigrants to assimilate into the American way of life. Not for them to change who they are or to leave their culture behind.

Outside of his public "clarification," Macdonald wrote an editorial highlighting the fiscal burden of immigration, and the disingenuous machinations of media looking to sell news, and political foes looking for the opportunity to wreak havoc, and even "extremist white liberals and their African surrogates" seeking to sow the seeds of conflict in Lewiston (Macdonald 2012). As in 2002, there were those who defended Macdonald as a well-intentioned and good person who did not intend to cause trouble (Thistle 2012b). As in 2002, there were those who asserted that he is a bigot and called for his ouster (Thistle 2012a).

In his attempt at clarification and self-exoneration, Macdonald made sure to mention all the ways in which he valued "new" Mainers and affirmed the benefits of community diversity. In a departure from the script as it had played out during the years of Mayor Laurier Raymond, Mayor Macdonald noted the rewarding personal relationships he had with Somali Lewistonians – people who were "like family." The new mayoral drama in Lewiston demonstrated both the ongoing risk of challenges to Somali inclusion and the significant progress that has been made. Even if the terms of solidarity and the mode of immigrant incorporation were still a point of contention and contestation, ten years into Somali settlement in Lewiston, there was no challenging Somali community membership.

A measure of achieved Somali inclusion was equally visible in changes in the people standing in support of the Somalis. In 2002, it was mostly non-Somalis who organized on behalf of the cause of Somali inclusion – generally white activists from community and religious organizations and speaking in support of Somalis. This time around, the public protest and organizing came largely from Somali Lewistonians who, like many other Lewiston residents, had acquired knowledge of the methods for and importance of confronting bias and inequality. Somali residents of Lewiston no longer required a Somali organization to broker their relationship to the city. Instead, they were frequently represented by successful and respected individuals – students completing their final year in Lewiston's schools and attending prestigious universities in the area, and adults who were now citizens and voters as well as the hardworking parents and people of faith they had earlier been considered.

For example, when asked to share his thoughts on Macdonald's endorsement of Somali assimilation, Hussein Ahmed, a community leader, business owner, and Somali Lewistonian, dismissed the mayor's view as a fringe perspective that reflected poorly on the entire city. In addition to highlighting the familiar form that diversity dramas take, Ahmed's comments also relied upon the fact of community membership. In 2002, Somali inclusion existed primarily as hypothetical – that Somalis should and would be able to belong. In 2012 the inclusive community was taken as given.

"I think one thing is very clear," Ahmed said. "This is a country where we have millions of people with different political ideologies, different religious theology but with one important sense of communal commitment that we have and that communal commitment is far more important than anything else." ...

"What will make me stronger is when I embrace my culture and have a community that is willing to accept my culture and I accept their culture," Ahmed said. "We will be a stronger Lewiston community and that's what I see and that's what is happening in Lewiston today." (Thistle 2012b, p. A1)

STRANGERS AND NEIGHBORS

Observing diversity in the city, Fischer (1999) discusses microsociological dilemmas, including uncertainty and anxiety in the face shared social norms and meaning systems, associated with living in a world inhabited by cultural strangers. Fischer delineates the ways in which the social order of the city is sustained in the face of diversity. In his assessment, urban social order depends upon social and residential segregation, a lack of trust, use of stereotypes, intimidation, and a "public etiquette" characterized by "proper manners such as 'selective inattention,' nonverbal cues of recognition, careful physical spacing, and what might be called 'elevator behaviour'"(Fischer 1999, p. 221).

Despite Fischer's emphasis on the metropolis, the difficult nature of life in a world of strangers is not confined to large cities. Gathering survey data in a variety of American communities, including Lewiston, Putnam (2007) finds that the social fabric in communities of all sizes is adversely affected by ethnic diversity. His research shows that people in diverse places have less trust in others, and less faith in the unselfish assistance and cooperation of their neighbors and their government. Community diversity is correlated with having fewer friends and being less happy and engaged in one's neighborhood.

Furthermore, while multiculturalism and diversity are often associated with the city, intercultural negotiation takes on added complexity in smaller places like Lewiston. Aided by the social distance and anonymity of life on the city street, urbanites experience the diversity of those around them at arm's reach. The underlying assumption of stranger-ness in city life is that the people one encounters on the subway and the sidewalk are unknown personally, no matter how racially, ethnically, and religiously different they may be. Places like Lewiston lack urban anonymity and significant residential segregation.

In Lewiston, the diverse stranger and neighbor are one and the same. Instead of depending upon segregation and anonymity, strategies for managing Lewiston's cultural difference centered upon shoring up the moral and symbolic boundaries of community, disseminating legitimated behavioral techniques and foundational theories of social life, and dispatching eruptions of disorder. A dominant cultural pragmatics of incorporation in Lewiston existed because, like the movement toward "verbal hygiene" noted by Cameron (2008), in the face of the "desire for order and meaning; setting language to rights becomes a surrogate for setting the world to rights" (Cameron 2000, p. 8). In the face of the heterogeneity of positions and perspectives – the uncertainty, moral and hermeneutical relativity, and unpredictability of cross-cultural life – standardized meanings and practices created a manageable reality of known facts and correct positions.

Evidence on the ground in Lewiston suggests that Somali inclusion is under way in the city, even as that inclusion is partial and not without costs and setbacks. Both enabled and constrained by the shared norms, practices, and boundaries established by the cultural pragmatics of incorporation, Somali and non-Somali residents of Lewiston could be relatively confident in their interpretations of situations and the behavior of others. Adoption of the perspective and practices laid out in this book assisted them as they struggled to control the impact and interpretation of their own speech and defended their stances as moral and worthy people who were part of a good community. Such relative control could be elusive to those, like Mayor Raymond and Mayor Macdonald, Ms. Smith, the mosque representatives writing against homosexuality, and Brent Matthews, whose undisciplined practices and perspectives were recast outside of their control and took meaning in relation to dominant epistemology and praxis.

Epistemology, praxis, and discipline underwrote the inclusion of immigrant newcomers; provided the framework for the moral constitution of welcoming community; and set the parameters for the performance of upright and anti-racist individual and subgroup identities. The dominant approach to incorporation also effectively erased or obscured difficult and material challenges to the negotiation of cultural difference, substituted appreciation of diversity for close contact, and precluded emphasis on the institutional aspects of inequality by viewing challenges to incorporation as the result of the behavior of dismissable separatists, bigots, and self-interested or psychologically limited individuals. As indicated by the dynamics documented in this text, contemporary multicultural epistemology and praxis are more than a moral good bringing greater solidarity and equality; they are also a moral and discursive power that can be just as coercive as emancipatory. Furthermore, inequality and exclusion are ongoing effects of the negotiation of cohesion; the establishment of moral standards and divisions, and the requirement of their performance leads to the exclusion of those who are unable or unwilling to toe the line.

Who has done this to the people of Lewiston? Why has it occurred? What are the interests being served in this tale? Who stands happily by, reaping the rewards of the dynamics uncovered in this research? Although it is certainly possible to identify inequality in the distribution of the costs and benefits deriving from the cultural system of incorporation, the following field note demonstrates that cultural-structural forms of power such as these can have a life of their own and serve as a tool that can be used by both the subjugators and the subjugated.

EVERYONE IS GREEK

I wandered downtown Lewiston in one of my first weekends of field research. According to Wednesday's paper, the First Annual Community Multi-Cultural Fair was to be held in the city's central park. I scheduled my arrival to coincide with dinner in hopes of enjoying some of the food I imagined would be available, some empanadas from the largely Latino Rural Workers Coalition sponsoring the event, perhaps, or maybe a first taste of the heretofore unexplored Somali cuisine.

After navigating somewhat uncertainly through the still unfamiliar streets of Lewiston, I arrived at downtown's Kennedy Park. To my surprise, the park was empty. There was no evidence of a multicultural fair in progress and nothing to indicate that I had missed it – no trash barrels full of leftovers, no tattered streamers or deflated balloons. It did not appear that I was early as the requisite people and stacks of tents, tables, and chairs for a pending multicultural fair were nowhere to be found.

A purchase of the *Sun Journal* and review of the calendar of events confirmed the time and location. Although the facts eluded me that day, I later learned that organizers of the multicultural festival had earlier announced the decision to postpone the event because of a lack of preparation. This particular event was not rescheduled during my time in Lewiston. However, I did attend a few other multicultural celebrations and potluck dinners offered in Lewiston by the Many and One Coalition, Lewiston High School, and the Rural Workers' Coalition in partnership with the Unitarian Church. All the same, on that September afternoon when I was new to the field, I found myself attending a non-event.

I felt at a loss in the face of the enormity of the task I had taken on in Lewiston – not just attending the multicultural fair but the entire undertaking of coming to know this unfamiliar community so as to be in the position to develop some useful insights into the social world. I walked down Lisbon Street, the city's primary thoroughfare, past a variety of storefronts, many empty and others sporting a hodgepodge of occupants including the public library, an ice cream shop, the chamber of commerce, a mosque, and a clothing boutique, "The International Shop." The shop was the only business open that Saturday afternoon so I entered. The tiny store was divided into two parts. Along one wall hung a variety of athletic apparel, Boston Red Sox, Celtics, and New England Patriots jerseys, including expensive retro-jerseys selling for more than $200 each, warm-up pants, and baseball hats. It was the type of clothing one might expect to see worn by men who dressed in sports fashions. On the other wall hung Somali clothing for women – a variety of flowing headscarves and dresses in bright and colorful prints. In observing the wares and layout of the store, I felt keenly that I had entered a culturally marked space, a store that did not sell the types of things someone like me usually purchases.

All the same, I was the only customer. I stepped up to the woman sitting behind the register. I took her to be Somali as her arms and head were covered in the manner typical of Somali women in Lewiston.

"Excuse me," I inquired, "I am here for the multicultural fair. Do you know anything about it?"

"No. I don't know," she replied. She said nothing more. I took a deep breath, letting the pause continue longer than I might otherwise. Maybe I should try to make conversation. That, after all, was why I was there, but the task seemed enormous on that first day with nothing being so

far what I expected and understood. Discouraged and feeling vulnerable
and awkward, I took my leave. Just as displeasing as the mystery of the
multicultural fair, I felt keenly that my inquiry in the international shop
revealed me as a stranger, yet another person "from away" seeking to
experience "diversity" in this town that was so tired of outsiders motivated to visit by an interest in local race relations.

I weighed my options and considered going back to my apartment. I
decided to make one last attempt at recovering the afternoon. I consulted
the newspaper again. In addition to listing the multicultural festival,
the calendar of events announced the annual Greek Festival at that the
Greek Orthodox Church across town. I drove from the old and crum-
bling downtown on the river to the new orderliness of the subdivisions
where the Greek Orthodox Church is situated. There was no missing the
place. The streets were filled with parked cars for some distance from the
church. I squeezed the car into an overlooked spot and joined the crowds
headed for the churchyard.

I still experienced the uncertainty and disquiet that had been resting
in my stomach since arriving downtown to find no evidence of the multicultural fair, a vague queasiness mistaken for pangs of hunger. Upon
entering the grounds, those feelings vanished. Here was the ethnic celebration I was expecting – a festival resembling in form the many church
fairs and St. Patrick's Day festivals of my youth. Activities at the Greek
Festival included church tours, drinks, and dancing at a tent labeled "The
Taverna," coffee and baklava at the bakery table, a large tent with rows
of metal folding chairs and tables covered with red and white checked
plastic for all those partaking of the Greek dinner – a large plate of
Greek dishes for $8.00, and a variety of smaller booths offering souvenir
T-shirts, "artifacts" from Greece, secondhand merchandise, home-made
crafts such as crocheted afghan quilts, and children's games and face
painting.

As I stood in line for dinner, an elderly gentleman distributing programs and selling raffle tickets pointed at my T-shirt. A gift from my sister
who was living at the time in Ithaca, New York, the bright green shirt
read, "Ithaca is Gorges."[1] As it was sitting atop my pile of clean clothes
when I dressed that morning, I put the shirt on. The elderly gentleman
smiled and asked, "Have you been to Ithaca?"

I grinned in return and nodded. "My sister went to school in Ithaca."

His smile faded a bit, "Ithaca, New York?"

[1] A pun on the town's topography.

"Yes," I answered.

"Well," he countered, "Ithaca, New York, is named after Ithaxa in Greece. It is a very important city in Greek history. Do you know why?"

I tried to maintain my grin despite my frustration in lacking relevant insider information. "No. Why?"

"Ithaxa is the home of Ulysses. He left his wife, Penelope, and his child in Ithaxa to go and fight the Trojan War. Have you ever heard of the Trojan War?"

This time I could answer in the affirmative. I read Homer's account of the Trojan War, *The Iliad*, in college. Satisfied, my interrogator moved on to sell raffle tickets to the next folks in line.

I arrived at the head of the queue, picked up a meal tray, and requested the spanakopita dinner. As he supplemented a hefty slab of the tasty spinach and feta cheese dish with hearty portions of salad, rice, and bread, the server took note of my T-shirt. "Have you been to Ithaca?"

This time I was prepared, "Well, this T-shirt is about Ithaca, New York, and I have been there, but I guess it is a pretty good shirt to wear today since Ulysses was from Ithaxa in Greece."

The server smiled broadly. "Ulysses! A very important man," he agreed.

I happily walked off with my substantial dinner to find a seat. The program for the festival boasted, "On this day ... Everybody is Greek." And, surely, as I sat down to my Greek meal wearing my "Greek" T-shirt listening to the Greek music emanating from the Taverna, I felt just Greek enough.

As an ethnographer in Lewiston, I learned much about immigrant incorporation by examining my own discomfort and isolation and the situations in which they arose. As I navigated the new world of Lewiston in those early days of research, I wrestled with uncertainty in the face of new routines, unknown people, and foreign social mores. The familiar form of the cultural festival offered comfort and confidence because I understood the scene and how I fit into it – I was there to partake of the food, listen to the music, and peruse the cultural artifacts. By happy accident and with a minimum of insider knowledge and experience, I successfully demonstrated that I was a friend of the Greek Orthodox Church and had even dressed for the event. The sense of being-in-the-right-place-ness that I established in this setting drew a sharp contrast with the anxiety and insecurity I had felt as I sought the nonexistent multicultural festival and entered the culturally marked International Shop, situations that I did not recognize as orderly and sensical and in which I did not know what to do and how I would be interpreted. My search for a recognizable form of engagement and the discomfort I experienced when lacking that form speaks to broader challenges experienced in diverse and immigrant communities characterized by face-to-face interaction.

In his well-known analysis of the panopticon as a mechanism that perfects the exercise of power, Foucault demonstrates that through the knowledge of constant surveillance, individuals come to monitor themselves. In such situations, the power of power is that it need not be imposed from without.

He who is subjected to a field of visibility, and who knows it, assumes responsibility for the constraints of power; he makes them play spontaneously upon himself; he inscribes in himself the power relation in which he simultaneously plays both roles; he becomes the principle of his own subjection. (Foucault 1977, pp. 202–203)

Furthermore, to speak of the power of the machine that is the panopticon renders the user insignificant.

Any individual, taken almost at random, can operate the machine.... Similarly, it does not matter what motive animates him: the curiosity of the indiscreet, the malice of a child, the thirst for knowledge of a philosopher, ... or the perversity of those who take pleasure in spying and punishing. The Panopticon is a marvelous machine, which, whatever use one may wish to put to it, produces homogenous effects of power. (Foucault 1977, p. 202)

Guided by Foucault, I suggest that we need not determine who is to blame or credit for that which is observed in this research. In Lewiston and beyond, individuals subjected to the strictures of the cultural landscape nevertheless attempt to harness its power in pursuit of recognition, self-interest, group goals, and communities marked by inclusiveness and equality.

We must, however, pause to recognize that, unlike the panopticon, the pragmatics of inclusion may be wielded by anyone, but some are more successful than others in this regard. Somali immigrants encouraged to adapt their culture and emphasize common ground with others in the community sacrificed a great deal and did so despite the intractable stranger-ness they carried as enjoyably diverse. Somali Community Services leaders, tainted by a presumed association with Islamic fundamentalism and Somali clannism, found themselves pushed out of public positions and out of work despite their claims to inclusivity and the appreciation of diversity. Historically excluded and economically marginalized members of the Franco-American underclass were discursively erased. The material concerns, cultural contributions, and language of this group were not valued as diversity. White Lewiston residents speaking with heavy Maine accents and referring to Somalis as Somalians might assert that they welcome newcomers and seek economic security for all city residents, but their claims were met with skepticism and without the presumption of goodwill. The more schooled someone was in dominant praxis, the more likely he or she was to perform inclusivity without incident. It is a common story, but in Lewiston the weight of power fell most heavily on those with the fewest resources for shouldering the burden.

References

Abbott, Andrew. 1997. "Of Time and Space: The Contemporary Relevance of the Chicago School." *Social Forces* 75:1149–1182.

Abdo, Geneive. 2006. *Mecca and Main Street: Muslim life in America after 9/11.* New York: Oxford University Press.

Agence France-Presse. 2010. "New President of Somaliland Fights for Recognition." *New York Times.* www.nytimes.com/2010/07/04/world/africa/04somaliland. html. July 3, 2010. Last accessed March 20, 2013.

Ahmed, Ismail. 2011. "Fragmented and Collaborative Leadership in a Changing Somali Community." Pp. 83–102 in *Somalis in Maine: Crossing cultural currents*, edited by K. Huisman, M. Hough, K. M. Langellier, and C. N. Toner. Berkeley, CA: North Atlantic Publishers.

Ajrouch, Kristine J. and Abdi M. Kusow. 2007. "Racial and Religious Contexts: Situational Identities among Lebanese and Somali Muslim Immigrants." *Ethnic and Racial Studies* 30:72–94.

Alba, Richard D. and Victor Nee. 2003. *Remaking the American mainstream: Assimilation and contemporary immigration.* Cambridge, MA: Harvard University Press.

2001. "Theorizing the 'Modes of Incorporation': Assimilation, Hyphenation, and Multiculturalism as Varieties of Civil Participation." *Sociological Theory* 19:237–249.

Alexander, Jeffrey C.. 2003. *The meanings of social life: A cultural sociology.* New York: Oxford University Press.

2006. *The civil sphere.* Oxford: Oxford University Press.

2010. *The performance of politics: Obama's victory and the democratic struggle for power.* New York: Oxford University Press.

Alexander, Jeffrey C., Bernhard Giesen, and Jason L. Mast. 2006. *Social performance: Symbolic action, cultural pragmatics, and ritual.* Cambridge, UK: Cambridge University Press.

Allport, Gordon W. 1954. *The nature of prejudice.* Cambridge, MA: Addison-Wesley.

Arthur, John A. 2000. *Invisible sojourners: African immigrant diaspora in the United States*. Westport, CT: Praeger.

Asch, Solomon. 1955. "Opinions and Social Pressure." *Scientific American* 193:31–35.

Bakhtin, M. M., Michael Holquist, and Caryl Emerson. 1986. *Speech genres and other late essays*. Austin: University of Texas Press.

Barna, LaRay M. 1998. "Stumbling Blocks in Intercultural Communication." Pp. 173–189 in *Basic concepts of intercultural communication*, edited by M. J. Bennett. Yarmouth, ME: Intercultural Press.

Barth, Fredrik. 1969. *Ethnic groups and boundaries. The social organization of culture difference*. Bergen: Allen & Unwin.

BBC News Magazine. 2012. "African Migrants Who Call America's Whitest State Home." Pp. 3:40. BBC News Magazine: BBC.

Bean, Frank D. and Gillian Stevens. 2003. *America's newcomers and the dynamics of diversity*. New York: Russell Sage Foundation.

Belanger, Damien-Claude and Claude Belanger. 1999. "French Canadian Emigration to the United States 1840–1930." In *Quebec History*. Montreal, QC: Marionopolis College.

Bell, Joyce and Douglas Hartmann. 2007. "Diversity in Everyday Discourse: The Cultural Ambiguities and Consequences of 'Happy Talk.'" *American Sociological Review* 72:895–914.

Bennett, James and Phil Nadeau. 2002. "Report to Governor Angus King: New Somali Arrivals and Other Issues Relative to Refugee/Secondary Migrants/Immigrants and Cultural Diversity in the City of Lewiston." Lewiston, ME: *City of Lewiston Executive Office*.

Bennett, Janet M. 1998. "Transition Shock: Putting Culture Shock into Perspective." Pp. 215–224 in *Basic concepts of intercultural communication*, edited by M. J. Bennett. Yarmouth, ME: Intercultural Press.

Berns-McGown, Rima. 1999. *Muslims in the diaspora: The Somali communities of London and Toronto*. Toronto: University of Toronto Press.

——— 2007. "Tradition and the Inner-City: Somali Women in Regent Park, Toronto." In *From Mogadishu to Dixon: The Somali diaspora in a global context*, edited by A. M. Kusow and S. R. Bjork. Trenton, NJ: Red Sea Press.

Besteman, Catherine. 2012. "Translating Race across Time and Space: The Creation of Somali Bantu Ethnicity." *Identities* 19:285–302.

Billig, Michael. 1991. *Ideology and opinions: Studies in rhetorical psychology*. Newbury Park, CA: Sage.

——— 1995. *Banal nationalism*. Thousand Oaks, CA: Sage.

Bjork, Stephanie R. 2007. "Diasporic moments: Practicing clan in the Somali diaspora." Ph.D. Thesis, University of Wisconsin, Milwaukee.

Blazak, Randy. 2001. "White Boys to Terrorist Men: Target Recruitment of Nazi Skinheads." *American Behavioral Scientist* 44:982–1000.

Bloemraad, Irene. 2006. *Becoming a citizen: Incorporating immigrants and refugees in the United States and Canada*. Berkeley: University of California Press.

Blumer, Herbert. 1958. "Race Prejudice as a Sense of Group Position." *Pacific Sociological Review* 1:3–7.

Bobo, Lawrence and Vincent L. Hutchings. 1996. "Perceptions of Racial Group Competition: Extending Blumer's Theory of Group Position to a Multiracial Social Context." *American Sociological Review* 61:951–972.

Boore, Abshir A. 2004. "Become One." *Lewiston Sun Journal*, p. A6.

Bouchard, Kelley. 2002a. "Lewiston Officials Talk with Somalis about 'Missteps'; They Say Services Will Continue, but Also Echo Fiscal Concerns Raised in the Mayor's Inflammatory Letter." *Portland Press Herald*, p. 1A.

2002b. "Lewiston's Somali Surge." *Portland Press Herald*.

Bowden, Mark. 1999. *Black Hawk down: A story of modern war*. New York: Atlantic Monthly Press.

Bragdon, Elaine Kemp. 2006. "George Washington Kemp of Leeds, Maine, 1832–1911." Pp. 83–85 in *Maine's Visible Black History*, edited by G. E. Talbot and H. H. Price. Gardiner, ME: Tilbury House.

Braverman, Amy M. 2002. "Keeping Their Religion: Richard Shweder and Students Study How Muslim-American Communitites Adapt Islam to U.S. Culture." *University of Chicago Magazine*, 94(6): 43–44.

Brubaker, Rogers. 2006. *Nationalist politics and everyday ethnicity in a Transylvanian town*. Princeton: Princeton University Press.

Camarota, Steven A. and Karen Jensenius. 2009. "Trends in Immigrant and Native Employment." In *Backgrounder* (monthly report–May). Washington, DC: Center for Immigration Studies. www.cis.org/articles/2009/back509.pdf. Last accessed March 30, 2013.

Cameron, Deborah. 2000. *Good to talk? Living and working in a communication culture*. Thousand Oaks, CA: Sage.

Central Intelligence Agency. 2009. *The World factbook: Somalia*. Washington, DC: Central Intelligence Agency.

Chernilo, Daniel. 2008. "Methodological Nationalism: Theory and History." In *Annual conference of the International Association of Critical Realism*. London: King's College.

Chmelecki, Lisa. 2003. "Jockeying for Power." *Lewiston Sun Journal*, December 14, p. A1.

2004. "Culture Clash." *Lewiston Sun Journal*, July 17, p. A6.

Collet, Bruce Anthony. 2006. "Migration, education, and perceptions of a national identity among Somali immigrants in Ontario, Canada." Ph.D. Thesis, Loyola University Chicago.

Community Building Planning Committee. 2003. Minutes: 3/11/2003, Lewiston, ME.

Department of Homeland Security. 2009. *2008 yearbook of immigration statistics*. Washington, DC: Department of Homeland Security.

Dillingham, Russ. 2006. "A Smile Is Her Umbrella." *Lewiston Sun Journal*, January 6, p. A1.

Dow, Whitney and Marco Williams. Independent Television Service, National Black Programming Consortium, Two Tone Productions., and PBS Home Video. 2004. "Two towns of Jasper." Alexandria, VA: PBS Home Video.

Duneier, Mitchell. 2001. *Sidewalk*. New York: Farrar, Straus and Giroux.

Edgell, Peggy, Joseph, Gerteis, and Douglas, Hartmann, 2006. "Atheists as 'Other': Moral Boundaries and Cultural Membership in American Society." *American Sociological Review* 71 (April): 211–234.

Elders of the Somali Community. 2002a. "Open Letter to Mayor Larry Raymond." October 6.

Elliott, Andrea. 2009a. "2 Somali-Americans Charged with Aiding Terror." *New York Times*, July 14, p. A13.

2009b. "A Call to Jihad, Answered in America." *New York Times*, July 11. www.nytimes.com/2009/07/12/us/12somalis.html. Last accessed March 30, 2013.

2009c. "Charges Detail Road to Terror for 20 in U.S." *New York Times*, November 24, p. A1.

2010. "The Jihadist Next Door." *New York Times Sunday Magazine*, January 31, p. 26.

Emmerson, Nick, Jennifer O'Connell, and Dan Peirson, producers. 2011. *All-American Muslim*. Film. Distributed by Discovery Communications.

ESPN.com news services. 2010. "Mich. School Practices 11 p.m. to 4 a.m." *ESPN. com*.

Esposito, John L. and İbrahim Kalın. 2011. *Islamophobia: The challenge of pluralism in the 21st century*. Oxford: Oxford University Press.

Ezekiel, Raphael S. 1995. *The racist mind: Portraits of American Neo-Nazis and Klansmen*. New York: Viking.

Fahrenthold, David A. 2006. "English Key to Jobs for Somalis, City Says." *Washington Post*, February 28, p. A3.

Faist, Thomas. 2000. *The volume and dynamics of international migration and transnational social spaces*. Oxford: Oxford University Press.

2009. "Diversity – a New Mode of Incorporation?" *Ethnic and Racial Studies* 32:171–190.

Fangen, Katrine. 2004. "The Need to Belong and the Need to Distance Oneself: Contra-identification among Somali Refugees in Norway." Pp. 78–88 in *Somalia: Diaspora and state reconstitution in the Horn of Africa*, edited by A. O. Farah, M. Muchie, and J. Gundel. London: Adonis & Abbey.

2006. "Humiliation Experienced by Somali Refugees in Norway." *Journal of Refugee Studies* 19:69–93.

Farah, Nuruddin. 2000. *Yesterday, tomorrow: Voices from the Somali diaspora*. New York: Cassell.

Fernando, Mayanthi L. 2010. "Reconfiguring Freedom: Muslim Piety and the Limits of Secular Law and Public Discourse in France." *American Ethnologist* 37:19–35.

Fetterman, David M. 1998. *Ethnography: Step by step*. Thousand Oaks, CA: Sage.

Finnegan, William 2006. "New in Town: The Somalis of Lewiston." *The New Yorker*, December 11, 2006, p. 46.

Ford, Richard. 2004. "Somali Pastoralists in Lewiston, Maine: Searching with Participatory Tools for a New Life." Pp. 59–77 in *Somalia: Diaspora and state reconstitution in the Horn of Africa*, edited by A. O. Farah, M. Muchie, and J. Gundel. London: Adonis & Abbey.

Foucault, Michel. 1977. *Discipline and punish: The birth of the prison*. New York: Pantheon Books.

Gardenschwartz, Lee and Anita Rowe. 1998. *Managing diversity*. New York: McGraw-Hill.

George, Alexander L. and Andrew, Bennett. 2005. *Case Studies and Theory Development in the Social Sciences*. Cambridge, Massachusetts: MIT Press.

Gettleman, Jeffrey. 2007. "The Other Somalia: An Island of Stability in a Sea of Armed Chaos." *New York Times*, March 7, p. 11.

2009. "Back from the Suburbs to Run a Patch of Somalia." *New York Times*, October 3, p. A5.

2010a. "More Troops for Somalia, but No Peace to Keep." *New York Times*, July 28, p. A10.

2010b. "Rare Haven of Stability in Somalia Faces a Test." *New York Times*, June 26, p. A4.

2010c. "Somali Town Embodies Enduring Sense of Loss." *New York Times*, September 16, p. A15.

2012. "A Taste of Hope in Somalia's Battered Capital." *New York Times*, April 4, p. A1.

Gettleman, Jeffrey and Mohammed Ibrahim. 2010. "Somali Militias Clash, Undermining New Strategy." *New York Times*, October 16, p. A6.

Glazer, Nathan. 1997. *We are all multiculturalists now*. Cambridge, MA: Harvard University Press.

Goodstein, Laurie. 2010. "Across Nation, Mosque Projects Meet Opposition." *New York Times*, August 8, p. A1.

Gottschalk, Peter and Gabriel Greenberg. 2008. *Islamophobia: Making Muslims the enemy*. Lanham, MD: Rowman & Littlefield.

Goza, Franklin. 2007. "The Somali Diaspora in the United States: A Socio-economic and Demographic Profile." In *From Mogadishu to Dixon: The Somali diaspora in a global context*, edited by A. M. Kusow and S. R. Bjork. Trenton, NJ: Red Sea Press.

Green, Joslyn 2009. "Refugees Unsettle the West." *High Country News*, October 26, pp. 14–17.

Hall, Jacquelyn Dowd. 1993. *Revolt against chivalry: Jessie Daniel Ames and the women's campaign against lynching*. New York: Columbia University Press.

Hamzeh, Ziad. 2003. *The Letter*. Film, 76 minutes. Seattle, WA: Arab Film Distribution.

Harkavy, Jerry. 2007. "Somalis Find New Lives, Adjustments in Lewiston." *Lewiston Sun Journal*, May 12, p. 1.

Hartigan, John, Jr. 1999. *Racial situations: Class predicaments of whiteness in Detroit*. Princeton, NJ: Princeton University Press.

Hein, Jeremy. 2006. *Ethnic origins: The adaptation of Cambodian and Hmong refugees in four American cities*. New York: Russell Sage Foundation.

Hernandez, Daisy and Kendra Field. 2003. "The Diversity Industry." *Colorlines* 6:23.

Herring, Cedric. 2009. "Does Diversity Pay? Race, Gender, and the Business Case for Diversity." *American Sociological Review* 74:208–224.

Hill, Miriam E. and Martha Augoustinos. 2001. "Stereotype Change and Prejudice Reduction: Short- and Long-Term Evaluation of a Cross-Cultural Awareness Programme." *Journal of Community and Applied Social Psychology* 11:243–262.

Hirsch, Arnold R. 1998. *Making the second ghetto: Race and housing in Chicago, 1940–1960*. Chicago: University of Chicago Press.

Hirsh, C. Elizabeth. 2009. "The Strength of Weak Enforcement: The Impact of Discrimination Charges, Legal Environments, and Organizational Conditions on Workplace Segregation." *American Sociological Review* 74:245–271.

Hodgkin, Douglas I. 2008. *Frontier to industrial city: Lewiston town politics 1768–1863*. Topsham, ME: Just Write Books.

Hoefer, Michael, Nancy Rytina, and Bryan C. Baker. 2009. "Estimates of the Unauthorized Immigrant Population Residing in the United States: January 2008." Washington DC: Department of Homeland Security.

Hopkins, Gail. 2006. "Somali Community Organization in London and Toronto: Collaboration and Effectiveness." *Journal of Refugee Studies* 19:361–380.

Hough, Mazie and Carol Nordstrom Toner. 2011. "L.L.Bean, Community Gardens, and Biil: Somalis Working in Maine." Pp. 169–189 in *Somalis in Maine: Crossing cultural currents*, edited by K. Huisman, M. Hough, K. M. Langellier, and C. N. Toner. Berkeley, CA: North Atlantic Press.

Huisman, Kimberlly A., Mazie Hough, Kristin M. Langellier, and Carol Nordstrom Toner. 2011. *Somalis in Maine: Crossing cultural currents*. Berkeley, CA: North Atlantic Books.

Huisman, Kimberly A. 2011. "Why Maine? Secondary Migration Decisions of Somalis in Maine." Pp. 23–47 in *Somalis in Maine: Crossing cultural currents*, edited by K. A. Huisman, M. Hough, K. M. Langellier, and C. N. Toner. Berkeley, CA: North Atlantic Books.

Huntington, Samuel P. 2004. *Who are we? The challenges to America's national identity*. New York: Simon & Schuster.

Huynh, My Tien. 2009. "Somali Independence Day Offers Culture, Food, Dance." *Lewiston Sun Journal*, June 23, p. A4.

Ibrahim, Mohammed. 2010. "Somali-American Is Named Prime Minister of Somalia." *New York Times*, October 15, p. A10.

Ibrahim, Mohammed and Jeffrey Gettleman. 2010. "Militant Alliance Adds to Somalia's Turmoil." *New York Times*, July 29, p. A10.

International Fund for Agricultural Development. 2007. "Sending Money Home: Worldwide Remittance Flows to Developing and Transition Countries." Report from the International Fund, Rome, Italy. www.ifad.org/remittances/maps/brochure.pdf. Last accessed March 30, 2013.

Jaworsky, B. Nadya. 2013. "Immigrants, Aliens and Americans: Mapping out the Boundaries of Belonging in a New Immigrant Gateway." *American Journal of Cultural Sociology* 1:221–253.

Jepperson, Ronald and John W. Meyer. 2011. "Multiple Levels of Analysis and the Limitations of Methodological Individualisms." *Sociological Theory* 29:54–73.

Johnston, David. 2009. "Militants Drew Recruit in U.S., F.B.I. Says." *New York Times*, February 24, p. A8.

Jones, Maggie. 2004. "The New Yankees." *Mother Jones* 29:64–69.

Joppke, Christian. 2009. *Veil: mirror of identity*. Malden, MA: Polity Press.

Kalev, Alexandra, Erin Kelly, and Frank Dobbin. 2006. "Best Practices or Best Guesses? Assessing the Efficacy of Corporate Affirmative Action and Diversity Policies." *American Sociological Review* 71:589–617.

Katz, Jack. 2001. "From How to Why: On Luminous Description and Causal Inference in Ethnography (Part 1)." *Ethnography* 2:443–473.

2002. "From How to Why: On Luminous Description and Causal Inference in Ethnography (Part 2)." *Ethnography* 3:63–90.

Kivisto, Peter. 2005. *Incorporating diversity: Rethinking assimilation in a multicultural age.* Boulder, CO: Paradigm.

Kivisto, Peter and Thomas Faist. 2007. *Citizenship: Discourse, theory, and transnational prospects.* Malden, MA: Blackwell.

Kleist, Nauja. 2007. "Ambivalent Encounters: Negotiating Boundaries of Somaliness, Danishness and Belonging." In *From Mogadishu to Dixon: The Somali diaspora in a global context,* edited by A. M. Kusow and S. R. Bjork. Trenton, NJ: Red Sea Press.

Koltyk, Jo Ann. 1998. *New pioneers in the heartland: Hmong life in Wisconsin.* Boston: Allyn and Bacon.

Koshen, Hawa Ibrahim A. 2007. "Strengths in Somali Families." *Marriage & Family Review* 41:71–99.

Kraska, James. 2010. "Freakonomics of Maritime Piracy." *Brown Journal of World Affairs* 16:109–119.

Kristof, Nicholas D. 2007. "A Land of Camel Milk and Honey." *New York Times,* February 27, p. 19.

Kron, Josh and Mohammed Ibrahim. 2010. "Islamists Claim Attack in Uganda." *New York Times,* July 13, p. A8.

Kurien, Prema A. 1998. "Becoming American by becoming Hindu: Indian Americans Take Their Place at the Multicultural Table." Pp. 409 in *Gatherings in diaspora: Religious communities and the new immigration,* edited by R. S. Warner and J. G. Wittner. Philadelphia, PA: Temple University Press.

Kusow, Abdi and Stephanie R. Bjork. 2007a. *From Mogadishu to Dixon: The Somali diaspora in a global context.* Trenton, NJ: Red Sea Press.

Kusow, Abdi M. 2004. "From Mogadishu to Dixon: Conceptualising the Somali Diaspora." Pp. 34–42 in *Somalia: Diaspora and state reconstitution in the Horn of Africa,* edited by A. O. Farah, M. Muchie, and J. Gundel. London: Adonis & Abbey.

Kusow, Abdi M.. 2006. "Migration and Racial Formations among Somali Immigrants in North America." *Journal of Ethnic and Migration Studies* 32(3):533–551.

Kusow, Abdi M. and Stephanie R. Bjork. 2007b. "Introduction: The Somali Diaspora in a Global Context." in *From Mogadishu to Dixon: The Somali diaspora in a global context,* edited by A. M. Kusow and S. R. Bjork. Trenton, NJ: Red Sea Press.

Kymlicka, Will. 2001. *Politics in the vernacular: Nationalism, multiculturalism, and citizenship.* New York: Oxford University Press.

2007. *Multicultural odysseys: Navigating the new international politics of diversity.* New York: Oxford University Press.

LaFlamme, Mark. 2006. "Inmate's Death Probed." *Lewiston Sun Journal,* June 1, p. 1.

Lamont, Michèle and Virág Molnar. 2002. "The Study of Boundaries in the Social Sciences." *Annual Review of Sociology* 28:167–195.

Lasch-Quinn, Elisabeth. 2001. *Race experts: How racial etiquette, sensitivity training, and new age therapy hijacked the civil rights revolution.* New York: Norton.

Lee, Maureen Elgersman. 2005. *Black Bangor: African Americans in a Maine community, 1880–1950*, edited by S. Senier, D. Ranco, A. Sweeting, and D. H. Watters. Durham: University of New Hampshire Press.

Leitner, Helga. 2004. "Local Lives, Transnational Ties, and the Meaning of Citizenship: Somali Histories and Herstories from Small Town America." *Bildhaan: An International Journal of Somali Studies* 4:44–64.

Leiva, Jose. 2005. "All Bundled Up." *Lewiston Sun Journal*, p. A2.

Lemke, Thomas. 2001. "The Birth of Bio-Piolitics: Michel Foucault's Lecture at the College de France on Neo-Liberal Governmentality." *Economy & Society* 30:190–207.

Levine, Ben, director and producer. 2003. *Reveil: Waking Up French!* Film, 103 minutes. Rockland, ME: Watching Place Productions.

Lewis, I. M. 2002. *A Modern history of the Somali.* Athens: Ohio University Press.

Lindkvist, Heather L. 2008. "The Reach and Limits of Cultural Accommodations: Public Schools and Somali Muslim Immigrants." In *Just schools: Pursuing equality in societies of difference*, edited by M. Minow, R. A. Shweder, and H. Markus. New York: Russell Sage Foundation.

Luling, Virginia. 2006. "Genealogy as Theory, Genealogy as Tool: Aspects of Somali 'Clanship.'" *Social Identities* 12:471–485.

Lumpkins, Charles L. 2006. "Civil Rights Activism in Maine, 1945–1971." Pp. 305–310 in *Maine's visible black history*, edited by G. E. Talbot and H. H. Price. Gardiner, ME: Tilbury House.

Lynch, Frederick R. 2002. *The diversity machine: The drive to change the "white male workplace."* New Brunswick, NJ: Transaction.

Macdonald, Robert E. 2012. "Enough Is Enough: Extremist Liberals Widen the Divide with Somalis." *Twin City Times* (Lewiston, ME), September 6, p. 5.

Marcus, George E. 1998. *Ethnography through thick and thin.* Princeton, NJ: Princeton University Press.

Marrow, Helen B. 2011. *New destination dreaming: Immigration, race, and legal status in the rural American South.* Stanford, CA: Stanford University Press.

Massey, Douglas S. and Magaly Sánchez. 2010. *Brokered boundaries: Creating immigrant identity in anti-immigrant times.* New York: Russell Sage Foundation.

Mazzetti, Mark. 2006. "U.S. Signal Backing for Ethiopian Incursion into Somalia." *New York Times*, December 27. www.nytimes.com/2006/12/27/world/africa/27africa.html. Last accessed March 30, 2013.

McDonald, Mark. 2009. "Record Number of Somali Pirate Attacks in 2009." *New York Times*, December 30, p. A9.

McKinley, Jesse and William Yardley. 2010. "Suspect in Oregon Bomb Plot Is Called Confused." *New York Times*, November 29, p. A17.

Menkhaus, Kenneth. 2003. *Somalia: A situation analysis and trend assessment.* Report released by the United Nations High Commissioner for Refugees, Geneva, Switzerland, August.

Michaels, Walter Benn. 2006. *The trouble with diversity: How we learned to love identity and ignore inequality.* New York: Metropolitan Books.

Milgram, Stanley. 1972. "The Familiar Stranger: An Aspect of Urban Anonymity." *Division 8 Newsletter, Personality and Social Psychology Section of the American Psychological Association.* Washington, DC: American Psychological Association, July.

———. 1974. *Obedience to authority: An experimental view.* New York: Harper & Row.

Miller-Idriss, Cynthia. 2009. *Blood and culture: Youth, right-wing extremism, and national belonging in contemporary Germany.* Durham, NC: Duke University Press.

Mohamud, Said. 2006. "Greater Understanding." *Lewiston Sun Journal*, July 15, p. A9.

Mott, Tamar. 2009. *African refugee resettlement in the United States.* El Paso: LFB Scholarly Publishers.

Nadeau, Phil. 2003a. "Lewiston Leads: Community Dialogue for Change Community Building Planning Committee Report to the Mayor and City Council: Group Report Findings and Recommendations." Lewiston, ME.

———. 2003b. "The Somalis of Lewiston: Community Impacts of Rapid Immigrant Movement into a Small Homogeneous Maine City." Paper presented at the Brown University Center for the Study of Race and Ethnicity, Providence, Rhode Island, August 14, p. 59.

———. 2007. "The New Mainers: State and Local Agencies Form Partnerships to Help Somali Immigrants." *National Civic Review* 96:55.

———. 2011. "A Work in Progress: Lewiston Responds to the Rapid Migration of Somali Refugees." Pp. 53–72 in *Somalis in Maine: Crossing cultural currents,* edited by K. Huisman, M. Hough, K. M. Langellier, and C. N. Toner. Berkeley, CA: North Atlantic Books.

Nagel, Joane. 1996. *American Indian ethnic renewal: Red power and the resurgence of identity and culture.* New York: Oxford University Press.

Omer, Hibo. 2007. "Get race out of the race." *Lewiston Sun Journal*, March 30, p. A8.

Omi, Michael and Howard Winant. 1986. *Racial formation in the United States: From the 1960s to the 1980s.* New York: Routledge & Kegan Paul.

Paluck, Elizabeth Levy. 2006. "Diversity Action and Intergroup Contact: A Call to Action Research." *Journal of Social Issues* 62:577–595.

Parker, James H. 1983. *Ethnic identity: The case of the French Americans.* Washington, DC: University Press of America.

Paul, Diane B. 1998. *The politics of heredity: Essays on eugenics, biomedicine and the nature-nurture debate.* Albany: State University of New York Press.

Peek, Lori A. 2011. *Behind the backlash: Muslim Americans after 9/11.* Philadelphia: Temple University Press.

Pendry, Louise F., Denise M. Driscoll, and Susannah C. T. Field. 2007. "Diversity Training: Putting Theory into Practice." *Journal of Occupational and Organizational Psychology* 80:27–50.

Perry, Alex. 2009. "Behind the Suicide Bombing in Somalia." *Time.* www.time.com/time/world/article/0,8599,1905730,00.html. Last accessed March 30, 2013.

Polgreen, Lydia. 2010. "A Question of Appearances: Obama Will Bypass Sikh Temple on Visit to India." *New York Times*, October 20, p. A6.

Portes, Alejandro and Ruben G. Rumbaut. 2001. *Legacies: The story of the immigrant second generation*. Berkeley: University of California Press.

Portes, Alejandro and Min Zhou. 1993. "The New Second Generation: Segmented Assimilation and Its Variants." *Annals of the American Academy of Political and Social Science* 530:22.

Portland Public Schools Multilingual & Multicultural Center. 2011. "Home Page." vol. 2011. "Letter to the Elders of the Somali Community." Portland, ME: Portland Public Schools.

Povinelli, Elizabeth A. 2002. *The cunning of recognition: Indigenous alterities and the making of Australian multiculturalism*. Durham, NC: Duke University Press.

Price, H. H. and Gerald E. Talbot. 2006. *Maine's visible black history: The first chronicle of its people*. Gardiner, ME: Tilbury House.

Putnam, Robert D. 2007. "E Pluribus Unum: Diversity and Community in the Twenty-first Century—The 2006 Johan Skytte Prize Lecture." *Scandinavian Political Studies* 30:137–174.

Raymond, Gino and Tariq Modood. 2007. *The construction of minority identities in France and Britain*. Houndmills, Basingstoke, Hampshire: Palgrave Macmillan.

Raymond, Laurier T. Jr. 2002. (Portland, ME). www.portlandschools.org/schools/multilingual/index.html. Last accessed January 24, 2011.

Rector, Amanda K. 2008. "An Analysis of the Employment Patterns of Somali Immigrants to Lewiston from 2001 through 2006." Augusta: Maine Department of Labor and Maine State Planning Office.

Reed, Isaac. 2011. *Interpretation and social knowledge: On the use of theory in the human sciences*. Chicago: University of Chicago Press.

Reitz, Jeffrey G. 2002. "Host Societies and the Reception of Immigrants: Research Themes, Emerging Theories and Methodological Issues." *International Migration Review* 36:1005–1019.

Reuters. 2006. "U.S. Says al Qaeda behind Somali Islamists." December 14.

Rhoades, Rex. 2004. "Another Letter in Lewiston." *Lewiston Sun Journal*, April 7, p. A6.

—— 2006. "Community Lessons in Tolerance." *Lewiston Sun Journal*, August 20, p. C8.

Richard, Mark Paul. 2008. *Loyal but French: The negotiation of identity by French-Canadian descendants in the United States*. East Lansing: Michigan State University Press.

Ricœur, Paul and George H. Taylor. 1986. *Lectures on ideology and utopia*. New York: Columbia University Press.

Roble, Abdi and Douglas F. Rutledge. 2008. *The Somali diaspora: A journey away*. Minneapolis: University of Minnesota Press.

Rytina, Nancy. 2009. *Estimates of the legal permanent resident population in 2008*. Washington, DC: Department of Homeland Security,

Said, Kadar. 2003. "A Split." *Lewiston Sun Journal*, December 28, p. A6.

Samatar, Ahmed I. 2004. "Beginning Again: From Refugee to Citizen." *Bildhaan: An International Journey of Somali Studies* 4:1–17.

Sandoval, Carlos, Catherine Tambini, Camino Bluff Productions, New Video Group, and Docurama (Firm). 2004. "Farmingville." *P O V 20th anniversary collection*. Docurama; Distributed by New Video, New York.

Sargent, David A. 2006. "Food, Fun Fill Festival." *Lewiston Sun Journal*, July 2, pp. C1, C2.

Scott, Ridley. 2001. *Black Hawk Down*. Pp. 16 film reels of 16 on 8 (ca. 143 min., ca. 12,870). Santa Monica, California: Revolution Studios.

Shandy, D. J. and K. Fennelly. 2006. "A Comparison of the Integration Experiences of Two African Immigrant Populations in a Rural Community." *Journal of Religion and Spirituality in Social Work* 25:23.

Shepard, Raynel Mary. 2005. "Acting is not becoming: Cultural adaptation among Somali refugee youth." Ed.D. Thesis, Harvard University, Cambridge, MA.
    2008. *Cultural adaptation of Somali refugee youth*, edited by S. J. Gold and R. G. Rumbaut. New York: LFB Scholarly Publishing.

Shibutani, Tamotsu and Kian M. Kwan. 1965. *Ethnic stratification, a comparative approach*. New York: Macmillan.

Shio, Thadeus Joseph. 2006. "Housing experiences of Somali immigrants in the Twin Cities, Minnesota: A housing careers perspective." Ph.D. Thesis, University of Minnesota, Minneapolis.

Sierra Club. n.d. "Sierra Club Maine Woods Campaign." Vol. 2011.

Singer, Audrey. 2004. *The rise of new immigrant gateways*. Washington, DC: Brookings Institution.

Skaggs, Sheryl. 2009. "Legal-Political Pressures and African American Access to Managerial Jobs." *American Sociological Review* 74:225–244.

Small, Mario Luis. 2009. "'How Many Cases Do I Need?' On Science and the Logic of Case Selection in Field-Based Research." *Ethnography* 10:5–38.

Smith, Philip and Alexander Riley. 2009. *Cultural theory: An introduction*. Malden, MA: Blackwell.

Somali Community Services of Maine Inc. 2003. "Prelimary Needs Assessment and Action Plan of the Somali Community in the Hillview Housing Project." Lewiston, ME.

Suarez-Orozco, Marcelo. 2002. "Everything You Ever Wanted to Know about Assimilation but Were Afraid to Ask." In *Engaging cultural differences: The multicultural challenge in liberal democracies*, edited by R. Shweder, M. Minow, and H. R. Markus. New York: Russell Sage Foundation.

Takaki, Ronald T. 1993. *A different mirror: A history of multicultural America*. Boston: Little, Brown.

Talbot, Gerald E. 2006. "Bangor, My Hometown." Pp. 96–102 in *Maine's visible black history*, edited by G. E. Talbot and H. H. Price. Gardiner, ME: Tilbury House.

Taylor, Charles. 2007. *A secular age*. Cambridge, MA: Belknap Press of Harvard University Press.

Taylor, Scott. 2004. "Somali Life in Lewiston." *Lewiston Sun Journal*, April 28, pp. B1, B4.
    2006a. "Somalis Feel Wary." *Lewiston Sun Journal*, July 6, p. 1.
    2006b. "'We Choose to Be Here.'" *Lewiston Sun Journal*, August 13, pp. A1, A4.

2012. "Mayor Won't Apologize to Somali Community; Says Statements Taken Out of Context." *Lewiston Sun Journal*, October 2, p. A12.

Thistle, Scott. 2012a. "Groups Call for Lewiston Mayor to Step Down." *Lewiston Sun Journal*, October 1, p. A1.

2012b. "Lewiston Mayor Says Comments Used as Political Weapon." *Lewiston Sun Journal*, September 26, p. A1.

Thompson, Becky W. 2001. *A promise and a way of life: White antiracist activism*. Minneapolis: University of Minnesota Press.

Thompson, Krissah. 2009. "An NAACP Chapter of a Different Hue." *Washington Post*, November 3, 2009, www.washingtonpost.com/wp-dyn/content/article/2009/11/02/AR2009110202850.html. Last accessed March 30, 2013.

Tice, Lindsay. 2006. "Mosque Incident Suspect Arrested." *Lewiston Sun Journal*, 5, p. 1.

2007. "Showing Another Side of Brent Matthews." *Lewiston Sun Journal*, pp. A1, A4.

Tienda, Marta. 1999. "Immigration, Opportunity, and Social Cohesion." In *Diversity and its discontents*, edited by N. J. Smelser and J. C. Alexander. Princeton, NJ: Princeton University Press.

"Times Topics: Piracy at Sea." 2010. *New York Times*, November 15. http://topics.nytimes.com/top/reference/timestopics/subjects/p/piracy_at_sea/index.html.

Umoja, Akinyele O. 1999. "The Ballot and the Bullet: A Comparative Analysis of Armed Resistance in the Civil Rights Movement." *Journal of Black Studies* 29:558–578.

United Nations High Commissioner for Refugees. 2009. "Statistical Snapshot: Somalia." Vol. 2009. Geneva, Switzerland: UN High Commissioner for Refugees.

U.S. Census, Bureau. 2000. "Census 2000 Summary File 3, Matrix PCT10." Vol. 2007. Washington, DC: U.S. Census Bureau.

2003. "DP-1. Profile of General Demographic Characteristics." Washington, DC: U.S. Census Bureau.

2008a. "Current Population Survey, Custom Tables." Washington, DC: U.S. Census Bureau.

2008b. "Table 1.1 Population by Sex, Age, Nativity, and U.S. Citizenship Status: 2008." Washington, DC: U.S. Census Bureau.

2009. "American Factfinder: Clarkston, Georgia." Washington, DC: U.S. Census Bureau.

2010. "American Factfinder: Wausau, Wisconsin." Washington, DC: U.S. Census Bureau.

2003. "American FactFinder: Lewiston, Maine." November 30. Washington, DC: U.S. Census Bureau.

U.S. Department of Labor. 2006. "Occupational Employment and Wages, May 2006 13–1079 Human Resources, Training, Labor Relations Specialists, All Other," edited by Bureau of Labor Statistics. Washington, DC: Department of Labor.

van Gelder, Elles and Ilvy Njiokiktjien. 2011. *Afrikaner Blood*. Documentary film, 8 minutes, 26 seconds. Released August 26. Johannesburg, South Africa: Frog in a Tent Studios.

Van Reeth, Douglas. 2007. "Montello Kids Get into St. Paddy's Day." *Lewiston Sun Journal*, March 17, p. A1.

Voyer, Andrea. 2011a. "Disciplined to Diversity: Learning the Language of Multiculturalism." *Ethnic and Racial Studies* 34(11):1874–1893.

2011b. "The Subjects and Objects of Multiculturalism." Paper presented at the annual meeting of the American Sociological Association, Las Vegas Nevada, August 20, 2011.

2013. "Notes on a Cultural Sociology of Immigrant Incorporation." *American Journal of Cultural Sociology* 1: 26–41.

Walsh, Katherine Cramer. 2007. *Talking about race: Community dialogues and the politics of difference*. Chicago: University of Chicago Press.

Warren, Robert Penn. 1957. *Segregation: The inner conflict in the South*. London: Eyre & Spottiswoode.

Waters, Mary C. 1990. *Ethnic options: Choosing identities in America*. Berkeley: University of California Press.

Waters, Mary C.. 1999. *Black identities: West Indian immigrant dreams and American realities*. New York: Russell Sage Foundation.

Waters, Mary C. and Tomas R. Jimenez. 2005. "Assessing Immigrant Assimilation: Empirical and Theoretical Challenges." *Annual Review of Sociology* 31:105–125.

Wilde, Melissa J. and Sabrina Danielsen. 2011. "Creating Heaven on Earth: Birth Control, Eugenics and Belief in the Social Gospel." Paper presented at the Yale University Center for Cultural Sociology, April 1.

Williams, Christopher. 2006a. "City Fired Man Charged in Pig's Head Incident." *Lewiston Sun Journal*, July 8, pp. A1, A9.

2006b. "Greene Woman Accused of Using Racial Epithets." *Lewiston Sun Journal*, July 12, pp. A1, A7.

2007. "Inmate Death: National Group Calls for New Investigation." *Lewiston Sun Journal*, January 27, p. B1.

Wimmer, Andreas. 2013. *Ethnic boundary making: Institutions, power, networks*. New York: Oxford University Press.

Wimmer, Andreas and Nina Glick Schiller. 2002. "Methodological National and Beyond: Nation-State Building, Migration and the Social Sciences." *Global Networks* 2(4): 301–334.

Wood, Peter. 2003. *Diversity: The invention of a concept*. San Francisco: Encounter Books.

Index

Somalia
  clan violence, 32
  history, 30–34
  piracy, 34
  Puntland, 34
  refugees from, 35
  role in war on terror, 15
  Somaliland, 34
  transitional government, 33
  turmoil, 15
Stevens, Gillian, 90n.5
Student Nonviolent Coordinating
    Committee, 119
Suarez-Orozco, Carola, 81
symbolic boundaries, 6n.4, 7n.5, 54,
    74, 78, 104. *See also* cultural sociology
    of immigrant incorporation
  excluding Somalis, 65
  of community, 71, 72

Takaki, Ronald, 118, 119
Thompson, Becky, 119
Tienda, Marta, 81
Toner, Carol, 20n.1, 42n.9, 43n.10
Town meeting, May 2002, 50–51, 80
train-the-trainer seminars, 11, 110–116
  description of, 114–115

language instruction, 120–125
links to Lewiston, 145
selection and observation, 113–114
Twin City Times, 72, 82, 83
Two towns of Jasper. *See* diversity training,
    in Lewiston
Two Towns of Jasper, The (film), 84
Umoja, Akinyele, 119

UNISOM I, 32
UNITAF, 33
United Nations, 32, 33, 34
University of Southern Maine, Lewiston-
    Auburn, 155

veil, the. *See* gender relations

Walsh, Katherine, 94, 94n.7
War on Terror, 33
Waters, Mary, 11n.8, 12n.9, 37,
    40, 72, 170
Welch, William, Chief of Police, 3, 76
Wood, Peter, 53n.2
World Church of the Creator
    meeting, 2, 73

Zhou, Min, 11n.9, 72, 81

F1